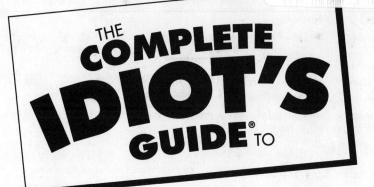

THE
COMPLETE
IDIOT'S
GUIDE® TO

# Vampires

*by Jay Stevenson, Ph.D.*

## ALPHA

A member of Penguin Group (USA) Inc.

## ALPHA BOOKS

Published by the Penguin Group

Penguin Group (USA) Inc., 375 Hudson Street, New York, New York 10014, USA

Penguin Group (Canada), 90 Eglinton Avenue East, Suite 700, Toronto, Ontario M4P 2Y3, Canada (a division of Pearson Penguin Canada Inc.)

Penguin Books Ltd., 80 Strand, London WC2R 0RL, England

Penguin Ireland, 25 St. Stephen's Green, Dublin 2, Ireland (a division of Penguin Books Ltd.)

Penguin Group (Australia), 250 Camberwell Road, Camberwell, Victoria 3124, Australia (a division of Pearson Australia Group Pty. Ltd.)

Penguin Books India Pvt. Ltd., 11 Community Centre, Panchsheel Park, New Delhi—110 017, India

Penguin Group (NZ), 67 Apollo Drive, Rosedale, North Shore, Auckland 1311, New Zealand (a division of Pearson New Zealand Ltd.)

Penguin Books (South Africa) (Pty.) Ltd., 24 Sturdee Avenue, Rosebank, Johannesburg 2196, South Africa

Penguin Books Ltd., Registered Offices: 80 Strand, London WC2R 0RL, England

International Standard Book Number: 978-1-59257-943-3
Library of Congress Catalog Card Number: 2008943368

11 10 09   8 7 6 5 4 3 2 1

Interpretation of the printing code: The rightmost number of the first series of numbers is the year of the book's printing; the rightmost number of the second series of numbers is the number of the book's printing. For example, a printing code of 09-1 shows that the first printing occurred in 2009.

*Printed in the United States of America*

**Note:** This publication contains the opinions and ideas of its author. It is intended to provide helpful and informative material on the subject matter covered. It is sold with the understanding that the author and publisher are not engaged in rendering professional services in the book. If the reader requires personal assistance or advice, a competent professional should be consulted.

The author and publisher specifically disclaim any responsibility for any liability, loss, or risk, personal or otherwise, which is incurred as a consequence, directly or indirectly, of the use and application of any of the contents of this book.

Most Alpha books are available at special quantity discounts for bulk purchases for sales promotions, premiums, fund-raising, or educational use. Special books, or book excerpts, can also be created to fit specific needs.

For details, write: Special Markets, Alpha Books, 375 Hudson Street, New York, NY 10014.

**Publisher:** *Marie Butler-Knight*
**Editorial Director:** *Mike Sanders*
**Senior Managing Editor:** *Billy Fields*
**Senior Acquisitions Editor:** *Paul Dinas*
**Senior Production Editor:** *Megan Douglass*

**Cover Designer:** *Bill Thomas*
**Book Designer:** *Trina Wurst*
**Indexer:** *Amy Lawrence*
**Layout:** *Brian Massey*
**Proofreader:** *Laura Caddell*

# Contents at a Glance

# Contents

# Introduction

Vampires beckon us out of our merely human existence. On a conceptual level, they break down the barriers between human and nonhuman and between living and dead, so that these basic distinctions lose their meaning. On an emotional level, they break down the distinctions between fear and desire. They terrify us and we love them for it!

At the same time, vampires symbolize some of the deepest and most delicate feelings that arise in response to our human connections with one another. They represent and embody the painful, parasitic impulses that sometimes take control of human relationships—relationships between lovers or among family members, among friends or enemies, and between rulers and their subordinates. And they hold out the promise—and the threat—of transformation. They could change us forever.

Their elusively symbolic power has made them hugely popular figures in legend and literature, pop culture and subculture. They appear in different contexts, changing in response to our shifting emotional and spiritual dilemmas. Killed, they come back; stripped of power, they learn new rules. Thus their history is closely linked to ours.

Vampires remain among the most persistently compelling of all legendary creatures. Despite their age, they are distinctly modern, every bit as much at home in a newly opened nightclub as a medieval castle. In fact only recently they have become more prevalent and significant than they have ever been.

*The Complete Idiot's Guide to Vampires* looks at these creatures, their nature, their history, and their impact, in the many different settings they have appeared, from ancient myth to modern media, as well as in their many guises—terrifying, seductive, deep and dark, glitzy and glamorous, weird and silly.

This book is divided into four sections:

**Part 1, "Points of Entry,"** talks about the many ways leading into the world of vampires, including history, literature, the occult, and pop culture.

**Part 2, "Gory Lore,"** discusses vampire legends from ancient times to today, including the superstitions and vampire scares of Eastern Europe and vampirelike myths from around the world.

**Part 3, "Out of the Coffin,"** relates vampires to the lives of the growing numbers of human beings today who identify with them, from role players and lifestylers to blood fetishists and clinical cases.

**Part 4, "Classic Vampires We Love to Hate,"** surveys the voluminous subject of vampires in literature from the Romantic period to today, including the work of John Polidori, Bram Stoker, and Anne Rice. We also take a look at early vampire films.

And to whet your appetite as you read, you'll unearth boxes filled with interesting dirt pertaining to the subject at hand:

**Grave Mistake**

Here you'll find faux pas, foolishness, and fallacies that have dogged the trails of those seeking to understand vampires.

**Dead Giveaway**

This feature supplies extra background information on subjects described in the text—the native soil, so to speak, of the vampire issues you're reading about.

**Cold Fact**

This box contains dark data of the strange-but-true variety to satisfy all the vampire trivia addicts.

**Stalk Talk**

Here, for the tongue-tied, you'll find definitions of vampire-related terms used in the book.

## Acknowledgments

Thanks again and always to the Central N.J. Scooby gang: TK, Cora, Matthew, Vic, and Stephanie, for books, articles, videos, websites, ideas, and feedback. Special thanks to Debra Roy for videos.

## Trademarks

# Part 1

# Points of Entry

Vampires are a bigger subject than most people realize, not only because their popularity has been surging recently like fresh blood from a jugular vein, but also because their history is so rich, multifaceted, strange, and ancient. Much more than a pale sucker behind an opera cape in a horror movie, the vampire is one of humankind's most fascinating terrors. So we owe it to ourselves to stick our necks out and find out what the excitement is all about.

There are many ways in to the world of vampires, as the chapters in this section show. Through history and legend, folklore and literature, pop culture, nightlife, and the occult, vampires yield a rich supply of food for hungry imaginations. And just so you don't make a mess when you feed, the subject is divided into sections like a TV dinner!

There's an overview, a look at undeath, a categorical breakdown of different vampire kinds, a chapter on relating to vampires from personal experience, and a look at the campy side of vampires. These chapters represent a range of approaches to the subject: historical, philosophical, occult, psychological, and silly! All of them should prepare you for the challenges that lie ahead in the rest of the book.

# Chapter 1

# Spadework

## In This Chapter

- ◆ Vampires in legend
- ◆ Literary vampires
- ◆ Vampires in movies and TV
- ◆ Vampires and reality

If you watch TV, go to the movies, read books, or give out Halloween candy, you probably have a pretty good idea of what vampires are supposed to be like: scary, fanged, humanlike creatures who return from the grave to suck the blood of their victims. This concept of vampires has been around for centuries, yet like so many old notions, vampires continue to have a powerful hold on people today. Their mysterious appeal will not die, but keeps coming back in new forms.

The endurance of the vampire myth is clear from all the books, movies, articles, websites, games, and nightclubs devoted to vampires these days. They come in all varieties. There may be a silly cartoon vampire on your breakfast cereal box, but there may be a sinister living vampire behind the disappearance of the child on the milk carton. Sometimes they're scary, sometimes funny, sometimes plainly make-believe, other times strangely real. And they seem to turn up when you least expect them.

The fact that vampires are so widespread and so various makes them extremely difficult to keep track of. Vampire lore from different times and places has a tendency to bleed together. It flows from many sources and is continually being replenished in different ways by those who fall under the vampiric spell. But despite the challenges posed by continual blending of old and new vampire lore, careful digging around by scholars has yielded recognizable remains of the origins, history, and development of the vampire myth. This chapter provides the bare bones of the story.

# Rising from Obscurity

Myths and legends telling of bloodsucking menaces can be found all over the world and are as old as fear itself. Practically all cultures have produced myths telling of monsters and demons who suck the blood of human victims. Today, such creatures are often called "vampires," regardless of where or when they come from. Originally, however, the word "vampire," and words like it, including *vampir, vepir, vopyr, upir,* and *lampir,* were used only in the countries of Eastern Europe, chiefly among the Slavic peoples where "spellcheck" hadn't been invented. But a creature just like the Slavic vampire was known in neighboring Greece as the *vrykolakas.*

> **Stalk Talk**
>
> The **vrykolakas** is not a cough lozenge, but a Greek vampire with essentially the same characteristics as the Slavic variety. The word comes from other words that may have meant "wolf pelt," or "werewolf." How or why this time it came to be applied to vampires is uncertain.

## Undeath of a Legend

It was in Eastern Europe that the one-and-only original authentic vampire got started. Scholars are uncertain about the origins of the Slavic vampire, which could have had many sources. Some scholars have made a convincing case that classical Greek and Roman legend fed old Slavic vampire lore. Others have argued that the Slavic vampire stems from legends brought to Eastern Europe by Gypsies from India. (As their name implies, Gypsies were thought to have come from Egypt, but in fact, they migrated to Europe from India.) Whatever their sources, there's no doubt that the original vampires were homegrown horrors, as native to Eastern Europe as overpaid CEOs are to the United States!

The vampire of Slavic legend was the start of the excitement that has led to all the vampire books, movies, TV shows, and Halloween costumes we're familiar with. But vampires underwent a few changes in the process of moving from their isolated native villages with names that are hard to pronounce to the starring role they play in popular culture. They have cleaned up their act a good deal. Now they are stylish, sexy, suave, and worldly. But they haven't always been.

*Au contraire.* Back in the old days in Eastern Europe, when vampires were still perfecting the art of victimizing the innocent, they came from humble peasant stock, walked around in a plague-infested condition, bloated with their own festering grave-juices and, beneath the stench of death, smelled like a barnyard. No doubt villagers used garlic as vampire repellant because it was the only thing around that smelled more strongly than vampires did! These early vampires menaced victims not through seduction but through physical violence and supernatural evil. And instead of piercing the necks of their victims with fangs, they used sharp, pointy tongues to draw blood from the area of the chest.

So actually the first vampires were bloodsucking hayseeds. At this point, if you're already a fan of vampire lore, you may be wondering about Vlad Tepes, the Wallachian prince, commonly known as Vlad the Impaler owing to his habit of making human shish kebob out of anyone he didn't like. Well, he was an actual historical person who lived before vampires became widely known outside of Eastern Europe. Information about Prince Vlad provided author Bram Stoker with background material for his famous vampire novel, *Dracula* (1897).

As a prince, Vlad was certainly no hayseed. But though he was something of a Slavic legend in his own right, he was almost certainly not the kind of guy the Slavic peasants had in mind when they told stories of bloodsucking corpses who returned from the grave. The polished, wealthy, aristocratic vampire made famous in *Dracula* and other stories was a literary invention and came later.

**Dead Giveaway** _____

Vlad Tepes, also known as Vlad Dracula and Vlad the Impaler, the ruthless and bloody fifteenth-century Wallachian prince, did not become part of vampire lore until Bram Stoker wrote his novel *Dracula* (1897), in which the modern vampire count is identified as the undead medieval tyrant. But although he was not a vampire in real life, Prince Vlad gains something from the comparison to Stoker's villain. Next to Vlad, in fact, Count Dracula is a sweet guy. According to some estimates, Vlad brutally tortured and murdered as many as 100,000 people wielding his medieval sword!

## New Monster on the Block

Greek and Slavic vampire legends were unknown to most of the world until late in the seventeenth century when reports were published throughout Europe telling of a rash of vampire scares and of the hunting and staking of real vampires! You see, the Slavic vampire legends were more than just scary stories told for amusement because nobody had Nintendo. The stories provided explanations for why people were dying in clusters.

During times of plague, when the death of one villager was followed by the deaths of others who knew that person, the people blamed vampires instead of the contagious disease. The idea was that the first dead body could not rest, but was compelled to return and destroy those closest to it—friends, neighbors, and family members. Naturally the villagers took action to prevent further killings. They identified the graves where corpses suspected of being vampires were buried. And they dug up the bodies and "killed" them again, sometimes by decapitation with a shovel, sometimes by burning the body, and sometimes through the technique made famous in the novel, *Dracula*, by driving a stake through the heart.

Word of the stakings got around and witnesses began writing reports about them that circulated throughout Europe. Pretty much everyone who could read and who had time to sit around and talk all day was reading and talking about vampires. Inquiring minds wanted to know: Could vampires be real?

**Cold Fact** _____

Vampire scares were reported in Austria, Hungary (including Serbia), Wallachia (just south of Transylvania), Prussia, Russia, Poland, and Greece between the years of 1672 and 1772. One such incident took place in Austria and was investigated by medical officers from the Austrian Army in 1732. Buried corpses suspected of being vampires were dug up and examined. According to official reports, some had fresh blood dripping from their mouths! Such reports caused a sensation throughout Europe.

## The Human Face of Horror

The Eastern European vampire mania continued throughout the eighteenth century and sparked a hot debate about whether vampires really existed. But the possibility that the undead could actually rise from the grave to suck the blood of the living turned out to be only a small part of the fascination vampires have continued to hold for people everywhere. Real or not, somehow they speak to us like no other legendary being; they resonate with our deepest fears and desires.

The "real" vampire scares in Eastern Europe attracted attention throughout the rest of Europe as the vampire incidents were documented and people debated whether the undead could attack the living. Eventually, however, the matter was laid to rest, except perhaps for the remaining isolated Slavic regions where the locals continued to entertain their traditional beliefs. But even as the fascination for real vampires began to wane throughout most of the world, vampires began to appear in literature as new and fascinating monsters ideally suited for the times.

# Poison Pen Pals

The first vampires to emerge in literature occurred in what literary scholars call the Romantic period. The Romantic movement aimed at achieving heightened and deepened imaginative experience through art and literature. Romantic literary conventions made a significant mark on the way people understand vampires.

Even today, many people see the vampire as a Romantic figure. Romantic poetry and fiction tended to be more self-evidently imaginative than before. The power of the human spirit to inhabit its own reality independently of scientific truths was an important Romantic theme as fantasies and feelings of all kinds came to be seen as important for their own sake simply as aspects of human experience.

## Honest to Goth

It's no accident that writers of the Romantic period incorporated vampires into their work. In writing about vampires, they struggled to come to terms with the complexities of human nature and experience—the fear, longing, doubt, and wonder that makes life so much more than scientific analysis can define. Romantic writers had, on one hand, the newly discovered concept of the Slavic vampire and, on the other, a rich literary legacy to draw on, including a recently developed genre of fiction known as *gothic*.

> **Stalk Talk**
>
> The word **gothic** has been used to describe everything from medieval architecture to twenty-first-century music. Gothic literature was a trend in eighteenth-century England characterized by eerie supernatural doings.

Gothic fiction emerged in England early in the eighteenth century as a quirky innovation aimed at middle- and upper-class women. Gothic tales centered on bizarre and supernatural occurrences involving things like haunted castles, crazy family members stowed away in the attic, depraved clergymen, and decayed aristocracy. Such stories weren't considered "serious literature" and didn't get much respect at first. When the Romantic period rolled around, however, gothic elements gained wider acceptance and were incorporated into much of the best fiction and poetry of the time.

> **Cold Fact**
>
> Literary historians often point to Horace Walpole's *Castle of Otranto* (1764) as the first gothic novel. There are no vampires in the tale, but there is a mysterious castle with trap doors, hidden passages, and portraits and statues that talk. All kinds of supernatural horrors take place, but it all works out in the end when the virtuous peasant Theodoro turns out to be the rightful heir of the castle and gets to marry the rich and beautiful Isabella.

## Chips off the Old Block

One familiar gothic/Romantic motif was the figure known today as the *femme fatale*, a sexy, seductive woman whose only reliable feature was the power to ruin—or actually end—the lives of the hapless men who fell in love with her. These bad beauties often had supernatural characteristics—they might be undead or transformed snake-demons—or they might simply be alluring yet cold. Either way, they provide some of the broader cultural context for the emerging literary vampire.

Another familiar character out of gothic and Romantic literature was the jaded, powerful, selfish aristocrat who always got his way and didn't care who he used or stepped on. He was typically suave yet strong-willed, capable of both brute force and subtle deception. This literary figure has many antecedents in history and literature.

These literary types, always menacing yet strangely admirable, became even more fascinating as vampires in the fiction of the eighteenth century. They also brought out the sexual and political implications of the vampire legend. The first extended prose vampire story was John Polidori's *The Vampyre* (1819), which was inspired by an unfinished novel by Polidori's one-time associate George Gordon, Lord Byron.

**Dead Giveaway** _____

Lord Byron wrote his unfinished vampire novel for an informal "ghost-story"–telling contest he proposed among a group of his friends while staying at the Villa Diodati in Switzerland in 1816. The most successful tale produced for the competition was Mary Shelley's *Frankenstein*, although Byron's tale turned out to be important as well. It inspired the first published vampire novel, *The Vampyre*, which was written by John Polidori but initially attributed to Byron. This story was highly praised when it first came out and before long was adapted a number of times for the stage. And the story of the contest in Switzerland was made into the movie, *Gothic* (1987) directed by Ken Russel.

Other vampire stories followed, most notably the "penny dreadful" (early pulp novel), *Varney the Vampire* (1847) by Thomas Prest and James Malcolm Rymer and "Carmilla" (1872) a short story of lesbian bloodlust by Joseph Sheridan Le Fanu. Though considered successful in their day, these works pale before the most influential vampire story ever written, Bram Stoker's *Dracula* (1897).

# Stage Frights

Starting in the early twentieth century, these oral and written vampire tales were turned into popular stage productions. In 1927, a stage version of *Dracula* became a hit on Broadway, starring Hungarian actor Bela Lugosi. As you may know, Lugosi starred in the classic Hollywood movie version directed by Tod Browning (1931). The movie was a smash, possibly and at least in part because it played on American *xenophobia*, or fear of foreigners, which was rife during the 1920s, '30s, and '40s. In fact, evil villains in the movies at this time were often foreigners. Lugosi's Dracula is about as foreign as they come!

Lugosi's Dracula soon became an icon of popular culture and vampire movies have been a cinematic staple ever since. Dracula himself has remained a feature film favorite, undergoing many striking incarnations. Here's a list of some of the more memorable films featuring Dracula and Dracula-like vampires.

**Stalk Talk**

**Xenophobia** is the unwarranted fear of foreigners, a condition that gripped many Americans during the first half of the twentieth century. As vampires moved from legend into fiction and film, many came to embody this fear. Dracula, especially, represents a parasitic alien, arriving from foreign shores to multiply his own kind and deplete his new country.

## Flicks of the Cape

◆ *Nosferatu* (1922)—classic German expressionist silent film directed by F. W. Murnau, loosely based on Stoker's tale, starring Max Schreck as the ugly, ratlike Count Orlock.

◆ *Dracula* (1931)—director Tod Browning classic, starring the immortal Bela Lugosi whose Hungarian accent, opera cape, and hair pomade have become vampire cliches.

- *Horror of Dracula* (1958)—Hammer Films' star Christopher Lee takes Dracula out of the castle and into the bachelor pad in a role he reprised in numerous sequels and spin-offs.

- *Blacula* (1972)—William Marshall stars as the African prince turned vampire set loose on Los Angeles in the 1970s.

- *Love at First Bite* (1979)—George Hamilton stars in this campy spoof set in New York City where Dracula meets folks far odder than himself.

- *Bram Stoker's Dracula* (1992)—Grand, lavish treatment directed by Francis Ford Coppola and starring Gary Oldman as a weird and flamboyant Count.

- *Shadow of the Vampire* (2000)—Willem Dafoe stars in this tribute to Max Schreck's performance in *Nosferatu*.

## Love-Hate Relationships

As this list indicates, the image of vampires has taken many turns in the twentieth century. This has been especially true during recent decades when vampire styles have included chic, funky, grungy, cute, creepy, and just about every other look and manner you can imagine. Amid the throng, however, two types of vampires have become especially popular with readers, movie-goers, and TV viewers.

The worldly, sensitive, conflicted vampires created by novelist Anne Rice have captured the imaginations of millions of readers since her first book, *Interview with the Vampire* was published in 1976. The book became the first of the series known as *The Vampire Chronicles*, recounting the experiences of vampires who seem more alive and human than most ordinary people. Rice remains the most successful of many popular authors of recent vampire fiction.

Then there are the hip but troubled young vampires of the movie *Buffy the Vampire Slayer* (1992) and the hit TV series based on the film. These teen fiends are vampiric embodiments of the many problems and challenges faced by high school- and college-age suburbanites. They demonstrate like no other evil beings why young adulthood can be hell!

**Grave Mistake** _____

Don't assume that the vampires Buffy slays are the first movie blood-
    suckers to stalk their prey disguised as California teenagers. Before
them came *A Polish Vampire in Burbank* (1986), and the vampiric scamps
of *The Lost Boys* (1987), a film filled with much of the same delightful
insouciant wit and sarcasm as the Buffy movie and TV show. In fact,
*The Lost Boys* served as an inspiration for *Buffy* creator Joss Whedon.

# True to Life

No outline of vampire lore would be complete without indicating some
of the ways reality and legend have influenced one another over the
years. The two currents can be difficult to tell apart sometimes. In fact,
there's a reciprocal relationship between legendary and fictional vampires modeled after real people and real people, in turn, modeling their
behavior after fictional and legendary vampires.

**Dead Giveaway** _____

One of the more significant differences between vampires out of
    Slavic legend and vampires as they appeared in eighteenth-century
literature is that literary vampires tend to be worldly and sophisticated
travelers while the legendary types restrict their activities to their native
villages. The most famous literary vampire, Dracula, has it both ways by
traveling around with boxes of dirt from his homeland. In fact, the myth
that vampires must sleep near their native soil was invented by *Dracula*
author Bram Stoker, but has been ignored by most other authors of vampire tales. Chelsea Quinn Yarbro is a notable exception. She describes
one of her vampires, St. Germain as having shoes with hollow heels
filled with soil from his native France.

## Role Models

As you know, the fictional character, Dracula, is modeled in part after
previous fictional vampires and vampirelike figures, as well as the his-
torical/legendary fifteenth-century Slavic prince, Vlad Tepes. And
Dracula is not the only literary vampire based on a historical figure.
Joris Karl Huysman's novel, *La-bas* (1891), is based on the life of a

fifteenth-century French marshal who fought with Joan of Arc before succumbing to an uncontrollable urge to torture children.

Ersabet (Elizabeth) Bathory, a seventeenth-century Hungarian countess, became notorious for torturing young girls and drinking and bathing in their blood in the attempt to preserve her youth. The Blood Countess, as she was known, helped inspire Le Fanu's short story, "Carmilla," as well as a number of B-movies of the 1970s, including *Countess Dracula* (1971) and *The Bloody Countess* (1973).

Vlad Tepes and Elizabeth Bathory remain the most spectacular and well-known of the "real life" vampires. But there are many others, including Victor Ardisson, "the Vampire of Muy," who, in the late nineteenth century, became erotically infatuated with corpses he dug up from the cemetery, and Peter Kurten, "the Vampire of Dusseldorf," a blood-drinking serial killer and rapist of the 1920s and '30s.

Occasionally, actual human killers model their murderous behavior on fictional vampires. In 1959 in New York, for example, a young man committed several murders while dressed in a Dracula costume. At his murder trial, he told the court he was a vampire. In Florida in 1996, a group of teenage vampire fanatics who practiced blood rituals and role-playing fantasies wound up killing the parents of one of the group members in the wake of a vampire ceremony.

In the twentieth century, vampiric behavior was recognized as a clinical psychiatric problem, also called Renfield's syndrome, after Dracula's famous victim in Stoker's novel. Symptoms include vampiric fantasies, drinking blood, drinking one's own blood (auto-vampirism), *necrophilia*, *necrophagia*, *cannibalism*, and sadism. A number of cases have been described in psychiatric literature.

> **Stalk Talk**
>
> There's a fine line separating definitions of the words **necrophilia**, **necrophagia**, and **cannibalism**. Necrophilia is an erotic attraction to dead bodies. Necrophagia is the urge to eat carrion and decaying corpses. Cannibalism is the practice of eating members of one's own species. Necrophilia and necrophagia are psychopathic conditions. Human cannibalism may be a deranged act, may be culturally sanctioned, or may be a desperate act of survival.

## Living the Dream

More recently, vampirism has become less of a disease and more of an alternative lifestyle. Dozens of websites celebrate vampirism and night-clubs throughout the world offer the vampirically inclined the chance to mix and mingle with their own kind. Role-playing games like *Dungeons and Dragons* and *Vampire: The Masquerade* enable players to inhabit virtual realities rife with vampires and other supernatural beings. Performers of rock music and other celebrities have modeled their stage personas after vampires. Many vampire societies have cropped up in recent years devoted to studying lore, investigating the paranormal, and simply basking in the pale glow of the ever-changing vampire legend.

As old and dead as vampires may seem, few people appear to be getting tired of them. They remain the world's most stylish and intriguing supernatural horror. Vampires today hold as great an appeal as ever and one way or another, more and more people are getting bit.

## The Least You Need to Know

- Vampiric beings appear in the mythology of virtually every culture.

- The first beings to be called "vampires" come from Slavic legend sometime during the Middle Ages.

- Vampires became famous throughout Europe in the wake of scares in the Eastern countries in which dead bodies thought to be vampires were dug up and staked.

- Writers of the first vampire stories drew on conventions of gothic and Romantic literature.

- In the 1931 movie *Dracula*, Bela Lugosi provided the recognizable look that has been commonly associated with vampires ever since.

- Vampires of fiction are often modeled on "real" vampires and vice versa.

# Chapter 2

# Come-Back Kids

## In This Chapter

- ◆ All about undeath
- ◆ Burial and the dead
- ◆ The hereafter
- ◆ Zombies, mummies, Frankenstein, and vampires

As you know, most vampires—all typical vampires, at any rate—are undead. That is, they died, but they got over it, partly. It's kind of a special situation. Many authorities regard undeath as a curse. Some, however, have suggested that it's pretty cool. You live indefinitely, have special powers, and feel a sense of independence from authority figures such as God. It's a mode of existence unlike any other.

Undeath isn't something people have always been aware of. Even so, it wasn't just discovered one day like Greenland or hang-gliding. Instead you could say it ripened over the centuries like dark fruit hanging from the tree of imaginary experience—fruit that was nourished by the strangely mingled waters of folk superstition, Christianity, and science.

This chapter is about undeath and the fictive and legendary beings who exist in that state. And it's about the religious and philosophical currents that have made undeath an intriguing and meaningful concept to mere mortals.

# Dead but Undaunted

To understand undeath in all its undeathliness, it helps to know a few things about belief in the afterlife. Mystics, occultists, and religious types from all times and places have commonly regarded death not simply as the end of life, but also as the beginning of a new mode of existence. Death is a transition, a crossing over from one state of being to another. Death is like a doorway between two worlds. Many have believed it is possible to pass through in both directions.

## Return to Sender

Since everyone has to die sooner or later, it's comforting to think that death is not the end of our existence. But belief in the afterlife does more than help people deal with the fear of their own death, it also helps those left behind adjust to their loss. Death disrupts not only the lives of those who die, but also the lives of the living. Belief in existence after death helps the living cope with this disruption and the accompanying grief.

Belief in the afterlife forges important connections and continuities between the living and the dead. There's the notion, for example, that how you live your life will determine what happens to you when you die. And there's the idea that people who cared about us in life are still watching over us from the next world. Somehow or other, something about the world of the living sticks with the dead, and something about the dead sticks with the world of the living.

Many myths, legends, folktales, and religious teachings tell of living people who visit the world of the dead. Several well-known Greek myths, for example, describe journeys to the underworld. The myth of Orpheus and Eurydice, for example, tells how Orpheus went to Hades in order to bring back his wife, Eurydice, to the world of the living. The heroic wanderer, Odysseus, also visits the underworld in his travels.

Much more common, however, are stories about dead people who visit the world of the living. The dead may return as spirits, ghosts, angels, zombies, vampires, or—according to the doctrine of reincarnation—living people, animals, and plants. In fact, there are dozens of names for the various sorts of beings who return from the next world to ours. A fancy term that covers most of them is *revenant*. A revenant is a being that comes back among the living from the dead.

 **Stalk Talk**

**Revenants** are beings that return from the grave, including spirits, ghosts, certain angels, zombies, and vampires.

Revenants return for many reasons—to help the living or to cause trouble, to accomplish the bidding of some higher power, or just to hang around because they aren't ready to move on to the next world. Interestingly, it's these unready deadies who loom largest in much folk belief. These are dead people who don't belong with us living folks, but are here anyway.

These malingering dead are sort of like little kids who won't get on the bus on their first day of school. They're so anxious about their new situation that they can't make the journey. It's understandable that they might feel this way. The hereafter can be an intimidating, unfamiliar place, fraught with who-knows-what weighty responsibilities and pitfalls! Fortunately, most cultures have figured out a way to prevent dead souls from coming down with the newly dead jitters and from hanging around here where they don't belong: a good send-off!

## All the Dirt on Burial

Burial, of course, is not just the use of human bodies for landfill, but a sacred rite. A French anthropologist named Robert Hertz went to a lot of funerals in places like Southeast Asia and Madagascar and noticed that the sacred mortuary rites of many cultures were a lot like initiation rituals such as birth, coming-of-age, and marriage rites. Herz said that many cultures regard the dead as people who have reached a new stage within society—not so much losing their place among the living as taking their place among the ancestors.

This attitude toward death and burial is especially common in tightly knit tribal and village societies. It's less common in larger, more developed settings where God is usually considered a more powerful and important spiritual force than the tribal ancestors. In small, isolated communities around the world, including many in the Slavic countries, the dead have been considered part of the social structure of the living.

**Dead Giveaway**

French anthropologist Robert Herz has shown that many tribal and village cultures associate the physical process of the decomposition of a dead body with the spiritual process of leaving the living community and joining the community of the ancestors. To celebrate this physical/spiritual process, many cultures observe "double obsequies" in which funerals take place in two stages spaced apart by up to several years. In the first stage, the newly dead body is buried. In the second stage, the remains are dug up, cleaned, and buried again. The dry, hard remains of a decomposed body indicate that the spiritual transition of the dead individual has been completed. This practice has been widely reported among many Eastern European communities.

## Straighten Up and Die Right

Burial rites help make the link between life and death clear to the whole society so that everyone understands the pecking order and lives up—or dies up—to their responsibilities. As with any social situation, however, things can go wrong and people don't always do what they're supposed to. Married people sometimes cheat on their spouses, kids sometimes disobey their parents, dead people sometimes return from the grave. It's all part of life and death. Communal rituals, however, help prevent these problems from cropping up. So a good burial is intended to keep the dead in their place in more ways than one!

Many communal rituals serve the purpose of preventing social problems from developing. Marriage rites, for example, help prevent people from cheating on or abandoning their partners. Coming-of-age rituals help prevent young people from shirking the responsibilities of adulthood. Similarly, if you believe in social continuity between the living and the dead, you could say that burial rites serve the purpose of helping the newly dead adjust to their situation. When the dead are properly initiated into the afterlife, they are less likely to hang around and cause trouble for the living.

The problem remains, however, that if something goes wrong with a burial rite, it is thought that something might also go wrong with the transition from the world of the living to the world of the dead. People with botched burials, in other words, risk getting kicked out of the "no longer with us" club. They become the afterlife equivalent of social misfits.

### Grave Mistake

Whenever you bury someone, it's nice to give them a good send-off with flowers, singing, epitaphs, and some refreshments for the living. But make sure the person you're burying is really dead! Vampire buffs have speculated that premature burial may have contributed to vampire legend in two ways: 1) it supplies obvious motivation for the buried person to "return" to the living and 2) the dying struggles in the coffin of someone buried alive can leave their body in a ghastly, contorted position others may interpret as "vampirish" in the event that the body is dug up.

In Slavic countries, this belief came into play in many of the old vampire legends. The Slavs observed many superstitions about how people should be buried and what could happen if all the rules weren't followed. The transition to the next world gets derailed, the dead don't make the journey to the other world, and then they come back and make trouble for the living. Some scholars say that the Slavs inherited this idea from the ancient Greeks. In any case, similar beliefs are evident all over the world.

# Pick Your Poison

Speaking in very broad terms, there are three kinds of unearthly troublemakers, each recognized and feared by different kinds of people:

1. Misfit revenants feared most by tribal and village communities

2. Undead monsters, feared most by modern people since the nineteenth century

3. Diabolical demons, feared most by those who believe in God and his enemy, Satan

# Zombie ...

Some undead monsters—notably vampires and zombies—probably started out as misfit revenants before hunkering down into undeath. In fact, zombies are similar to vampires in many ways. According to Haitian tradition, zombies are dead people who have been reanimated by voodoo magic.

Voodoo is a religious cult that combines native beliefs with beliefs brought over from west Africa, together with a sprinkling of Catholicism thrown in for good measure. Like Slavic Europe, Haiti was a place where many belief systems combined. Christianity coexisted more or less uncertainly with the traditional beliefs of various groups. The word "zombie" comes from "nzambi," a Congolese word for spirit. Voodoo priests called bokors work the zombie-making magic. When a bokor turns a dead person into a zombie, the zombie becomes the bokor's slave.

**Cold Fact** _____

Zombies are popularly thought to have no will or consciousness of their own. This characteristic has made the zombie a recent focus of interest among analytic philosophers who are interested in the theoretical implications of life without consciousness. Some philosophers trace the roots of this issue back to Descartes, who suggested that animals lack consciousness, acting and reacting automatically on the basis of physical stimulus.

The people most susceptible to being made into zombies are misfits in society—those voted least likely to succeed in the afterlife. It is said that if you are lazy in life, you may be too lazy to make it quickly to the next world. If so, you may be targeted by a bokor who will perform a magic ritual to keep you among the living even though you have died.

# ... And Son

As you know, many zombies moved from Haiti to Hollywood, where they have frequently appeared in horror movies. One of the reasons zombies are popular as movie menaces is that, like vampires, they are undead. Undead beings are horrific in ways other revenants (like ghosts and spirits) are not. In addition to zombies and vampires, Frankenstein-type monsters and mummies are familiar undead faces, popular in movies as well as in books since the European Romantic period of the early nineteenth century.

The undead monsters we know from books and movies, however, are somewhat different from the misfit creatures who return to the world of the living according to the folklore of tribal and village societies. The misfit revenants of folklore, quite frankly, don't have the same dark, evil zing possessed by their more modern counterparts.

It's not that folklore misfit revenants aren't charming characters. No doubt they have many fine qualities that those of us living in the age of fast food and cyberspace will never know. But the fact is, for that deep down dark dirty glamorous evil, you have to look to the modern undead monsters—especially the vampire. The vampire and other undead creatures, unlike misfit revenants, bask in the demonic light of the diabolical, yet they are not exactly damned to hell as demons.

## Passing Fancy

It appears likely that misfit revenants became undead monsters only after isolated tribal and village communities came into contact with Christianity. Christianity supplies a conception of the afterlife that differs sharply from the community of ancestors' view. Under God, no one is a misfit. Everyone has somewhere to go when they die—either to Heaven or to Hell.

According to the Christian worldview, revenants from Hell are not mere misfits, but demons or damned human souls. Semi-Christian Slavic villages may have accepted this view only partly and may have attempted to reconcile it with native traditional burial practices. To an extent, Christianity may have cast the whole purpose of traditional burial rites into doubt. As burial rites became confused, there may have been an increase in mixed up send-offs and a resulting increase in potential revenants. And the status of these revenants may have been subject to confusion as well. Were they damned souls or ancestral misfits? Or both or neither?

In areas where mainstream Christianity took hold and dominated religious thinking, vampires and similar undead creatures weren't a real problem. Instead, demons, damnation, and witches were the predominate fear. In areas where Christianity is only one aspect of a larger religious mix, undeath makes sense as an imaginative expression of spiritual and religious uncertainty.

**Cold Fact** _____

Various ideas about the spiritual state of vampires have been put forward: They have no souls. They are damned. Their immortality is a spiritual curse, as is their inability to commune with humanity. All these things make sense, given a Christian belief in the immortal soul. Ironically, failing to believe in the immortal soul can be regarded as a spiritual curse as well, a curse to which scientific thinking has doomed many modern people!

## Crossing the Divide

The next step in the evolution of the undead vampire took place when isolated village communities (in which Christianity was still on its way) came into contact with a cynical civilized world (in which Christianity was just on its way out). Both cultures shared a borderline belief in Christianity, so both cultures were similarly predisposed to be fascinated by undeath as an in-between state that is not quite damnation and not quite mere misfit revenant.

It didn't take long before this fascination on the part of the civilized world found expression in the form of novels and plays and, later, in movies and TV shows. Vampires are special to the modern world. After all, civilized society has encountered countless unearthly beings in the process of absorbing (vampirizing?) traditional societies around the world, but none of these other creatures has held anything close to the fascination for civilized types that vampires hold. Because, in general, while many of us may be unsure about the whole God thing, we hear vampires speaking to us from beyond the grave.

# Monster Mash

Undead beings are especially intriguing to modern people in part because of the subtle influence of science on belief. Of course science doesn't recognize or support the existence of the undead, but it doesn't recognize or support the existence of any other unearthly state either, and that's the point. Science seems to have doomed mortals to wander the earth deprived of an unearthly state, despite the fact that our mortal condition often feels downright unearthly. So even though modern people who believe in science may not actually believe in undead creatures, the idea is compelling.

## Creating Monsters

Undead vampires are monsters, unlike revenants from Hell who are either damned souls or demons. The difference between demons and monsters is subtle but significant. Demons are *diabolical*, traditionally deriving their evil characteristics from their opposition to God. Monsters are *supernatural*, deriving their evil characteristics chiefly through their opposition to the natural order of things. Of course, the terms aren't mutually exclusive. Supernatural beings are often diabolical as well.

The difference between diabolical demons and supernatural monsters stems from a major historical development. At a pivotal time in history, mainstream European occult belief underwent a paradigm shift from an emphasis on demons to an emphasis on monsters. This was when empirical scientific thinking became widely accepted. It all fell into place by the eighteenth century during the period in European intellectual history known as the Enlightenment, or the Age of Reason. Vampires, in fact, got in beneath the ground floor of this development.

> **Stalk Talk**
>
> Diabolical and **supernatural** are terms that imply two different conceptions of evil. Diabolical evil opposes God while supernatural evil opposes nature. Demons are generally diabolical beings while monsters are generally supernatural. The distinction, however, is not sharp and absolute, since God and nature are often thought to be on the same side!

One of the main ideas that caught on during the Enlightenment was that humanity could improve itself through reason, overcoming weaknesses and limitations associated with "nature." Together with this rationalist hope arose a corresponding fear of exceeding natural limits. Supernatural undead monsters express this fear.

In contrast, prior to the Enlightenment, during the Middle Ages and later the Renaissance, human beings were considered basically complete and unchangeable by nature. But humans were faced with an important choice between the divine powers of good (God and the angels) or the infernal powers of evil (Satan and the demons). Those who chose to ally themselves with evil were witches and sorcerers, people who made bargains with demons and attempted to summon them through black magic.

### Grave Mistake

Don't assume that all cultures understand their vampires in relation to the traditional Judeo-Christian concept of God or the scientific concept of nature. Vampire Princess Miyu, currently popular in Japan and catching on in the rest of the world, occupies a reality derived in part from Buddhist belief. She and her kindred vampires guard the boundaries between the world of gods and demons and the world of humanity.

One important difference between demons and monsters is that monsters are more closely related to human beings and less directly concerned with God. Monstrous vampires are not typically considered the inhabitants of hell, but of the grave. They exist in a supernatural undead state rather than an infernal diabolical one. Remember, though, the legend of undead vampires grew in part out of legends of demons and witches, so the line distinguishing the two is often a blurry one.

## A Horror for Our Time

The idea of the undead vampire combines the sense of social alienation conveyed by misfit revenants with the sense of evil and depravity conveyed by demons. You could say they are so out there that even God doesn't care whether they go to Hell! Undeath, in short, is Hell for people who don't really believe in God. It's a perfect horrific state for creeped-out modern people.

Undeath resonates wickedly with the existential alienation of moderns who don't feel they belong. Like alienation, undeath is strange and unpleasant, but also special. In fact, the modern vampire is a lot like philosopher Friedrich Nietzsche's Ubermensch, or "superman," who lives apart from the herd because he is so much better than anyone else is.

**Grave Mistake**

One of the most common misconceptions about vampires is that the Romanian word nosferatu means "not dead." Not true. It means plague-carrier. The term is occasionally applied to vampires, most notably in the classic German silent film, *Nosferatu, eine Symphonie des Grauens* (1922).

# Modern Monsters

At the risk of beating an undead horse, it should be stressed that the idea of undeath is a modern one. It originated in the nineteenth century after science had started to make people feel distant from God and when the Romantic period started to make people feel distant from science. The fact that vampires go back at least to the Middle Ages tends to obscure the relatively recent beginnings of the idea of undeath, but undeath is a modern concept nonetheless.

# Stay-Fresh Packaging

Undeath is a physical state that science can't explain, so no one could imagine it before science came along to fail to explain it. The physical— as opposed to the spiritual—aspects of undead creatures sets them apart. You could say fear of the undead is part of an obsession with physical reality that is generated and fueled by science. In a scientific world, spiritual beings just don't matter that much. So, if you want to scare people as an unearthly creature in a scientific world, you'd better come equipped with a physical body!

Take mummies, for example. Few creatures, living, dead, or otherwise, are as ancient as mummies. But no one ever imagined a mummy stomping down the street wrapped in its bandages in pursuit of love or revenge before the nineteenth century. Of course, the fact that British archeologists and others started gathering up Egyptian mummies and bringing them to museums at this time contributed to the undead mummy mystique. Science not only brought the mummies to the civilized world, it also made them scary.

**Dead Giveaway** _____

Mummies can be found in Hollywood movies, ancient tombs, and in nature as well. A mummy is any dead body that has been preserved from decay, either deliberately through embalming, or accidentally, as when a body is preserved in ice or in tar pits. The ancient Egyptians preserved the bodies of their rulers as mummies, apparently in the belief that this would enable them to live on in the afterlife. Potions supposedly concocted from mummy's flesh were sold in Europe for magical and medicinal purposes well into the Renaissance period. In the nineteenth century, when European explorers began collecting mummies for museum exhibits, spiritualists began spreading stories of ancient curses protecting the mummy's tomb. Hollywood has picked up on these stories in a big way.

## Back to the Drawing Board

But of course, the most obvious scientific embodiment of undeath is Frankenstein's monster. He shows most clearly that undeath was created in a laboratory. As you may remember from the previous chapter, *Frankenstein* is the monstrous progeny of British author Mary Shelley, who wrote the novel as part of the famous ghost-story contest involving Lord Byron and John Polidori in 1816 in Italy. (Polidori wrote *The Vampyre* for this contest.)

Frankenstein's monster is put together with the parts of various newly dead corpses that Dr. Frankenstein digs up from the cemetery. The creature appears normal in every way, but he doesn't quite fit in. Shelley's novel has a lot to say about what it's like to be a monstrous outsider—lonely, misunderstood, feared, and despised. The cold, scientific processes that brought him to life and account for his existence aren't enough for him. He wants to be part of the human community, but he doesn't belong. The tale, of course, has become a classic horror story for many of the same reasons that have made vampires popular.

## The Least You Need to Know

- ◆ Undeath is not quite damnation and not quite merely failing to fit in.

- ◆ Undead creatures come from regions where mixed belief predominates and Christianity is only partially accepted.

♦ Vampires, zombies, mummies, and Frankenstein's monster are all undead creatures that have become familiar from books and movies.

♦ Undeath resonates with many modern spiritual problems, including the problem of not believing in spirituality!

# Chapter 3

# Blood Types

## In This Chapter

- ◆ Vampirology
- ◆ Vampire classification
- ◆ Spirit vampires and monstrous vampires
- ◆ Human vampires and alien vampires

It's hard to be a vampire watcher if you don't know the rules, and few creatures are governed and explained by more rules than vampires are. In fact, new rules are enacted all the time. Practically every time another pulp novelist writes another vampire thriller, he or she invents a whole additional set. It's getting so a vampire can't even brush its fangs after a meal without having to go through some special occult procedure.

Will sunlight kill it? Will a cross frighten it away? Can it survive on animal blood or must it have human victims? Not only do different authorities say different things about these matters, but different vampires within a single story or virtual world may obey different rules. Keeping up with all of them can be a bewildering task, made all the more challenging because different sources often use different terminology.

And of course, the different kinds of vampires keep multiplying. Demonic vampires, psychic vampires, astral vampires, changed alive vampires—each has its own particular characteristics.

# Bloody Study

*Vampirology*, the "science" of vampires, is a popular subject these days. There are lots of folks out there working out the rules of vampire behavior, schemes of vampire classification, essential vampire characteristics, and the history and structure of vampire society. As more and more vampires arrive on the scene, new theories emerge to explain them.

### Stalk Talk

**Vampirology,** the study of vampires, is a subdiscipline of demonology, which is older and has had more practitioners than its bloodsucking subset. Unlike demonology, which once enjoyed a certain degree of official support from the Church, vampirology has no major institutional underpinnings outside of fan clubs and research societies.

## It Takes All Kinds

People who study vampires are about as various as vampires themselves. Many vampirologists are occultists, interested in explaining vampires in terms of a broad system of supernatural or paranormal beliefs. For example, there was Franz Hartmann (1838–1912), who explained vampires in a way that makes sense given the peculiar metaphysical principles of Theosophy. (You can read more about Hartmann later in this chapter, and also in Chapter 9.) Other vampirologists are scholars like the eccentric Montague Summers (1880–1948, no relation to Buffy Summers!), who collected and wrote exhaustively on everything he could find on the subject.

Vampirologists may be fans of popular culture, crime buffs, psychologists, or vampire wanna-bes. All it takes is a little imagination and an avid interest in the subject to start collecting and spinning off ideas. In fact, many of the best vampirologists are writers of fiction—people who know how to make the imaginary seem real.

It's common in most vampire stories, whether in written form, in movies, or on TV, to devote some time to explaining what vampires are, how they came to be that way, what their powers and weaknesses are, and so on. Many stories, of course, stick more or less to the traditional and legendary views. But there's plenty of innovation as well. Some of the most thought-provoking vampirological ideas can be found in stories. Many more are set forth in role-playing games, where vampires inhabit virtual worlds.

The problem is, people have dreamed up so many different kinds of vampires over the years that it's difficult for them all to coexist in the same reality. Thus vampirology is not a hard science, but an attempt to impose order on legends, superstitions, speculations, and strange twists of fate. As a result, classifying vampires is a little bit like mapping your nightmares. Wrong turns seem to come with the territory. Nevertheless, if you steep yourself in vampire lore long enough, certain patterns begin to emerge. You get a sense of the history, the basic varieties, and the possibilities for new kinds. Either that or you go absolutely nuts!

**Dead Giveaway** _____

Demonology was recognized as a serious study during the Middle Ages, with books on the subject written by experts such as priests. One such book is the now infamous *Malleus Maleficarum* (Hammer of Witches). Written in 1484 by two friars, this book was sanctioned in 1486 by Pope Innocent VIII and was subsequently used as a guide by members of the Inquisition to identify, torture, and execute witches. It also describes some of the demons witches supposedly summoned, but the real emphasis was on ferreting out human enemies of the Church. Vampires as such are not discussed in the *Malleus*, although there is information on the vampirelike demons, the succubae and incubae. The first book on vampirology treats the Greek vampire, the vrykolakas. This was written in 1645 by a cleric in the Greek Church named Leo Allatius.

## Cloudy Concepts

A long-standing point of confusion in understanding vampires is the demon-vampire question. Vampires are often defined as a particular kind of demon. At the same time, they are often distinguished from demons. Most fans of *Buffy the Vampire Slayer*, for example, will tell you that demons and vampires are different creatures with separate sets of characteristics, even though they may be in league together. Consult folklorist Montague Summers, on the other hand, or psychologist Ernest Jones, and the distinction sometimes breaks down. These guys tend to ignore the difference between demonic and nondemonic vampires.

And there are other gray areas. Are all vampires undead? Can they be living creatures? Is it possible to be born a vampire? Can they be ghosts? Can they be aliens from another planet? The short answer to these questions is that the familiar mainstream vampire inherited from Slavic legend and popularized in books and movies is the undead, reanimated corpse of a former human being—not born that way, not from planet Drakulon, not simply alive, nor a ghost, nor a demon. In general, this traditional undead vampire has awakened the most interest, attention, and terror.

The longer answer is that vampire lore is living mythology. People continue to use the vampire concept in new ways, combining it with new ideas and incorporating it into new realities. So to really understand vampires, it helps to see them in various contexts, not just stomping around the Transylvanian castle or sleeping in the coffin that opens from the inside.

## Leagues of Their Own

Vampires can be divided conveniently into four main groups based on what sort of creature they are:

1. Spirit vampires

2. Monstrous vampires

3. Human vampires, and

4. Alien vampires

Remember, these distinctions aren't written in stone and not every vampirologist recognizes these terms. What's more, certain vampire types may straddle two or more categories. For the present purpose of classification, however, it makes sense to see spirits, monsters, humans, and aliens as different groups, each capable of sending delegates to the United Vampire Assembly.

Within each of these main groups exist several other vampire varieties. Monstrous vampires, for example, include the undead, the changed alive, and the born vampires. You'll see as we go along.

### Grave Mistake

Don't assume that all vampire buffs use the same terminology or interpret terms the same way. They don't. People use the term, *psychic vampire*, for example, to mean different things. It refers to the disembodied spirit or astral body of a living person when this spirit is sent out to menace others. It also refers to living people who drain others emotionally.

# Bad Spirits

Spirit vampires have many significant advantages over the other kinds. They are not weighted down with physical bodies, which means that they can't be killed with a stake to the heart. In fact, many say they can't be killed at all, though some claim they can be destroyed or controlled through magic.

Of course, not all spirits are spirit vampires. Spirits are any creatures that can exist without physical bodies. They are often thought capable of passing through material barriers, appearing or disappearing at will, and floating or flying through the air. They are often considered immortal and indestructible. Some have the power to take possession of material bodies, either living or dead, and to appear in various forms. Spirits can be human souls or divine or demonic powers. Spirit vampires, then, can be either bloodsucking human ghosts or bloodsucking demons.

## Shady Characters

Ghostly vampires are the vampiric spirits or souls of human beings. They may be the spirits of dead or living people. The belief that all human beings have spirits or souls is common to many cultures. These spirits separate from the body at death. After separating from the body, souls ordinarily depart from our physical world to inhabit a realm appropriate to their kind. Sometimes, however, they remain on Earth as ghosts and, in rare cases, as vampiric ghosts.

Vampiric spirits may be capable of separating from the body before death as well. Many cultures recognize shamans, who are medicine men or women capable of sending their spirits out on mystical journeys. Typically, these journeys are voyages of discovery. Sometimes, however, disembodied spirits go out to seek revenge. Living people who send out their spirits on evil errands are commonly identified as witches. Their spirits, however, are occasionally identified as vampires.

### Stalk Talk

**Astral vampires** are the disembodied spirits of living people who send them out to prey on others. The phenomenon of astral vampirism was offered as an explanation for the Slavic vampire scare by occultist Franz Hartmann.

The occultist Franz Hartmann set forth a version of the idea that living people could have vampire spirits. He called them *astral vampires* and he suggested that the astral vampire phenomenon actually accounts for the Slavic belief in undead vampires. Here's how his thinking goes:

The Slavic vampire scares generally took place during times of plague, when it was necessary to bury the dead quickly to control the contagion. Under these circumstances, people were sometimes buried alive. To survive in the grave, these people sent out their spirits, or astral projections, to procure nourishment from living people. Instead of visiting the Quickie Mart, they visited friends and family and sucked their blood. In this way, Hartmann proposed one incredible superstition as a way of clearing up another!

## Hell's Angels

Occultists and theologians have offered various theories about whether, how, and when divine and demonic spirits were created. Some say they are uncreated, existing for all time. Others say God created them as angels, some of whom fell from grace to become demons. Others say all spirits—including evil spirits—represent a higher, evolved form of human consciousness.

Though the word "demon" can be used to refer to the spirits of all cultures, demons have figured with special prominence in the Judeo-Christian tradition, which generally regards demons as fallen angels. As fallen angels, demons typically reside in Hell when they are not visiting the human world to tempt or terrorize ordinary mortals. Demons can also be understood independently of the Judeo-Christian worldview as malevolent, nonhuman spirits.

### Cold Fact

Some demons of the Judeo-Christian tradition started out as gods worshiped by rival religions. Baal, for example, was originally an ancient Phoenician sun god. His cult spread and became a threat to the early Jews who claimed Baal worship involved sex and child sacrifice. By the time the Christian gospels were written, the god Baal is known as Beelzebub, the prince of demons.

In the history of the world's folklore, demonic spirits predate vampires. Some of these demons, however, resemble vampires so closely that they have come to be called vampires. Prominent examples are the demons of seduction: the incubae (singular, incubus) and succubae (singular, succubus). Incubae and succubae, male and female demons respectively, were known throughout Europe and recognized by the Church during the Middle Ages. They appeared at night to have sex with people as they slept. They accounted for wet dreams, nightmares, and unexplainable pregnancies. They did not suck blood, but they did leave their victims feeling drained, used, exhausted, and sinful.

*Incubae*, *succubae*, and related demons were known by many different names throughout Europe. In Eastern Europe, they were commonly known as *moras*. Mora lore merged with vampire lore in some regions, so moras were sometimes considered vampires.

### Stalk Talk

**Incubae** and **succubae** are demons known to the European Middle Ages who stole in upon sleeping men and women by night and had sex with them. "Incubae" and "succubae" are Latin terms, but these demons were also known by other names specific to various countries, including "**mora**," a term used in Eastern Europe where the concept merged with vampire lore. Slavic legend sometimes distinguished between living and undead moras.

In *The Vampire Chronicles*, Anne Rice declares that vampires are actually cases of demonic possession. In this world, the demon Amel took control of the soul and body of the Egyptian Queen, Akasha, who became the first vampire. When Akasha was killed, the demon moved on to a new body. If the demon is destroyed, all the vampires will die.

# Meet the Monsters

Unlike the demonic vampire, the monstrous vampire is not a spirit but instead a former human being who has been changed into an evil anomaly. The monstrous vampire includes the traditional vampire of European legend and literature—Dracula and all vampires like him. Monstrous vampires may be undead like Dracula, changed into vampires while alive, or born vampires. Traditionally, undead vampires have received most of the attention, but the others are interesting, too.

## Beyond the Grave

Undead vampires, of course, are more than just parasitic bloodsuckers in human form. They have that special something, a macabre, supernatural quality that sets them apart. The fear of getting drained like a strawberry daiquiri is only one aspect of the terror we feel in their presence. The other part of it is the creepier fear of dying and awakening again as monsters ourselves.

As cool as this undead threat clearly is, some people get tired of the musty cobwebs-and-tombstone ambiance that usually comes with the undead vampire. Few people spend much time in graveyards these days, so vampire fans are finding it easier to relate to vampires who are less coffin-bound. These are the born vampires and the changed alive.

## Still Ticking

Some sources say that it is possible to be born a living vampire. According to Slavic legend, the child of two illegitimate parents can fall into this category. According to more recent lore, you can be born a vampire by having vampire parents or by being the offspring of a woman who was bitten by a vampire while pregnant. This distinction, for example, figures into the plot of the action vampire thriller, *Blade* (1998), starring Wesley Snipes, based on the Marvel comic book series, *Blade the Vampire Hunter*. In the movie, born and undead vampires vie with one another for power.

**Grave Mistake**

Many sources suggest vampires can reproduce pretty much like ordinary biological creatures—by having sex. According to Gypsy lore, for example, vampires can mate with human mortals. And of course, many vampire films portray vampires as lustful. This view, however, is not the last word. Vampires have their own unique method of propagating their kind that satisfies their particular cravings like nothing else. Many—including vampire author Anne Rice—suggest vampires are not particularly interested in sex.

Some say human beings may change into vampires without dying first. As with undead vampires, changed-alive vampires typically get that way after being bitten by another vampire. Or there may be some other supernatural explanation. Medical explanations—including genetic mutation and blood disease—are increasingly popular, following the lead of Richard Matheson's novel, *I Am Legend* (1954), in which blood-infecting bacteria turns people into vampires.

# Vampires Are Us

Many vampire authorities stress that vampires are not human. Often, this point needs to be made precisely because vampires look and act very human and, in most cases, used to be human. In the novel *Dracula*, for example, when Arthur confronts his undead fiancée Lucy, he wants to embrace her. Dr. Van Helsing reminds him, for his own safety, that she is no longer human. Vampires are often so seductive that their potential victims stand a better chance of survival if they realize what inhuman monsters they are up against.

The fact is, however, that a large part of the appeal and the terror vampires hold over human beings has to do with their tendency to blur the distinction between human and nonhuman nature. In many respects, vampires are all too human. They are needy, vulnerable, strong-willed, proud, deceitful individuals. They have feelings, preferences, and a sense of humor. If they weren't undead, (or ghostly, or alien) they would be almost impossible to distinguish from human beings who happen to go around sucking blood.

> **Cold Fact** _____
>
> Vampire stories typically use supernatural characteristics to indicate that vampires are not human. Dracula, for example, cannot be seen in a mirror, can change into a bat, a wolf, or mist, and can crawl head-first down the sides of buildings. These features distinguish him from humanity more than many of his more striking traits, including his deviousness, cruelty, bloodsucking, and even his aversion to garlic!

And actually, yes, there are human beings who go around sucking blood. What's more, there are human beings who don't suck blood, but resemble vampires in other respects. Some of these people consider themselves to be actual vampires. Others do not, but have been considered vampires by others. As I said, the distinction is a blurry one. And the lines can be drawn and crossed in many ways. It may help, though, to remember that human vampires are not demons, not aliens, and are nonsupernatural.

Here's a list that will give you a sense of the range of human beings who have been referred to as vampires:

◆ Figures from history and legend said to have habitually drunk human blood, most notably Prince Vlad Dracul Tepes and Countess Elizabeth Bathory.

◆ Famous psychotic serial killers who fetishized the blood of their victims, including Victor Ardisson and Peter Kurten.

◆ People who drink their own blood or the blood of consenting donors because it gives them a pleasurable feeling of excitement. Some of these people have been diagnosed as neurotic or even psychotic. Others are apparently emotionally healthy and lead otherwise normal lives.

◆ People who embrace kinky alternative lifestyles, go to "vampire" clubs, wear fangs and (sometimes) drink human blood—all in good clean fun.

◆ Metaphorically, anyone who uses, manipulates, or drains others. Extortionists, for example, are sometimes called vampires. Also heartless, seductive women were commonly called "vamps" during the first half of the twentieth century. Remember the song, "Hard-hearted Hannah, the vamp of Savannah, GA"?

◆ People afflicted with a rare genetic disease known as porphyria, the symptoms of which include acute sensitivity to light. This disease has been offered as an explanation of how vampire legends got started.

> **Grave Mistake**
>
> Some porphyria patients in recent years have felt embarrassed and inconvenienced as a result of the highly speculative theoretical link between the disease and vampirism. Don't assume porphyria patients are vampires. They're not.

## Worlds Apart

Finally (almost), we come to vampires from outer space. Why not? Check out the spaghetti sci-fi horror flick, *Planet of the Vampires* (1965), directed by Mario Bava. This film is actually better than you might think! Or try *Lifeforce* (1984), based on the novel, *The Space Vampires* (1976) by Colin Wilson.

The most famous alien vampire is Vampirella, the curvaceous femme fatale from the planet Drakulon. She first appeared in 1969 as a comic book heroine created by Forest J. Ackerman, an obvious take-off of another comic-book character, the French Barbarella, created by Jean-Claude Forest.

## Going Bats

And of course, there's still one more kind of vampire that is neither demonic, monstrous, human, nor alien: the vampire bat. This bat, *Desmodus rotundis*, lives in Central and South America. It is a small flying rodent that feeds off the blood of larger mammals by nicking them and lapping with their tongues. Their saliva contains a strong anti-coagulant for optimum flow.

Like the legendary creatures they are named after, vampire bats hunt at night, often preying on their victims while they are asleep. Vampire bats are small, so they rarely kill those they feed off—usually pigs, horses, or cattle, though they have been known to bite people. Although it is not found in Slavic countries, the vampire bat got its common name in the eighteenth century, around the time when Slavic undead vampires were making their mark on the rest of the world. They are hideous in appearance; not even the babies are cute!

**Grave Mistake**

Slavic legend does not say that vampires can morph into vampire bats. Vampire bats got their name only after Slavic vampire legends became widely known. In fact, they are found only in the New World, not in Europe. Traditional vampires more commonly changed into wolves. Bram Stoker has Dracula changing into a large bat, but does not specify what kind. Vampire bats, in fact, are small, except for an extinct, prehistoric species named, appropriately enough, *Desmodus draculae*.

## The Least You Need to Know

◆ Vampirology is the ongoing "science" of vampire history, description, and classification.

◆ Spirit vampires are disembodied predators including ghost vampires and demon vampires.

◆ Monstrous vampires are nonhuman vampires with bodies, including undead, changed alive, and born vampires.

◆ Human vampires are nonsupernatural and include any and all of the many different sorts of people who call themselves vampires or have been so called by others.

◆ Alien vampires appear mostly in comic books and movies merging sci-fi and horror.

# Chapter 4

# Deep Feelings at Stake

## In This Chapter

- ◆ Relating to vampires from personal experience
- ◆ Vampirism as unwanted, unrequited, and parasitic love
- ◆ Vampirism as risque sexuality and as bereaved love
- ◆ Vampirism as political corruption and social evil

People relate to vampires on all kinds of levels. Lots of us get vicarious thrills from watching them in films and on TV and reading about them in books. Many people identify with vampires, dressing up in vampire attire and going out to mingle in nightclubs with other children of the night, or assuming vampire personas as they log on to Internet chatrooms to indulge in some dark and colorful group fantasies. And yes, in rare cases, people imitate vampires in psychotic and criminal ways.

We all have our own levels of interest in vampires, whether mere casual curiosity or feverish fixation. But regardless of whether the interest is idle or intense, people relate to vampires because vampires relate to us. Their nature and characteristics are reflections of our own. In understanding them we develop a better understanding of ourselves.

Often, vampires supply astonishingly apt representations of complex feelings, ideas, and interpersonal situations. These feelings, ideas, and situations can be both subtle and important, and difficult to understand and talk about. Indeed, it's possible to go through life with problems you didn't know you had but which suddenly become clear to you after an encounter with a vampire. This chapter talks about some common but vexing problems that vampires can help us understand. In the process, it suggests why so many mere mortals can relate to vampires so easily.

# Pangs and Fangs

At one time or another, everyone experiences sharp, painful, yet poignant and bittersweet pangs in life. Sometimes we feel victimized by vampiric forces beyond our control. Other times we feel it's our own fault and, like a staked vampire, we got what was coming to us. And at other times, like a vampire killer, we feel we must make some dire sacrifice to rid ourselves of attachments that, though dear to us, are harmful. In all cases, the vampire concept often captures the experience perfectly.

**Grave Mistake** _____

Don't get sucked into believing that vampires and vampire killers are polar opposites. Usually they have strong affinities with one another—similar characters and characteristics. Often they are rivals for the heart of the victim. Sometimes they are even blood relations. Blade, the vampire hunter from the Marvel comic and the movie, is the son of a vampire, as is the dhampir, a supernaturally-endowed vampire killer from Gypsy legend.

## De-Crypting the Codes

From the victim's point of view it's all very simple. There's a mysterious magnetism. Then there's the bite. Then the sucking. Something dies; something lives on. There's a change, a burial and then finally, when you think it's all over and forgotten, there's an uncanny return.

This mysterious vampire magnetism stands for any dangerous desire you feel for something that can hurt you. The bite and the sucking are the unfortunate consequences. Death, survival, and change are how you respond to those consequences. Burial is putting the experience behind you. The return is what you can't put behind. You still desire; you still risk dire consequences. And you risk becoming so embroiled in your dangerous desire that you turn into a vampire yourself!

This scenario is incredibly similar from the vampire's point of view. Instead of magnetism, the dangerous desire is bloodlust. Instead of the bite and the sucking, the consequence is a stake through the heart.

Finally, from the perspective of the vampire killer, there's only painful awareness and grim resolve to do what must be done. Poetic, huh? Creepy, too. That's life. If you've ever wanted something and gone after it only to have it turn around and bite you—or to find that *you* have bitten *it*—or decided that, at all costs, the biting must stop—then you know what I'm talking about.

It seems that whatever people become most afraid of and most strangely attracted to stalks the earth as a vampire in our collective imaginations. Vampires stand for things that people love and hate simultaneously, and they stand for the problem of being torn by the pull of powerful, contradictory feelings. This is why so many people can relate to vampires even though they may fear them at the same time.

### Cold Fact

Norine Dresser, a teacher of folklore at California State in Los Angeles prepared a questionnaire and administered it to 574 high school and college students in the mid-1980s asking whether they believed it possible that real vampires exist. Twenty-seven percent answered yes. Speaking of real vampires, an article appearing in *The New York Times* in November 2000 quoted an estimate that about 1,000 vampire "lifestylists" (people who dress up like vampires and go out to nightclubs) are active in New York City.

## Common Blood

Vampires and vampirism can function as an imaginary or psychological expression of what can go wrong when our most powerful human desires go haywire. They offer an explanation or warning about what can happen when people's desires are frustrated, or when people give in to their dangerous desires despite the dire consequences. We all want love, life, and power. In wanting these things, we all risk hate, death, and exploitation. To understand vampires is to understand this predicament.

Not all intense desires, however, are captured equally well by the vampire concept. If you can't go bowling often enough, for example, and you risk messing up your life because you're a bowl-aholic, the vampire concept may not speak to your problem in a very compelling way. The same thing holds if you like pickled herring more than you should. There's just not a lot of supernatural mileage in these problems. That's why few people wake up in the middle of the night screaming from nightmares of being pursued by the evil pickled herring demon!

Interpersonal problems, however, are another story. Family problems, love problems, problems with society; these issues can get so creepy that only vampires can do justice to them. A vampire's supernatural characteristics often symbolize common, mundane, interpersonal problems—problems that can feel very creepy but are actually familiar and all-too ordinary.

### Dead Giveaway

Vampires and vampirelike creatures from the folklore of many cultures often represent terrifying images of family relationships gone wrong. Many cultures recognize bloodthirsty mother figures who prey on children. Examples include the empusa from ancient Greece, the strix from ancient Rome, the langsuyar from Maylasia, the cihuateteo from Mexico, the aswang from the Philippines, and the ancient Babylonian demon known as Lilith. Many of these legendary demons were said to have started off as human women with children who died and dealt with their bereavement by attacking other people's babies. Horrific father figures are common in folklore, too, but these usually take the form of flesh-eating ogres rather than bloodsucking vampires.

The creepiness of many ordinary problems results at least partly from the tendency of good things and rotten things to get muddled up together. This often happens in close interpersonal relationships—good and bad mingle and blend like the blood of a vampire and its victim. And like problems involving an inextricable mix of good and bad, vampires are themselves evil creatures with powerful attractions.

# Fatal Attractions

While vampires evoke many emotions, one of the things they stand for most powerfully is dangerous sexual attraction. Often this connection is pretty obvious, as when a victim is sexually attracted to, and then killed by, a vampire. There's nothing too subtle about death by hickey. But more subtly, vampires also represent things that can go wrong with human love and sex in everyday life.

One of the things about love that really bites is unrequited love. If you love someone who doesn't love you back, that person can seem inhuman. Conversely, being pursued by some creep also bites. If you want someone to leave you alone who insists on following you around, that person can seem inhuman. Anyone who is either too aggressive or too cold in love can seem—and may even feel—at least a little vampiric.

## Prowlers

Lot's of people—typically guys—crave sex but have a hard time connecting emotionally with those who attract them. They can seem pretty creepy to anyone they're interested in. They lurk, they leer, they may even stalk. Powerful as their feelings are, they may not want others to know about them. Like vampires avoiding sunlight or ducking under their capes, they try to avoid detection.

Obviously, these people are uncomfortable with their feelings and uncertain about how to deal with them. What may, in fact, be a healthy sex drive may feel wrong, strange, and scary. A good illustration of this problem in vampire terms can be found in the book for young adults, *Thirsty* (Candlewick Press, 1998) by Matthew T. Anderson, in which the challenges of going through puberty with all its changes and longings are symbolized as the supernatural problem of becoming a vampire.

**Dead Giveaway** _____

A Fool there was and he made his prayer
(Even as you and I)
To rag and a bone and a hank of hair
(We call her the woman who did not care)
But the fool he called her his lady fair
(Even as you and I!)
...
The Fool was stripped to his foolish hide
(Even as you and I)
Which she might have seen when she threw him aside—
(But it isn't on record the lady tried)
So some of him lived but the rest of him died—
(Even as you and I!)
—from "The Vampire," by Rudyard Kipling

## Femme-pires

Strangely, it's often hard to tell who's the vampire and who's the victim. While, from one perspective, guys who go after women who aren't interested in them can seem like vampires, from another perspective, it's the uninterested women who are vampires—or "vamps" as they were commonly referred to early in the twentieth century.

The analogy between unrequited love objects and vampires is at the heart of a poem by Rudyard Kipling called "The Vampire." There's nothing remotely supernatural about the poem, just an attractive, insensitive woman and a poor shmoe who can't help trying to get her to like him. But the similarities between vampires and uncaring females is made clear.

When someone you're interested in doesn't respond to you, they can seem as cold as death, yet not dead. And they have a strange power over you. Of course, they may not particularly want to suck your blood, but it can feel like they are draining you somehow. Vampires, like unrequited love objects, may have a powerful sexual attraction but are not themselves predominantly interested in love or sex. Getting involved with either one can be dangerous and painful.

As in any good vampire story, the situation can keep you guessing about what is real and what isn't. In many relationships between vampire and victim, it can be unclear whether the vampire is really evil or whether the victim is imagining things. The same can hold true in unrequited love. Maybe you've fallen under the spell of the cruelest person on earth, or maybe it's all in your mind.

**Cold Fact**

People who are paranoid often think they are being persecuted. On the other hand, people who are persecuted often get told they are just paranoid! It's often hard to tell a real victim from someone who is confused. Uncertainty about whether a victim's perceptions can be trusted is a standard suspense-producing feature in countless tales of mystery and horror, including vampire stories.

Maybe you've built up false, imaginary ideals about someone you're crazy about. If that person doesn't live up to those ideas, you may think he or she is undergoing sudden, mysterious changes. They may become as vicious as a wolf, as flighty and elusive as a bat, or not quite all there, like mist. (Similarly, Dracula turns into these things in Bram Stoker's novel.)

# Playing With Matches

In addition to unrequited love, vampires also symbolically express the problems of ...

1. Exploitive relationships in which one of the partners is a user.

2. Sexual taboos, in which both lovers are involved in kinky doings not widely accepted by society.

3. Bereaved love, in which one of two lovers has died.

## Used Goods

Sadly, people in relationships sometimes exploit one another for all kinds of reasons. People who use their partners are, like vampires, human parasites. They demand things that they do not give in return.

Love and support, for example, are basic components of any good love match, but when these things only flow in one direction, one partner gets drained sooner or later.

Users in a relationship can be overbearing, demanding, tyrannical masters. To their more submissive partners it can seem like they have superhuman strength, much as vampires possess. Or they can be sneaky, subtle, and deceptive. They are often hard to detect. They don't see themselves for what they are, like vampires that leave no reflection in the mirror. A number of self-help books have been written comparing troubled love matches to the vampire/victim relationship. Take a look at Chapter 15 to find out more on the subject.

## Taboo Turn-Ons

Vampires also symbolize sexual taboos. *Dracula*, remember, was written in England during the Victorian period, notorious as being a sexually repressed time. Sex was not a polite topic of conversation. As people repressed their sexuality, sexual fantasies rose to the surface in bizarre, sometimes disturbing ways. Few scenes out of literature are as disturbing as the scene in *Dracula* when Arthur drives a stake through his undead fiancée on the night they were to be married. It's horrible yet distinctly erotic.

### Dead Giveaway

The Thing in the coffin writhed; and a hideous, blood-curdling screech came from the opened red lips. The body shook and quivered and twisted in wild contortions; the sharp white teeth champed together till the lips were cut, and the mouth was smeared with crimson foam. But Arthur never faltered. He looked like a figure of Thor as his untrembling arm rose and fell, driving deeper and deeper the mercy-bearing stake, whilst the blood from the pierced heart welled and spurted up around it. His face was set, and high duty seemed to shine through it; the sight gave us courage, so that our voices seemed to ring through the little vault.

And then the writhing and quivering of the body became less, and the teeth ceased to champ, and the face to quiver. Finally it lay still. The terrible task was over.

—Lucy the vampire getting staked in *Dracula* (1897)

Readers have been debating about what this gruesome scene might symbolize ever since it was written. A Victorian fear of sex? A blend of lust and hatred toward women? A breaking down of conventional sexual barriers? (Lucy is "set free" from the curse of being a vampire.) Some readers have suggested that Lucy the vampire seems to enjoy being staked. If so, the scene represents the ultimate sadomasochistic fantasy.

Vampirism can symbolize every and any form of sexuality that is frowned on by mainstream society. Homosexuality is a recurrent theme in much vampire literature and film where vampire/homosexual analogies range from graphically obvious to scarcely perceptible. Vampires, like gays and lesbians, are different from most people and bond in slightly different ways. They are commonly misunderstood and feared by others. As a result, some homosexuals, like most vampires, have had to be secretive, revealing their true natures only to a select few.

For decades, homosexuality, like vampirism, has been wrongly regarded as a social ill, a kind of contagion that can spread to infect "normal" people. This idea resonates with the familiar notion that vampirism spreads from the vampire to his or her victim. Drug use, incidentally, is regarded in this way today and some vampire tales have picked up on this. In the movie *The Lost Boys* (1987), for example, Michael Emerson is pressured by some vampires into drinking bottled blood, loses touch with reality, gets hooked, and becomes a vampire himself.

> **Cold Fact**
>
> Not all homosexuals are open about their sexuality. Similarly, not all those who dress up as vampires and go out to nightclubs are open about their lifestyle. Much as homosexuals who go public say they are "out of the closet," lifestyle vampires who are open about their vampiric pursuits say they are "out of the coffin"!

## Love and Death

As you can see, vampirism resonates strongly with all kinds of problems pertaining to love and sex: unwanted love, unrequited love, parasitic love, taboo love, misunderstood love. And there's another important problem: bereaved love. Whenever love and death come together, vampires are likely to appear.

If you love someone who dies, it's not easy to stop loving them. Your undying love, like a vampire's immortality, can be both a curse and blessing. You may have longings and fantasies for your loved one to come back to you—and perhaps take you with them. Or you may feel distressed by the hold they continue to have on you, especially since you no longer have a hold on them. This can make it difficult or even impossible to carry on with life. You can feel drained of energy and disenchanted with the human world.

To get on with your life, you may need to forget your dead partner somehow, or rid yourself of his or her memory. This can feel like "killing" your beloved a second time. And despite your efforts, he or she may keep coming back!

**Dead Giveaway**

During the Middle Ages in Europe it was common to save various tokens and reminders of human mortality, including human skulls and other bones, hourglasses, scythes, and paintings and poetry on the theme of death. These were called *memento mori*, which is Latin for "remember you must die." The purpose of saving them was to reflect on them and become prepared for death. Some memento mori were poems inviting male readers to think of beautiful women not as the living, attractive people they were, but as the corrupted corpses they were destined to become.

The theme of the departed lover returning from the grave as a vampire occurs in *Dracula* when Lucy returns to Arthur. This theme is also the subject of many old folktales and occurs in the long poem, *Thalaba the Destroyer* (1801), by Robert Southey. Thalaba is a hero who faces many supernatural threats, including a vampire in the form of his deceased newlywed bride, whom he destroys.

# Lonely Hearts in Circulation

Experience with problems like these may account for much of the intense interest vampires hold for many people. Having been through, or heard about, a complicated and painful situation in life, people can feel especially fascinated by imaginative expressions of those situations in the supernatural form of vampires. They recognize kindred spirits in vampires, vampire killers, and vampire victims. This recognition has been catching on in such a big way that vampires and vampire fans have achieved a group identity in recent years.

## Painful Wisdom

Whether you encounter these challenges directly in your own life or indirectly in the lives of those around you, vampires can help you understand them, perhaps deal with them, and possibly be prepared for them if and when, vampirelike, they come back. The notion that knowledge of vampires can help you is catching on these days. Many fans of *Buffy the Vampire Slayer*, for instance, feel personally empowered by Buffy's example in understanding, and standing up to, the supernatural menaces she faces, as well as the mundane social challenges those menaces often represent. And through it all she's still a good pal to her friends.

> **Cold Fact**
>
> The ranks of "good" vampires in fiction, movies, and TV have exploded over the past several decades. They include Angel from *Buffy* and the *Angel* spin-off, *Vampirella*, Nick Knight from the *Forever Night* TV series, and Miyu, Vampire Princess from Japanese video and TV.

Time was, however, when psychologists regarded fascination with vampires and vampire victims as a sign of perversion or neurosis. Ernest Jones, a Freudian psychologist, expounded this view back in the early 1930s. He regarded vampiric fantasies as fundamentally perverse, resulting from repressed desires that resurface in abnormal ways. This idea helps explain vampire-related neurosis and psychosis as well as vampire copy-cat crimes in which criminals feel inspired to do evil by vampires.

In recent years, vampires are increasingly recognized as sympathetic figures and the increasing numbers of people who identify with them are considered imaginatively engaged in resolving common human challenges. According to this view, a passionate interest in vampires can lead people through and beyond life's difficulties. Much as vampires are said to possess privileged knowledge of dark secrets, vampire enthusiasts often have an understanding and acceptance of human nature and experience, with all its pitfalls. Instead of representing repressed sexuality, vampires are coming to represent an emergence beyond sexual stereotypes. Vampire fans tend to be comfortable with all forms of sexual and personal expression.

## Blood Red Tape

Part of the open attitudes currently embraced by many vampire fans has to do with the fact that vampires in popular consciousness are no longer the lone wolves they were once thought to be. In movies, stories, websites, as well as among nightclubbers and in chat rooms, vampires are recognized as highly social creatures. Though they may remain individualistic, they flock together in parties, nests, cults, keeps, and clans. Their relationships are often highly structured, involving special roles such as masters, minions, and retainers. As social beings, their symbolism may remain sexually charged, but can also emerge as fundamentally political.

Much as lone vampires with their lone victims symbolize problems related to intimate and personal sexual desire, vampires in groups symbolize problems in the larger society. Although vampires are only recently coming into their own as political symbols in a big way, their political significance has been recognized for over a century. Karl Marx, most notably, characterized capitalist society as essentially vampiric when he wrote in *Das Kapital*, "Capital is dead labor which, vampire-like, lives only by sucking living labor, and lives the more the more labor it sucks." Similarly political humorists of the nineteenth century sometimes referred to the ruling classes as the "vampirarchy" rather than the "hierarchy."

More recently, vampirism has been strongly associated with the Communist regime of the Romanian dictator Nicolae Ceausescu and its aftermath. "All Dracula's Children," a short story by vampire fiction writer Dan Simmons, is set in Romania in the wake of the Ceausescu regime, as is Caryl Churchill's play, *Mad Forest* (1996), which includes a poignant dialog between a vampire and a dog. In both works, vampirism is associated with political corruption and a vicious cycle of economic and social exploitation.

**Dead Giveaway**

Under the leadership of Communist dictator Nicolae Ceausescu (1967–1989), Romania became a brutal police state. Conditions became intolerable, and in 1989 a revolution took place with the support of the army. Ceausescu and his wife, Elena, were executed on Christmas day on live TV broadcast throughout the country. Sadly, Ceausescu's overthrow failed to lead to stability in the region, which has remained torn by economic collapse, as well as ethnic conflict. Since the fall of his regime, Ceausescu has been compared in literature and popular imagination to Count Dracula, while modern Romania has been seen as a place conducive to vampire activity.

## Morbid Hordes

These days, vampires in movies and stories point to all kinds of political and social problems. Here's a list of some of them:

- Political conspiracies—vampires are deceptive and secretive even in groups.

- Political corruption—corruption is also what happens to dead bodies!

- Racial tensions—vampires are a group apart.

- Greed—vampires can't get enough of what they want.

- Ambition—vampires have indomitable wills.

- Pollution—vampires are heedless of the common good and destructive on a large scale.

- AIDS—vampires are an epidemic unto themselves.

- Organized crime—vampires band together in lawless gangs.

- Business monopolies—vampires bleed the competition dry!

- Cult activities—vampires aren't your typical church-goers!

To all the problems and evils they represent, vampires bring an aura of mystery and power, combined with the suggestion that bad things have their attractive side. Thus they make compelling sense of issues that might otherwise seem merely ugly and depressing. It's no wonder that, instead of recoiling in horror from vampires so many people feel the urge to come closer ... closer!

## The Least You Need to Know

- Vampires often represent problems of everyday existence, especially interpersonal ones.
- Vampires can resemble unwanted lovers and unresponsive love interests.
- Vampirism can represent parasitic relationships and taboo sexuality.
- Vampires can represent the memory of deceased loved ones.
- Vampirism can represent a host of social and political problems from AIDS to xenophobia.

# Chapter 5

# Vamp Camp

## In This Chapter

- ◆ The Lugosi legacy
- ◆ Campy shows
- ◆ Really bad movies
- ◆ Campy collectibles

No, in spite of its title, this chapter isn't about basic training for vampires. "Camp" is an attitude, an aesthetic, an unavoidable quality that rises to the surface whenever consumer culture gets carried away with itself. It often happens when funny and serious get mixed up together, but it is more than just making fun of something. It can be a sophisticated appreciation of not-so-sophisticated things, or a blatant, public celebration of something that people ordinarily think of as private. Camp is hyping your cake and eating it, too. It's missing the point on purpose.

How about a Venus de Milo action figure? Kids can learn to appreciate classic antiquity and pretend she knows kickboxing! Or how about a theme park based on well-known diseases? That bipolar disorder roller coaster is one wild ride! And you know it's only a matter of time before they come out with cigarette-flavored ice cream for that refreshing smokeless after-dinner treat! When people have a sense of humor about what they like, they have campy tastes.

It's inevitable that people are going to have fun with things that aren't "supposed" to be fun. This makes campy vampires a dead certainty. Many vampires, vampire shows, and vampire-related consumer goods are so campy it's scary. Books, too, believe it or not. I heard there's even a *Complete Idiot's Guide to Vampires!* To think anyone would read such a thing!

# Getting to Know You

Vampires fascinate us with their strangeness and, fascinated, we bask in their mysterious presence until gradually, mysterious though they are, they become familiar. Everyone knows all about them, they become popular, appear in great books and movies, then in not-so-great ones, then in downright lousy ones, then great ones again. They are represented in art and used in advertising. They're so readily visible you get used to seeing them standing out in the crowd.

At some point, people start to notice the irony of shrouded, secret, night-stalking vampires becoming common, everyday entities. And we even start to imagine them in the context of our ordinary work-a-day world.

Without completely stripping them of their supernatural qualities, we imagine them living by the same rules, regulations, and routines the rest of us follow: going to work, going shopping, going "out for a bite." And suddenly, what was once terrifying becomes funny. The familiar legends start to pick up new wrinkles. Some say, for example, that Dracula *had* to come back from the dead because he was buried in a rented tux!

> **Cold Fact**
>
> Dracula has a reputation for good grooming and personal hygiene, so he makes a great spokes figure for personal grooming products. He has even appeared in ads for—of course—hair tonic and—what else?—mouthwash.

## Role Model

The first vampire to become really familiar—and who remains by far the best-known vampire figure—is Bela Lugosi's Dracula. Bela was

great in the 1931 movie *Dracula*, directed by Tod Browning. His interpretation of that role was so compelling that he got everyone to see
vampires his way, at a time when few people had seen many vampire
movies before. He made such a mark as the undead Count that it became
virtually impossible to look at Lugosi again without thinking of Dracula.

**Grave Mistake**

Don't assume Dracula has always been the best-known vampire. Prior
to 1897 and the publication of Bram Stoker's *Dracula*, the most
famous vampire of stage and story was Lord Ruthven, the Byronesque
vampire of John Polidori's story, *The Vampyre* (1819). Polidori's tale was
adapted for the stage many times during the nineteenth century, first in
France, later in England, and then in Germany where it was staged as
an opera. Lord Ruthven was less of a cold-blooded fiend than Dracula
and more of a subtle disrespect of family values. The tale has recently
been republished by Oxford World Classics.

Lugosi continued to act for the rest of his life, but was almost invariably
typecast as a villain. He reprised his role as Dracula several times,
including once in the horror film spoof, *Abbot and Costello Meet
Frankenstein* (1948), considered one of the comedy team's best films.
Lugosi plays Dracula turned mad scientist who wants Lou Costello's
brain for his monster.

Lugosi evidently enjoyed his status as a camp icon. Over the course of
his career following *Dracula*, he did much to reinforce the idea that
vampires can be as comfortable in the sun as underground. At his
funeral, his body was publicly displayed in the coffin, wearing his
Dracula cape!

So the Lugosi character came to represent what vampires look like:
black cape, widow's peak hairline, dark hair parted down the middle
and combed back, thin lips, penetrating stare. And just as Lugosi was
the best-known Dracula, Dracula was by far the best-known vampire,
thanks to the Bram Stoker novel. Lugosi's familiar look meant Dracula,
and Dracula's familiar name meant vampire.

**Dead Giveaway**

Lugosi's last film is the infamous affront to celluloid, *Plan 9 from Outer Space* (1959), directed by Ed Wood. The film is commonly hailed as the worst movie ever made, in part for its lack of production values. For example, tombstones are obviously made of cardboard and bend visibly as characters brush past them. Lugosi plays a sort of vampire figure who is brought to life by aliens who want to take over Earth. The actor died, however, before the filming was completed, so Wood recruited an understudy who hid his face behind a cape to disguise the fact that he wasn't Lugosi. The obvious ruse fails miserably, however, since the understudy is much taller than Lugosi! The film is so lame it became a cult favorite and helped inspire the bio pic of the director's career, *Ed Wood* (1994), starring Johnny Depp in the title role.

# Bela Ringers

The Lugosi look and the Dracula name are so easy to identify that people have been vampirizing them ever since to gain recognition. Here's a list of some variations on the theme.

For kids:

♦ Bunnicula—veggie-sucking bunny from the popular children's book, *Bunnicula: A Rabbit Tale of Mystery* (1996) by James Howe.

♦ Count Chocula—for those big sweet tooths, the General Mills breakfast cereal with a brown, Lugosi-style vampire on the box. You'll find it next to Franken Berry and Boo Berry cereals.

♦ Duckula—originally a character in cable TV's *Danger Mouse* cartoon show, *Duckula* became a spin-off.

Not exactly for kids:

♦ *Blacula*—1972 movie starring William Marshall as the eighteenth-century African prince-turned vampire and set loose on L.A. in the '70s.

♦ *Rockula*—1989 film about a 300-year-old teen vampire in search of babes as well as blood.

**Cold Fact** _____

The first-ever full-length movie feature for the hearing impaired in which all the dialog takes place in sign language is the vampire movie *Deafula* (1974), in which a theology student becomes a vampire and goes on the prowl after his classmates. This later-day silent film stars and was written and directed by Peter Wolf.

Definitely not for kids:

◆ Jacula—Sexy vampire queen from a popular erotic Italian comic book series of the 1970s.

◆ *Gayracula*—1985 film featuring a homosexual vampire set in L.A.

◆ Dragula—transvestite vampire from a 1973 film and from a 1994 pornographic feature.

◆ Draghoula—Jewish scientist turned transvestite vampire from the 1994 film.

◆ Spermula—(1976) If you have to ask, you don't want to know!

# Pale Imitations

And the parade of happy vampire camp-ers continues. It's interesting to note, however, that vampires in movies—scary and otherwise—pretty much died out during the '40s and '50s. Then, in the post-war era, Hammer Films came out with a zestier, sexier spate of vampire films, featuring Christopher Lee as a swinging bachelor vampire in search of technicolor blood. The Hammer films, for the most part, were not self-consciously campy, but they helped revive vampire popularity and paved the way for vampires who were.

## Spooky Spoofs

Camp sensibility often involves the ability to recognize and enjoy clichés. The Lugosi-esque Dracula and all of his vampiric trappings have become just about the oldest clichés in Hollywood. As you can imagine, if you haven't already seen firsthand, lots of vampire movies make fun of the familiar Dracula business. Some, like director Roman Polanski's *Fearless Vampire Killers* or *Pardon Me, But Your Teeth Are in My Neck* (1967) manage to be funny and scary at the same time. Others, like *Dracula: Dead and Loving It* (1995), starring Leslie Nielson as a suave-looking but clumsy Count, are just silly.

Sometimes movies get humorous mileage out of unexpected juxtapositions of the modern world with traditional gothic ambience, as in *Transylvania 6-5000* (1985) starring Jeff Goldblum as a reporter who is glad to find that Dracula's castle is an establishment that accepts credit cards. Other times, humorous potential is teased out of the old ideas, as in *Love at First Bite* (1979) when the scientist-vampire hunter and Dracula try to hypnotize one another.

### Stalk Talk

Hopping vampires have become familiar to fans of Chinese martial arts/vampire movies. These vampires hop as a feature of their non-human, supernatural identity. They first appeared in the popular Hong Kong horror/comedy, *Mr. Vampire* (1986) and have been popping up ever since. If a good guy sees them, he can stop them in their tracks temporarily by holding his breath.

Sometimes one set of clichés isn't enough, so movies combine vampire-schtick with other familiar gimmicks. There's the gothic western, *Billy the Kid Vs. Dracula* (1966), the Italian sci-fi horror film, *Planet of the Vampires* (1965), and *Rockabilly Vampire* (1997) featuring a blood-sucking Elvis look-alike. And keep an eye out for Hong Kong's greatest vampire flick, *Mr. Vampire* (1986) where martial arts meet Asian gothic comedy/horror. The film, which has spawned many sequels, features the now famous *hopping vampires*, so-called for their unusual means of locomotion.

## Greasy Kid Stuff

A campy angle the whole family can enjoy involves vampires and/or vampire hunters as members of the family, often kids. Especially well-known are Lilly and Grandpa from the 1960s TV show, *The Munsters*, which relates the adventures of a typical suburban family who happen to be gothic horror characters. More obscure is the low-budget horror/ heart warmer, *A Polish Vampire in Burbank* (1986) in which a young (comparatively) vampire comes of age and cuts his teeth on his first kill.

*The Lost Boys* (1987) is a more serious, but still funny version of the family theme. It features a half-vampirized family compared in the film to a "bloodsucking Brady Bunch" and preteen vampire hunters equipped with squirt guns loaded with holy water and garlic juice. And speaking of garlic, it's tough to be a vampire around teenagers. The Dracula in *Monster Squad* (1987) found this out the hard way when he bit into a pizza and had his mouth singed by the garlic!

*Once Bitten* (1985), starring a young Jim Carrey as a naive vampire victim is an especially silly attempt to bring vampires into the world of teenagers. And then of course there's the "way lethal," way campy *Buffy the Vampire Slayer*. Buffy is so hip to both the supernatural and mundane worlds that she can spot a vampire in a crowd of classmates by its bad fashion sense.

# Horrible Horror

As delightful as vampire films can be, the painful truth is that they are not always of the best quality. In fact, many of them suck! Bad acting, bad screenwriting, bad photography, editing, and special effects do not necessarily prevent a movie from getting produced and released, especially if that bad movie is a vampire movie. Vampire flicks include some of the worst movies ever made. Sometimes they're so bad, it's hilarious.

## Vicious Cycle

Hilarity is often in the eye of the beholder. It can take a delicately honed film sensitivity to be able to appreciate the finer points of a lousy movie. Not everyone can pick up on all the ways a horror movie can be funny without intending to be. Nevertheless, there are enough bad film aficionados out there to keep the bad moviemakers in business.

In fact, as long as people go to watch bad movies, movie producers will keep making them. Put some big guy in a cape or a rubber suit and get some good-looking women in negligees or torn dresses, bang out a script (monster comes to life, monster menaces victims, monsters meets horrible death) splatter lots of ketchup and maybe some slime, and start rolling the film. If you get new ideas or change your mind once you've started, just make changes as you go and hope it all comes together somehow in the editing room. Anything left on the cutting room floor can be spliced into the sequel!

**Dead Giveaway**

The salad days of exploitation horror film were in the 1960s, when theaters commonly ran "B-movies" between showings of the main feature. Typically low-quality, low-budget productions, 1960s-era B-movies have since become a staple of late night television, especially in the horror genre. Many of the stock features of B-movie horror films have been revived in recent years by independent movie producers specializing in low-budget campy bad taste horror films. Troma Entertainment and EI Cinema with its Shock-O-Rama and Seduction Cinema branches are prominent examples. Both companies produce over-the-top schlocky horror films with lots of gore, nudity, and cheesy effects. EI also releases older exploitation flicks. Both have numerous vampire films in their catalogs.

# Lesser Evils

Here's a roster of just a few of the many vampire films that have distinguished themselves by their low quality:

- *Plan 9 from Outer Space* (1959)—Touted everywhere (including in a sidebar that appears in this chapter) as the worst film ever made.

- *Atom Age Vampire* (1961)—A mad scientist invents a serum that turns him into a monster, the better to harvest fluids from female victims that will enable him to make his disfigured girlfriend beautiful.

- *Billy the Kid Vs. Dracula* (1966)—Dracula messes with the wrong hombre in this clunker. BYO humor.

- *Vampire Beast Craves Blood* (*Blood Beast Terror*) (1967)—A woman turns into a bloodsucking moth.

- *Legend of the Seven Golden Vampires* (1974)—The first vampire movie made in Hong Kong pits Dracula against Peter Cushing as Van Helsing assisted by a squad of kung fu experts. The U.S.

distributors thought it was so bad they wouldn't release it here, but it eventually made it into the States under the title *The Seven Brothers Meet Dracula* (1979). Despite the lack of plot, some people like it!

◆ *Sorority House Vampires* (1997)—Silly titillation for teens as zombie-style vampires menace a sorority.

**Grave Mistake**

Campy vampire films run the sex-and-violence gamut from practically wholesome to downright sick. When selecting viewing material, be sure it's appropriate for the people who are going to watch it. Because horribly gory and/or pornographic vampire films sometimes try to be campy, it's a good idea to keep in mind that a humorous title doesn't necessarily indicate an innocent film!

# I *Must* Have You!

While some are content to watch campiness unfold on screen, others must possess it for themselves. Vampire-related items make popular collectibles as a visit to the vampire list on eBay makes abundantly clear. You can fill your bookshelves, equip your video library, decorate your house, augment your wardrobe, and get all kinds of stuff to take with you to your grave.

## Bad Goodies

Someone was auctioning off a cute little Ziggy doll—with fangs! Someone else had a Russ Troll for sale—with fangs! Someone else was selling a stuffed plush Bugs Bunny—with rabbit teeth, actually, but he had a vampire cape!

Much as you gotta love these cuddly cutey-pies, none of them has anything like the vampirish magnetism of this one Dracula-headed Pez candy dispenser that was up on the virtual auction block. Bidding had already reached a surreal $132.50 with several days to go. Evidently Dracula can still bleed some people dry!

**Cold Fact** _____

Bugs Bunny squares off against the vampire, Count Bloodcount, in the Warner Brothers cartoon short, "Transylvania 6-5000" (1963), not to be confused with the 1985 feature film of the same title. It seems Bugs is traveling in Transylvania when he stops for the night at the Count's castle.

And there are all kinds of accessories for making your crypt a home, including a Bela Lugosi clock, a Buffy light switch cover, and a coffin coffee table. And how about a Dracula windsock floating out on your front porch? To let people know you're undead and well there were address labels ornamented with blood-dripping fangs. And to keep the traffic under control there was a sign that says "Bat Crossing" and another that says "Vampire Parking." And of course there were enough posters, videos, books, and comic books to bury an army of vampires.

## For the Gory Gourmet

There's a growing selection of items on eBay and elsewhere to help the undead live the good life. For those with a taste for solid food, there are a number of vampire cookbooks. For instance, there's the *Count Dracula Chicken Cookbook* (Adams Press, 1970) by Jeanne Youngson (Dracula served chicken to Jonathan Harker on his first night in castle Dracula). And *The Dracula Cookbook of Blood* (Mugwort Soup Publications, 1993), which includes recipes from around the world that call for blood, as well as a few bat dish recipes. And for food that bites back, try vampire hot sauce from Louisiana.

And of course there's vampire wine—blood red, naturally and made and bottled—no kidding—in Transylvania (which is now actually part of Romania). In fact, if your blood lust is tinged with wanderlust and political conditions permit, you can arrange to stay in the Golden Krone Hotel in Bistritz, Romania, where, according to the novel *Dracula,* Jonathan Harker stopped for a meal on his way to the Count's castle. You can also visit various buildings associated with Dracula's real-life prototype, Vlad the Impaler. Or if Romania is too far away, you can traverse the "Dracula Trail" in Yorkshire, England, and see the sights mentioned in Stoker's novel.

Before you go, you'll want to make sure you look your best in a new set of custom vampire fangs, a rakish set of claws, a cape, and blood red or black lipstick. And if you drive to the airport, you'll want to get a vampire-fang grille cover for the front of your car to show it can suck more than gas.

**Grave Mistake**

If you go outside, don't forget the sun block! You'll want SPF 300 or higher to keep from shriveling up! Actually, vampires have been represented as sun block users by day in at least two films: *Blade* (1998) starring Wesley Snipes, and *Sundown: The Vampire in Retreat* (1990), a vampire/Western starring David Carradine.

## The Least You Need to Know

♦ The most easily recognizable vampire clichés harken back to Bela Lugosi's Dracula in the classic Tod Browning film of 1931.

♦ The camp aesthetic often stems from a mix of horror and familiarity.

♦ Bad vampire films that are unintentionally funny are relished by movie watchers with campy tastes.

♦ Vampire collectibles can command high prices, but they lend a distinctive touch to any room.

♦ The good life, vampire-style, is available with help from cookbooks, food and wine purveyors, and your local travel agent.

# Part 2

# Gory Lore

Vampires are what legends are made of—legends being those timeless, amazing stories that many people have taken to be true. Often they raise more questions than they answer, such as "how and why did people think this stuff up?" And just as often they speak to something inside us that understands without question and says, "I hate it when that happens!"

Vampire legends come from all over and from way back. And they have a way of getting tied in with the legends of other horrific beings. It almost seems that whenever you find yourself on the wrong side of the tracks in Never Never Land, you'll run into vampires along with the other rough customers in the neighborhood.

While vampire legends are ancient and international, most come from Eastern Europe where vampire lore was part of the way of life—and death! Vampire lore is so powerfully compelling that it has often shaped the ways people think and behave. And while it has shaped the lifestyles of cultures very different from ours, much of it is still remembered today and gets woven into the stories, games, and fantasies of modern people.

# Chapter 6

# Earthy Types

## In This Chapter

- ◆ Slavic vampire lore
- ◆ Vampire names
- ◆ Causes, characteristics, and remedies
- ◆ A vampire tale

"Traditioooooooooon, tradition!" What if all the characters in *Fiddler on the Roof* had a strange fixation with dead bodies stemming from a deep-seated uncertainty about the proper way to dispose of a corpse? The song, "Sunrise, Sunset" would take on a whole new meaning! "Is this the little corpse I buried …" Or how about "Vamp-hunter, vamp-hunter, catch me a catch!" Well, aside from the music and Jewishness, it's a rough idea of what traditional Slavic vampire lore is like.

Not that all of it exactly hangs together. In fact, it includes many diverse traditions from Greece to Russia and from Germany to Turkey. It hearkens back past our ability to trace it into the Middle Ages and continues right up into the early decades of the twentieth century. Sometimes it asserts Christian values and beliefs, other times it defies them. Sometimes it's funny, sometimes it's exciting, often it's just weird, but it's always macabre.

But through it all, the tale spinners, rumor spreaders, nightmare mongers, and panic panderers followed a simple, iron-clad rule in contriving Slavic vampire lore: Invent the rules as you go. In fact, the rules governing folkloric vampires are mostly arbitrary and inscrutable. It's not always garlic and crosses like in *Dracula*, but might be the hem of a shroud, a bowl of millet, or a strange sleeping position.

# What's in a Name?

Apparently, the people who named vampires could not stop stirring their alphabet soup. Spelling options extend far beyond vampire and vampyre. Linguists drive themselves crazy trying to figure out how the various terms for vampire, found throughout Eastern Europe, may have shifted and spread over the years.

### Grave Mistake

Believe it or not, the first vampires were definitely not called "vampires." They may have been called something like "upirs" or "oburs." The English word "vampire" probably came from a German rendering of the Serbian word, "vampir." In fact, though, "vampir" was only one of many traditional words for the creatures we call vampires.

Vampir and upirnina are Serbian. Upir is Russian. Upior and upierz are Polish. Vepir, vapir, and ubour are Bulgarian. Lampir is Bosnian and Croatian. All of these terms are linguistically related to one another and were used to identify the creatures we know as vampires.

Here's another set of linguistically related terms used to describe vampires: Vrykolakas is Greek. Vurkolak is Turkish. Vukodlak is Serbian. Volkodlak is Croatian. Varcolac is Romanian. Originally, all these words meant something like "wolf pelt." Many say that these terms were used to identify werewolves, although there is scholarly disagreement on the issue. In any case, regardless of the original meaning, all these terms have since been used as synonyms for vampires.

And vampires have been known by still other names as well, depending on where you go. Moroi and strigoi were used in Romania. Nachzehren and doppelsauger were used in Germany. Vjesci was used in Poland. And all of these terms mentioned so far are just the most commonly used ones!

# Scattered Remains

The fact that names for vampires are all so different in various places gives you an idea of how different vampires themselves can be. Vampires from Slavic folklore take many forms and exhibit a variety of feeding habits, powers and weaknesses, origins, choice of prey, and ways to be killed. They come from different sources and contexts too— religious cults, folktales, and superstitions. Nevertheless, there are some common elements holding most vampire lore together.

## Small Town Vamps

Picture an isolated little village in Eastern Europe with a few farmers and their families, a miller, a blacksmith, a couple of merchants, and maybe a priest. Now and then a soldier or two may wander through. An old witch, wise grandma, or a hermit may live outside of town in the surrounding forest. Everyone goes about his or her own business, more-or-less carefree, until suddenly, unexplainably, people start dying.

**Dead Giveaway** _____

An Armenian legend tells of a vampire named Dakhanavar who preyed on anyone rash enough to reside in the valleys around Mount Ararat where he lived. (Mount Ararat is famous to Christians and Jews from the story of Noah's Ark.) He dispatched his victims by sucking their blood in their sleep—not from their necks, but from the bottoms of their feet! One day, a couple of surveyors figured out a way to foil the vampire. They counted all the valleys—366—and then lay down to sleep. To protect themselves from the foot-sucking vampire, they each lay with their feet underneath the other's head, so when the vampire came to them, he couldn't find their feet. Frustrated, he went off and was never heard from again!

Instead of running to the village clinic for their plague shots, the surviving villagers immediately think of vampires. There are no telltale fang marks in anyone's neck (Slavic vampires often pierce their victims with their tongues and may not leave a wound), but people may feel weak and have black marks on their skin. Wives may dream their dead husbands visited them by day or by night. The vampire may work his evil magically while remaining in the grave. Or he may rise out of the grave as mist before transforming again to a solid body. Or he may simply dig himself out the hard way—gopher-style, or possibly by pushing his coffin lid up ahead of him.

The vampire may have been seen in the form of an animal such as a dog or a bull. Or it may appear as the skin of a bull filled up like a bladder with blood. The vampire may also be a werewolf, a witch or sorcerer, a ghost or spirit, or a flesh-eating *ghoul*. A ghoul is a creature from Islamic cultures in the Middle East, distinguished by its habit of eating human corpses.

In addition to sucking blood, the vampire may kill with the evil eye or some other form of magic. It may kill out of pure evil or it may want its loved ones to join it in the grave. In rare cases it may set out to punish wrongdoers, such as those who break promises. The vampire may kill livestock instead of people, or may simply make strange scary noises or destroy and disorganize people's property. Sometimes it returns to have sex with its former spouse. But in any case, when people start dying in groups, there's no doubt in anyone's mind that a vampire is the problem. Who else would feel a supernatural compulsion to kill them?

> **Stalk Talk**
>
> A **ghoul** is an unearthly creature from the Middle East who eats the flesh of the dead. In Islamic countries, doing so is considered not merely gross, but deeply sacrilegious as well. Ghouls are demons that often masquerade as ordinary people and even marry unsuspecting princes or princesses until they are discovered and magically vanquished.

# Weeding Out the Riffraff

The first step is to identify the bloodsucking culprit. Sometimes there are special vampire hunters who have supernatural vampire-hunting powers. People born on Saturday are sometimes thought to be able to spot vampires. Then of course there's always guesswork and conjecture!

Was anyone strange buried before the spate of deaths? Did anything strange happen at someone's burial? Often little things will stick out in people's minds as being out of the ordinary, and one of these will provide the clue as to who is refusing to lie quietly in his or her grave.

Just to be sure, the townspeople might take a white horse to the grave-yard and lead it over the graves. If it refuses to cross someone's grave, they've got their vampire dead to rights. Then it's only a question of what to do about it.

Someone asks grandma; some-one else asks the priest. If a sol-dier is in town on furlough, they might ask him. Grandma sets out a hawthorn branch, some millet, some garlic, rearranges the furni-ture, or plants a sunflower by the door. The priest says prayers, sprin-kles holy water around the grave. The soldier sticks his sword into the grave and stays up at night watching in the graveyard.

**Cold Fact**

One reason people thought garlic would ward off vampires was because vampires were associated with the stench of death that some people thought caused disease, or the supernatural maladies brought by vam-pires. In overpowering the evil smell associated with vampires, people thought gar-lic had power over the vam-pire itself.

If the vampire story is a folktale, the vampire will be outwitted and destroyed by one of the villagers or soldiers, who then live happily ever after. Perhaps the soldier will steal the vampire's coffin lid and keep the vampire at bay until dawn when it falls down lifeless. Or perhaps it will be destroyed through an elaborate and improbable series of magic tricks.

Folktales say victims may be brought to life again by pouring their blood back into their wounds or onto their ashes. Or they may be car-ried in their coffins out of their houses through underground passage-ways, enabling them to rise from the grave as flowers that then turn back into human beings. Or perhaps a hermit will know where a lizard with a magic herb in its mouth can be found, which will restore vam-pire victims to life. Or if a piece of the vampire's shroud is burned over hot coals, the smoke may revive the victims.

If, however, the vampire is the result of superstition, the people keep worrying. They hope a vampire hunter will kill it, or that it will be eaten by a wolf, but how likely is that? But although folktales always have happy endings, real life can leave you guessing. People often deal with their daily fears by developing superstitions, including supersti-tions about vampires. Many become convinced they will be the next to die. They hear things, see things, feel funny. So the townsfolk take more aggressive action. They dig up the vampire.

# Blood Evidence

Often, the villagers are amazed to find the vampire strangely undecayed and red in color. More shockingly, it may appear to be bloated with blood. Perhaps it lies face down in its coffin or shows some other sign of having moved. It may have been chewing on its shroud.

What the villagers do next ranges in severity from tucking the vampire in by pinning its shroud to the bottom of the coffin to slash-and-burn destruction of the corpse and the grave. Some vampire remedies include placing things inside the coffin such as nails, coins, flax seed, or a fishing net. If the corpse is found lying upside down, it may be turned right side up. Or if it's found right side up, it may be turned upside down.

More drastic steps include cutting the sinews in the corpse's legs or cutting off the head—typically with a spade. The mouth may then be stuffed with garlic and placed at the corpse's feet. And of course there's the good old stake through the heart. Traditional sources seem to prefer hawthorn wood. Or the heart may be pulled out and burned. The entrails may be pulled out and burned, too. Heck, the whole body may be burned. Some of the ashes may be fed to surviving relatives to protect them from harm or to prevent them from becoming vampires themselves.

After it's all over, the grave may be destroyed. Or the bones left over from cremation may be sprinkled with wine and reburied. A priest may be on hand supervising the proceedings. Or priests may be on hand trying to prevent the proceedings from taking place at all! There are no universal rules.

**Dead Giveaway** _____

You might think that a vampire who has been staked, gutted, hamstrung, beheaded, and cremated would be taken care of for good, but this isn't always the case. According to one vampire story, the vampire's belly is filled with birds, snakes, and maggots. When the vampire is being cremated, the villagers have to make sure none of these creatures escape, since the vampire might be inside them!

# Turn for the Worse

So how do vampires get to be that way in the first place? Contrary to popular belief, victims did not usually become vampires themselves in Slavic lore. It's usually some other cause that sets the vampire in motion. Although the answer differs from case to case, it most often has to do with the way an individual is born, dies, or is buried:

- ◆ Birth—if you are born with the birth membrane (caul) over your head; if you are the illegitimate child of an illegitimate child; or if you are born with teeth, hair, or a red birthmark, you may come back as a vampire after death.

**Dead Giveaway** _____

A belief circulated among certain Slavic peoples who moved to Germany is a creature called a doppelsauger (double sucker). If a child was weaned but returned to its mother's breast, it would never be satisfied, but would seek out breast nourishment even in the grave after death by attempting to chew on its own breast. By doing so, the creature would supernaturally weaken any living relations. To prevent this, a coin could be placed in the mouth of the corpse, or a barrier placed between the mouth and the breast. If these precautions aren't taken, the body must be dug up and its head chopped off!

- ◆ Death—if you die unbaptized; commit suicide; leave unfinished business; are killed by a vampire; die unexpectedly, violently, unattended, or through unexplainable causes, you may come back as a vampire.

- ◆ Burial—if you are not buried, buried without the proper ceremonies, buried at a crossroads, buried with your shroud touching your mouth, or if a cat jumps over your corpse before you are buried, you could come back as a vampire.

In fact, the Slavs were worrywarts about these issues. And they continually second-guessed themselves, inventing new rules and superstitions about what could happen if this or that burial rite was or was not performed. But there are plenty of other ways to come back from the grave as a vampire. For example, you can become a vampire if you are a witch, a werewolf, or a heretic in life, or if you have two hearts.

# Tale from the Crypt

A number of Russian vampire stories were collected and published in the mid-nineteenth century by a Russian folklorist named A. N. Afanasiev. One of these, called *Upir* (Vampire), is about the adventures of a Russian Buffy-type named Marusia, who lived long ago and far away in an enchanted kingdom. Here's how the tale might read today.

## Strings Attached

Back in Marusia's day they had St. Andrew's Feast celebrations instead of high school proms. It was at a celebration that Marusia met this really hot-looking guy. They danced together and hung out, and the guy was really generous with his money. He bought everyone wine and gingerbread, which isn't so bad a combination as it sounds. Anyway, he was young, rich, and handsome, and he seemed to have honorable intentions, because he asked Marusia to marry him.

**Cold Fact**

Many folktales—especially the ones about girls—are concerned with family tensions and how to escape them. Of course, the easiest way for a traditional village girl to escape her family is by getting married.

As a matter of fact, Marusia would rather have married a young, rich, handsome man with honorable intentions than become a famous movie star or win the lottery. It's kind of a folktale thing.

So anyway, she said "Dah," which may sound like a flippant way of saying "of course, you idiot," but is actually Russian for "yes." "But tell me," she went on. "Where do you live?"

"I come from all over," he answered and winked slyly. "Well, be seeing you," he said and started to leave.

"Wait a second," Marusia responded and went to button up his jacket. Secretly, without the man's noticing what she was up to, she took out a spool of thread, made a loop, and fixed the loop over one of the man's jacket buttons. "Glad we could *hook up*," she said oh-so-dryly as the man rode off, unraveling thread as he went.

Anyway, after picking up the thread of the plot, so to speak, Marusia found herself standing outside a church. Inside she could hear what we'd recognize as a boom box playing a Black Sabbath tape, so she guessed some depraved Satanic ritual was being performed. She put a ladder up to a window to see what was going on.

Inside she saw her fiancé munching on the forearm of a corpse as though it were corn on the cob. Then he dug into the ribs. What Marusia saw next filled her with horror: a sign that clearly said, "no eating in church." As you might imagine, Marusia began to have second thoughts about marrying him. She started to move back down the ladder, but she slipped and scratched the window before recovering her balance. The young man heard the noise and turned just in time to see a shadow through the window moving out of sight.

**Cold Fact**

Some folktales tell of brushes with undeath and lucky escapes. For example, a soldier encounters two vampires, either of which would have killed him had they not gotten into an argument and destroyed one another. Another tale tells of a man saved from a vampire by his dog. Unfortunately the dog later turned against the man for not helping it.

The next day, the young man went to visit Marusia. She had just started to work up a way to let him down gently when he asked her, "Were you at the church?"

Caught off guard, she stammered and said "No."

"Did you see what I was doing?"

Marusia knew she had been found out, but she stuck to her lie. "No," she said again.

"Guess what," the man responded. "By the time you see your mother again, she'll be dead."

"Or I could fix you a sandwich." Marusia answered, but it was too late. The man had already left. And sure enough, when Marusia went to find her mother, her mother was dead. The next day, the man came back and asked the same questions. Marusia had a stubborn streak, so she gave the same answers. So the young man told her her father would die. And her father did die.

You might think that Marusia would start to realize that saying "no" wasn't the best way to deal with her flesh-eating boyfriend, but she had that folktale thing going, so she said "no" once again and the man told her that she would die before the following night. Things looked bad. She was an orphan, doomed to an imminent supernatural death, and engaged to a messy eater.

### Grave Mistake

It's wrong to lie, especially if you're the heroine in a folktale! You'll wind up with a serious guilt complex! Notice that Marusia lies repeatedly and is repeatedly punished for it. Repetition is a frequent device in folktales. Often it serves to reinforce the lessons in the story. In the story of Marusia, repetition drives home the message that it's important to tell the truth—or else!

So she decided to go see her wise old grandma for some advice. "Well," said Grandma, "whenever I find myself engaged to a flesh-eating murderous vampire who's going to kill me, I just tell the priest to dig a tunnel underneath the doorway so my coffin can be carried through it. Then I have them bury me at the crossroad like a common suicide or heretic. You might give it a try."

"Thanks, Gram, I will," said Marusia.

Marusia had a heck of a time persuading the priest to do as her grandmother suggested. She told him she was having the doorway painted to look nice for the wake, but it wouldn't be dry in time, so he would have to dig the tunnel. Then she said her cause of death would be suicide, so they would have to bury her at the crossroad. There was a lot of red tape, but she managed to work everything out just before she collapsed dead into her coffin.

### Dead Giveaway

Notice the story of Marusia seems wrapped up in unresolved religious issues. Strangely, the priest helps Marusia take unsanctioned measures to thwart the vampire. It's hard to imagine a real priest going along with them. Later, the grandma—rather than the priest—gives Marusia some holy water to keep the vampire at bay. This could be seen as sacrilegious use of holy water. And why does the vampire eat the corpse in the church? To desecrate the sacred house of God or to suggest that ordinary villagers can't always trust what goes on there? In fact, the tale's ambiguity reflects an actual ambiguous relationship between folk and religious belief in Eastern Europe. Sometimes folk belief drew on religious doctrine and sometimes the two were opposed.

## Flower Power

Several weeks later, a rich, young, handsome man with good intentions—not the vampire—happened to be riding by on his horse. He paused for a moment at the crossroad, deciding which way to go, when he noticed a lovely flower growing there. He dismounted and dug up the flower, roots and all, and brought it back with him to his castle.

That night, the flower turned into a beautiful girl. Having honorable intentions and all, he asked her to marry him. "Dah" she said, "as long as we never have to go to church. I had a bad experience there once." The young man agreed and they were wed. After a couple of years they had two children and lived happily ever after.

At least, they would have, but …

One day, one of Marusia's husband's clients was in town to offer Marusia's husband an important contract, so everything had to be perfect and Marusia had to be all obedient. Marusia's husband insisted that she go with him to church in order to impress his client. Marusia didn't like the idea, but what could she do? She went into the church and there, sitting on the window ledge was her old fiancé the flesh-eating vampire.

"Were you at the church last night?" He asked.

"No!" she said.

"Did you see what I was doing?"

"No!" she said again.

"Guess what?" he responded. "Your rich, young, honorably intentioned husband and your two children will die." And they did.

As you might imagine, Marusia was really starting to feel steamed. She went to her grandmother, who gave her some holy water in a little glass bottle and told her to be a good little girl and always tell the truth. "Right," Marusia answered. "I get the picture."

But Marusia was stubborn and didn't think the truth or the holy water would actually work. So when the vampire showed up the next day and asked her the same questions, she whipped out a wooden stake she was carrying up her sleeve and with a spinning, backhanded kung fu move,

**Grave Mistake**

Grandma doesn't always know best! In some vampire tales, only the vampire itself knows how it can be destroyed. The hero's job is to trick or force the vampire into revealing its secret, then rally the townspeople to put the measure into action.

she staked him in the chest and he disintegrated into dust. But before he crumbled, she dumped the holy water out of the bottle and collected some of the vampire's blood. She took the blood and poured it over the ashes of her husband and two children and restored them to life.

And Marusia's husband's client was too scared not to give him the contract.

## The Least You Need to Know

♦ Vampires were known by many names throughout Eastern Europe, including upir, vukodlak, and vjesci.

♦ Slavic vampire legends reflect an obsessive anxiety about death and the proper way to dispose of a corpse.

♦ When someone becomes a vampire, the cause is often traced to a peculiarity of birth, death, or burial.

♦ Rules governing the creation, prevention, and destruction of vampires are extremely flexible and vary widely from case to case.

# Chapter 7

# Long in the Tooth

## In This Chapter

- ◆ Ancient vampires and proto-vampires
- ◆ Lilith
- ◆ The baital, rakshasa, and churel from India
- ◆ The lamia, empusa, and mormo from Greece
- ◆ The Roman strix

Everybody knows vampires have been around a long time. Their history, however, is difficult to trace. On the one hand, it's shrouded in mystery. On the other hand, it's bedazzled by the glare of modern-day vampire hype. Sometimes it even seems that Slavic vampires are like young children with an unknown father. Everybody is pointing the finger at some ancient demon or other as the source of the vampire family.

Virtually no one outside of Eastern Europe had even so much as heard of vampires until the seventeenth century. Prior to that time, no one thought of lumping all the world's ancient blood-sucking demons into a special category. Now, however, folklorists and vampire fans are finding ancient vampires under every pot shard and broken marble column, trying to shed old light on the comparatively recent vampire phenomenon. In digging up vampires from the ancient past, some seek connection to larger, trans-historical truths. But they risk trivializing the beliefs of ancient and alien cultures very different from their own.

Amid the confusion, however, are some compelling theories about how the Slavic vampire may have evolved out of ancient sources. These ancient bloodlines may show the early stages of many of the more striking characteristics of the vampire clan. In doing so, they lend greater depth to Slavic vampire lore.

# Old Bats

Folklorists and vampire buffs have identified a number of ancient sources that may have contributed to the Slavic vampire legend. Many ancient demons, witches, and ghosts resemble Slavic vampires in intriguing ways. In some cases it's hard to tell whether these beings actually became incorporated into original Slavic vampire folklore or whether any resemblance is merely coincidental. Either way, a number of creatures from ancient times are commonly identified by scholars and others as "vampires," proto-vampires, and vampirelike.

## A. K. A. Vampire

Sometimes, the similarities are only skin deep. If a demon has fangs, for example, someone will call it a vampire, regardless of any other considerations. The Hindu goddess Kali is a hideous female sometimes represented with fangs. In addition, she has been worshiped with sacrifice, and is said to become intoxicated by drinking blood. Calling Kali a vampire however, as people sometimes do, doesn't really shed much light on this fearsome goddess, who has many important nonvampire characteristics.

She loves flesh as much as blood, for example, and is one of many manifestations of the Tantric deity, Shakti, the consort of Shiva. In some ways, it is an act of Western arrogance to consider this Hindu deity in terms imported from Slavic folklore. Do Hindus go around referring to Satan, the supremely evil Judeo-Christian-Islamic dark power, as just another one of the Hindu rakshasas?

On the other hand, while the vampire label may not do much for Kali, Kali does a lot for vampires. She enriches vampire lore considerably, bringing fresh blood to the vampire party. She can help people think about vampires in a new light. And heck, she's really cool and so are vampires. So there you go!

In addition to appearance and bloodthirstiness, two more characteristics typically attract the vampire label to non- and pre-vampiric ghosts and demons. The concept of undeath is one, although this is rare in ancient lore. (As you'll see later in this chapter, an ancient Greek ghost named Philinnion falls into this category.) The other characteristic is a human set of emotional issues, especially spite, lust, and revenge.

> **Dead Giveaway**
>
> If you're writing a factual report explaining the Hindu goddess Kali, calling her a vampire will only confuse things and obscure important differences. On the other hand, if you're writing a story about vampires or cooking up a vampire role-playing scenario and you want to bring Kali in as one of the flock, go for it!

Demons who disguise themselves and become involved in people's love lives and family lives are often called vampiric. In fact, there are an astonishing number of seductive, baby-killing female demons from all over the world who fit the vampire profile. You know what they say: "Wild women don't get the blues!"

## Scary Mothers

As creatures out of myth and legend, vampirelike beings have always provided ways of coming to terms with the traumas associated with birth and death. Many of the most ancient of all bloodsuckers are demonic female beings that prey on children. They provide folk-explanations for childhood deaths and serve as powerful symbols of what can go wrong with the mother/child relationship.

For example, there's the ancient Mayan (modern-day Mexican) monster, the *cihuateteo*. These creatures are women who died in childbirth and return from the grave to prey on living children by night. They resemble ordinary women except they are unusually pale. There are female child-killing demons from other ancient cultures, too, including the *langsuyar* from Malaysia. Such demons may have served in part to frighten women into upholding the responsibilities of wifedom and motherhood, lest they, too, become monsters.

## Out of Eden

It's pretty clear that neither the cihuateteo nor the langsuyar influenced Slavic vampire folklore. There is a similar evil female demon, however, who has been associated with the origins of the Slavic vampire. This is Lilith, an ancient demon best known, perhaps, from Jewish legend as the first wife of Adam who fled the Garden of Eden to become a night-stalking bloodsucker of newborn babies.

**Grave Mistake**

Don't assume that waving a cross will protect from all vampires! The fact that Lilith and other ancient vampirelike beings predate Christianity has been offered as an explanation for why crosses and holy water have no effect on some vampires. Clearly vampire lore comprises Christian as well as non-Christian influences, some of which predates Christianity.

Lilith is among the oldest known demons in world folklore and she's still going strong as a modern vampire and occult figurehead. She is obliquely referred to in the Sumerian *Epic of Gilgamesh*, which was written on clay tablets around 2000 B.C.E., but is best known from the Jewish Talmud. She was an important figure in Jewish legend throughout the Middle Ages, as we know in part from the many charms and amulets inscribed with magic formulas intended to keep Lilith away. Like many other divine and demonic beings of the ancient world, Lilith was sometimes recognized as an entire class of creatures, called lilitu or liliths.

## Death Mask Face Lift

Lilith has enjoyed something of a revival in recent years. She is recognized as a potent symbol, if not as an actual deity, by contemporary occultists. And she appeared as a character in the Marvel comics series, *The Tomb of Dracula* in the 1970s. More recently, she was woven into the premise of the role-playing game, *Vampire: The Masquerade* in which she is a key factor in the origin of vampires.

Lilith has a good deal in common with a vampire named Akasha from Anne Rice's well-known series of novels, *The Vampire Chronicles*, especially *Queen of the Damned* (1988). Like Lilith, Akasha hails from ancient times in the Fertile Crescent and brings together demonic powers and vampiric attributes. Akasha was an Egyptian queen who was assassinated. Just as her soul was leaving her dying body, she was possessed by a demon named Amel. Akasha became the first vampire in Rice's fictive universe and the fate of all other Ricean vampires is linked to hers.

**Cold Fact** _____

The ancient Hebrews considered blood a sacred substance and they forebade drinking the blood of animals. The words, "the blood is the life," found in the Biblical book of Deuteronomy (12.23), reaffirm this creed. They are repeated in Bram Stoker's novel *Dracula* by the raving, insect-eating lunatic, R. M. Renfield, Dracula's hapless minion.

# Indian Bloodlines

Some scholars believe that the Slavic vampire may be based, at least in part, on ancient demonic beings from India. There is little direct evidence for this connection, but it is possible that Indian legends were brought to the Balkan Peninsula in southern Europe by Gypsies (as their name implies, Gypsies were thought to have come from Egypt, but in fact, they migrated to Europe from India) or by Arab traders.

## Baital Tales

Indian lore is crowded with unearthly beings, many of whom are said to congregate in, or rise from, graveyards. In general, they do not feed specifically on human blood, although many eat human flesh. The rakshasas, for example, are ghoulish, flesh-eating demons who haunt graveyards and interfere with sacred rites of good people.

Another interesting creature is the baital, a former dead person who resembles a small human with wings like a bat and a tail like a goat who may sometimes be found hanging upside down from trees in graveyards. A baital is a central character in the collection of Indian tales,

*Baital-Pachisi,* or "25 tales of a baital." Most of these tales were translated by Sir Richard F. Burton and published in 1870 under the title, *King Vikram and the Vampire.*

**Dead Giveaway** _____

Distinctions among vampirelike creatures from different cultures sometimes get lost in translation. Some non-European menaces bear such obvious similarities to the European vampire that writers who translate their stories into European languages simply refer to them as "vampires." For example, when the English writer Richard Burton translated into English a group of Indian tales centered around a king named Vikram and his encounter with a kind of demon known as the *baital,* he called the work *King Vikram and the Vampire* (first published in 1870). Similarly, British classicist Bickley Rogers uses the word "vampire" to refer to an ancient Greek demon called the *empusa* in his translation of Aristophanes's *The Frogs.*

The baital who tells the tales is mischievous rather than bloodthirsty. His supernatural condition enables him to subtly mock the great king in ways a mere mortal would not dare to do. As a result, the baital teaches Vikram some valuable lessons in humility. These lessons, in fact, are passed along in the tales themselves, which are both fantastic and humorous.

## Seeds of Tradition

Like the Eastern Europeans who gave rise to vampire legend, Indians recognize a wealth of burial customs and superstitions. Among these is the belief that a mother who dies in childbirth poses a threat to the family from beyond the grave. She may come back as an unearthly menace known as a churel or a jhakin.

Various ritual procedures have been practiced to keep these creatures in their graves including:

♦ Driving nails into the ground above the grave

♦ Breaking the feet or chaining them together before burial

◆ Scattering millet seed along the path to the burial ground (the churel is compelled to stop and count the seeds, which takes it at least until daylight)

Interestingly, versions of these procedures were also practiced in Eastern Europe to prevent vampires.

# Vampires Going Greek

Still clearer lines of influence leading from ancient times to Slavic legend can be traced back to Hellenic Greece. The lore and mythology of classical Greece contains many unearthly beings, stories, and beliefs that may well have contributed to the idea of the Slavic vampire. These include seductive demons and an amorous undead.

## Final Fling

One ancient Greek tale tells of a dead woman who returns from the grave not as a spirit, but as an embodied revenant. Although she is not exactly a vampire, her story sets a fitting macabre tone for the Slavic vampires that were to come. The tale, as you can imagine, has become important to vampire scholars. It is reported by a freed Greek slave called Phlegon, who lived during the time of the Roman Emperor Hadrian.

Phlegon's story tells of a dead woman who returned from the grave for some post-mortem hanky-panky! Her name is Philinnion and she's sort of an undead version of Cinderella, except that instead of turning from a princess back into a poor stepdaughter she turns from a sexy babe back into ... well, here's the story:

**Cold Fact** _____

Phlegon's tale of Philinnion and Machates is an intriguing and singular account of an ancient undead revenant. Unfortunately, the account survives only as a fragment, part of the beginning having been lost. The missing portion may have contained useful information for interpreting the unusual story.

Philinnion is the young, deceased daughter of some householders, who appears before a young man named Machates who was visiting her parents for a few days. One day the parents happened to mention their dead daughter to Machates, who answered that he had just spent the night with a woman of the same name. He showed them a ring she had given him. It had belonged to their own dead daughter.

### Dead Giveaway

Philinnion was an undead body who, unlike vampires, didn't drink blood. Strangely, however, Homer's *Illiad* tells of disembodied human spirits who do drink blood. It seems that the hero, Odysseus, has some urgent business to discuss with the shades of the dead, especially with the dead prophet, Teiresias. The problem is, the dead spirits don't have enough physical strength to speak loudly enough to be heard. So Odysseus digs a pit and sacrifices a herd of sheep, letting their blood flow into the pit. When the spirits drink the sheep's blood, they gain enough strength to hold up their end of the conversation.

The parents forced themselves to remain calm until they had investigated the matter. They staked out the hallway that night and, sure enough, their daughter appeared, about to slip through the door of Machates's room. "Philinnion!" they cried. "What are doing out of your grave?"

"What does it look like?" Philinnion responded with an expression that seemed to say "Parents can be so stupid about what goes on when boyfriends are in the house!" "As a matter of fact," she went on, "I pulled some strings in the underworld and arranged to come back for a few nights, but I had to promise I wouldn't let you see me. Now that you have seen me, I have to turn back into a hideous rotting corpse. Bye!"

And she fell to the floor, a hideous, rotting corpse like she said. The householders raised a cry of alarm, so that first the servants and then the townsfolk arrived on the scene. The mob decided to open up Philinnion's grave and found there was no body in it, pretty much proving that the woman-turned-corpse was Philinnion. And to clinch it, they found a ring that Machates had given her, sitting on the bier.

Even though the townsfolk were basically pretty open-minded and had nothing personal against dead people, they were uncomfortable with the idea of love relationships between living and dead, so they burned Philinnion's body to put a stop to the whole thing. And that was the end of the story, except for Machates, who couldn't stand being a loose end of the plot, and so he killed himself.

## Home Wrecker

In addition to non-blood-drinking undead corpses and blood-drinking disembodied spirits (described in the sidebar), ancient Greeks recognized several vampiric demons who may sometimes have sucked blood, although actually they were just mean, vengeful, and seductive. Those most frequently identified as possible vampire prototypes are Lamia, Empusa, and Mormo. Although these are individual demons, they also represented demonic varieties, so you could have a bunch of lamiai, several empusae, and numerous mormolykiai. Who says Greek grammar is tough?

Lamia, the best known of the three, was a Libyan princess who had a fling with Zeus who, as you may know, was ruler of the Gods on Mount Olympus. It was a pretty serious fling, because Lamia had several children as a result. Hera, Zeus's wife, found out about it and took custody of the kids. Lamia got upset and went on a rampage, killing as many children as she could get her hands on until she became transformed into a snake demon. Her snakiness, however, didn't prevent her from seducing men and robbing them of their strength and killing them.

## Lawson Found

Ancient Greek myths, tales, and rituals appear to have had many of the elements that later went into the Slavic vampire. All you need to do is take these stories and the ideas behind them, mix them together, let them sit for a few centuries, mix in some Christianity and local superstition and *voilà!* Vampires. This is more or less the argument, at any rate, of the book, *Modern Greek Folklore and Ancient Greek Religion* (1910) by classicist and folklorist John Cuthbert Lawson.

Lawson attempts to explain the development of the Greek vampire known as the vrykolakas, which is essentially the same as the Slavic version, comparing it to the revenants of classical times. Lawson is a pretty smart guy, but he's kind of biased against modern vampires, preferring just about anything that came out of "the grandeur that was Greece" in pre-Christian times. If he were alive today, he'd probably rather watch Hercules than Buffy!

# When in Rome

A close connection appears to exist between Slavic bloodsuckers and a certain class of demonic spirit from ancient Rome named for the screech owl. This is the *strix* (plural, *striges*), a demon with a woman's head and the body of a bird of prey, capable of attacking sleeping infants and seducing men. The word "strix," which also means owl, appears to be related to *striga*, a Latin word that became the Italian word, *strega*, which is now used interchangeably with the English word "witch."

**Grave Mistake** _____

Sometimes it's a mistake to impose rigid categories on mythic and supernatural beings. In the folklore of some countries, the distinctions between such creatures as witches, vampires, ghosts, and wolfmen can be quite blurry. In addition, a "witch," or a "vampire" from one region may have different characteristics from analogous witches and vampires from other regions. The point is, you just never know what sort of creature is going to put the bite or the hex on you!

In some accounts, the Latin striga is a living human being capable of drinking human blood. It's easy to see how a version of the striga could have turned up in the Slavic region of Europe. During the second century C.E., the Romans founded a colony in the midst of the Slavic countries. The colony took hold and came to be named Romania after the people who founded it. At some point, the bloodsucking Romanian striga merged with the concept of the Slavic vampire. Related terms, including shtriga, strigoi, and strigon, have been used in the Slavic region, especially Romania, to refer to vampires.

# Iran from Vampires

Still another likely source of Slavic vampire lore are some of the religious beliefs from ancient Iran. These beliefs appear to have existed in Eastern Europe side by side with Christianity and local folk beliefs throughout much of the Middle Ages. They are important in the history of vampires not so much because they recognize specific demons, but for what they say about the relationship between evil and death.

## Faith Buffet

Scholars say the Slavs may have encountered Iranian beliefs at various times in history: some before they migrated to Eastern Europe, others waiting for them when they arrived, and still others after they had been there a while. Despite their common origin in Iran, these beliefs took the form of different religions. What's more, they were probably practiced in a variety of different ways in Eastern Europe, together with other beliefs. You might say the region was something of a spiritual smorgasbord.

Here are three incarnations of Iranian-based religion that have made their mark in Eastern Europe:

> **Cold Fact**
>
> Nineteenth-century Russian folklorist A. N. Afanasiev advanced a theory that the Slavic vampire stems from a local pre-Christian god or demon who lives in the sky and controls the weather, sucking rain from the clouds much as vampires would later suck blood from human beings.

- Mithraism—an ancient sect adopted by many Romans as the Roman Empire spread East based on the worship of the Sun God Mithra.

- Manicheanism—a dualist (good vs. evil) religion founded by a prophet named Mani (216–274 C.E.) who attempted to combine the teachings of Jesus, Buddha, and the Iranian prophet Zoroaster.

- Bogomilism—a heretical Christian sect founded by a Slavic priest named Bogomil based largely on Manichean ideas and practiced in Eastern Europe from the ninth to the fourteenth centuries.

## Demon Magnets

The extent to which these Iranian-influenced religions made a mark on Slavic vampires is difficult to assess, since very few writings have been found to document them. It seems likely though, that something of the Manichean and Bogomilist attitude toward dead bodies enters into the picture. In these religions, dead bodies were seen as spiritually unclean and therefore evil.

Unclean things attract evil spirits. We know the Manicheans practiced careful burial rites to avoid unnecessary contact with unclean corpses and the evil spirits that are attracted to them. This attitude toward dead bodies may well have influenced Slavic vampire lore, in which dead bodies are virtual breeding grounds for troublesome supernatural doings. Unfortunately, we may never know just when, how, or if this idea took hold.

## The Least You Need to Know

- Ancient ghosts and demons often get labeled as vampires because they suck blood, seduce human beings, or commit spiteful murders.

- Lilith is one of the oldest known demons brought into the vampire fold from Jewish legend.

- The baital is a whimsical and witty vampirelike being from India, who appears in the collection of tales, *King Vikram and the Vampire*.

- Vampiric demons from ancient Greek lore include the lamia, the empusa, and the mormo.

- Ancient Rome has contributed the stryx, a demon and witch, to vampire lore.

- Ancient Iranian religious belief may have influenced Eastern European attitudes toward dead bodies.

# Chapter 8

# Suckers from All Over

## In This Chapter

◆ International and multicultural vampires

◆ Vampirelike creatures from world folklore

◆ Vampires and colonialism

◆ Vampires in international pop culture

Vampirelike beings have been identified and described in the folklore of cultures from around the world. Even today, Western travelers encounter new lands and new legends and discover intriguing similarities between local stories and superstitions and those familiar from Slavic vampire legends. Whether or not you see these non-Slavic creatures as, in fact, vampires, as many observers are increasingly inclined to do, a look at them can give you a clearer sense of how the vampire bug takes hold and spreads, as well as some of its mutations.

In addition to the vampirelike creatures discovered by folklore collectors in their travels from place to place are vampires that arise at the point of contact between Western and non-Western cultures. Whenever strangers pour into town, people are apt to get worried and spread rumors. Under these circumstances, some particularly scary and interesting vampires have been born. It seems that vampires have been used as psychological weapons in the cultural conflicts between different groups of people.

But vampires can also help bring people together. Many non-Western cultures have embraced the Slavic and Hollywood vampire as their own. In the process, they give the vampire a new, local flavor, blending it in with local traditions and, in some cases, even local vampirelike menaces.

# Eastern Beasts

We might as well start, for no special reason, in the Far East, where many cultures have generated and maintained proud traditions of bloodsucking terror. Notable examples are from China, where folkloric menaces have appeared in classic Chinese literature, and Malaysia, where vampiric beings have hidden holes in them like piggy banks—the kind you don't have to smash to get your change out of!

## Death Breath

The Chinese recognize an undead menace called the chiang shih. Like Slavic vampires, the chiang shih possesses unearthly strength and can maintain its undead state by feeding on the living. And it may have long, sharp fingernails capable of making deep lacerations in living flesh.

**Dead Giveaway** _____

Terms of comparison between non-Slavic vampirelike creatures and the full-blooded Slavic vampire vary from case to case. Of the many vampirelike creatures from around the world, all menace humanity, most do so through seductive means, and many suck blood. Few, however, are undead. The chiang shih from China is one of these few. Known from the legend and literature of Dynastic times long before the rise of Communism, the chiang shih is a dead body that isn't ready to call it quits. And it can kill living people just by breathing on them.

The Chinese traditionally believe that all people have two souls, a higher soul and lower one. At the time of death, the higher soul leaves the body to join with the ancestors. The lower soul, however, sometimes hangs around inside the corpse where it is liable to do mischief. The malingering lower soul can absorb energy through sunlight or moonlight if the body is left exposed to open air by day or night, and in this way can gather the strength to rise again.

## Four Beddings and a Funeral

One of the best known Chinese chiang shih stories was written during the Ch'ing Dynasty by P'u Sung-ling (1640–1715). You might think of Sung-ling as something of an Edgar Allan P'u! Anyway, he wrote a popular collection of stories called *Liao-chai chih-i*, or *Strange Tales from a Chinese Studio*. In one of these stories, four travelers stopped at an inn late at night. The innkeeper told them he had no vacancies and he could not give them a room. But the travelers pleaded with him, explaining that they were too tired to go on without rest. They offered to take any spot on the floor the innkeeper could provide. They also offered him lots of money.

So, reluctantly, the innkeeper took their money and showed them to a room where a dead body was lying behind a curtain. "This was my daughter-in-law," the innkeeper explained. The travelers shrugged and immediately lay down and went to sleep.

Before long, however, one of the travelers was awakened by the loud snoring of the other three. He thought about waking them to make them stop, but decided against it, since he was out-numbered. But just then, he heard the curtain rustling. He looked and saw the pale corpse of the innkeeper's daughter-in-law draw back the curtain and stand above the snoring sleepers one by one. As the chiang shih stood above each sleeper, the snoring stopped.

The wakeful traveler was too scared to move. Fearing that the slightest noise would attract the chiang shih, he hid under his covers without moving. The chiang shih returned behind the curtain. Gathering his courage, the traveler crept out of bed and went to each of his companions in turn, shaking them. But they would not awaken.

Suddenly, the chiang shih emerged again from behind the curtain and lunged after the traveler, who shrieked and ran out of the room with the chiang shih running after him. He ran as fast as he could, but the chiang shih ran faster and quickly—but not too quickly—caught up with him. He fell down in front of a tree and fainted just as the monster lunged at him with its long, sharp fingernails.

The traveler woke from his stupor the next morning to find the dead body of the innkeeper's daughter-in-law standing directly over him. She had driven her fingernails so deeply into the trunk of the tree that she couldn't pull them back out. Eventually, the fingernails had to be cut off and plucked out of the tree with pliers.

The body was quickly buried. (Unlike Slavic vampires, chiang shihs cannot dig or float themselves out of their graves after they've been buried.) The three travelers in the room were found dead and they were buried, too. The surviving traveler remained a nervous wreck for many months and never fully recovered from the experience.

> **Cold Fact** _____
>
> A Japanese folktale tells of a vampirelike cat who kills the beautiful concubine of a prince and takes over her body. Each night when the prince came to visit, the cat in the form of the concubine would weaken him. Eventually the cat was discovered, but it escaped and had to be hunted down again. A one-act play based on this folktale called *The Vampire Cat* was written in English in 1918.

# Hole-y Horrors

Malaysia is a Far Eastern land especially rich in fear-inspiring folklore that's rife with menacing not-quite-human creatures. Two stand out as particularly interesting:

1. Penanggalens—evil spirits that take possession of women and turn them into predatory witches. They fly around by uprooting their heads from their bodies with the guts attached, which dangle beneath them as they fly!

2. Langsuyars, also known as pontianaks—former women who died in childbirth and return to suck the blood of children. They wear their hair long to disguise a big hole in their backs.

According to one story, a husband and his wife were both suspected penanggalens. One day an enterprising young hero put the matter to the test. He waited outside the couple's house at night and, sure enough, their heads detached from their bodies and flew off into the darkness, trailing their guts after them. The young hero switched the bodies while the heads were away, putting the husband's body where the wife's was and vice versa. When the heads came back, they fixed themselves onto one another's bodies. The switch didn't do them any real harm, but it proved to everyone who saw them that way that they were penanggalens!

Pontianaks are much like many other demonic moms turned bad, some of whom were described in the previous chapter. They are unique, however, in that it is possible to tame them. All you have to do is cut off their long hair and fingernails and stuff them into the hole in their backs. Then they can live for an indefinite period of time as reasonably well-adjusted members of society!

**Cold Fact**

The traditional pontianak has merged in Malaysian popular culture with the Slavic vampire imported from Hollywood. During the 1950s and '60s a number of Malaysian-made horror films were produced, featuring blood-sucking pontianaks.

# Black Magic

As we continue to survey vamp-kind from China to Peru, our next stop is west Africa, where many vampirelike menaces have not only made their home, but have made the journey across the Atlantic to South America and the West Indies on slave ships. In general, the creatures that most closely resemble Slavic vampires are not undead, or even spirits of the dead, but living witches who prey on their enemies in a variety of ways.

## Crafty Characters

Folklore concerning witches is widespread in west Africa. Witches are said to learn their sorcery in secret and to live unrecognized in their communities. Motivated by spite, jealousy, greed, or revenge, they attack their victims in various ways, frequently by sapping them of essential bodily fluids or energy.

In pre-colonial Yoruba society in Nigeria, witches were typically described as wives of men who had two or more other wives. These witches jockeyed for position in the family pecking order by sucking the blood of their husbands and of the children of their cowives. They did this with the help of magic that prevents their victims from detecting them. Yoruban witches learn their craft from their mothers. Or they may gain entry into a coven, or group of witches, by bringing an offering, such as a young child, which is then eaten by the whole group. Women may become witches against their will if they are tricked into eating human flesh or drinking human blood.

> **Cold Fact** _____
>
> If you're married to a witch, be sure to keep close track of your family jewels! Some Yoruban witches are said to be capable of borrowing their husbands' sexual organs and using them to have sex with other women! The extracurricular activity makes the husband impotent.

## Soul Food

A little to the north of the Nigerian Yoruba tribe live the Hausa tribe of Niger. The Hausa tell of vampirelike witches known as "soul eaters." As their name implies, they feed on human souls, causing their soul-deprived victims to waste away. Sometimes the soul eaters have the bodies of their victims for dessert!

Soul eaters are ordinary human beings that have swallowed magic beans or stones that give them the power to steal other peoples' souls. Soul eaters, like Slavic vampires, are shape-shifters, often stalking their victims while inhabiting the shape of an animal. Their animal form often has a peculiarity about it. A soul-eating dog, for example, may have no tail or may howl in a strange manner. When their victims notice these strange things, they become so startled that their souls momentarily leap out of their bodies. At that moment, the soul eater will snatch the disembodied soul and keep it trapped inside a jar until dinner time.

Soul eaters can also snatch souls simply by touching their victims or by touching their victims' shadow. Sometimes soul eaters can catch souls by standing downwind of their victims. They are difficult for ordinary humans to detect, but fellow soul eaters can recognize each other right away. Although most of them are bad, there are a few good soul eaters who protect the community against their evil counterparts.

### Dead Giveaway

Perhaps the foremost authority in multicultural vampires is Montague Summers, a one-time Anglican priest who left the Church of England and moved to southern Europe for many years, where he did research for his many books on vampires and witches and where he claimed he was ordained a Catholic priest. At least one of his editors, however, has cast doubt on this claim, speculating that Summers was actually revolving in occult circles and exploring non-Christian spirituality instead of working toward the Catholic priesthood. Summers, then, may have been playing on both sides of the religious fence! In any case, thanks largely to Summers's authoritative work, many vampire scholars have been inclined to accept with little question the notion that the "vampire" is a multicultural phenomenon recognized the world over.

# South of the Border

Mexico and Puerto Rico have some interesting vampiric traditions, too. Some of these traditions hearken way back to before the Spanish conquest. Others are almost literally hot off the presses. It seems that human and animal blood really hits the spot whether you're an ancient Aztec blood god or an escaped genetic experiment from outer space!

## Gods' Blood

The ancient Aztecs recognized their own version of the vampirelike mother-turned-bad demon found in many parts of the world. These were the cihuateteos, who started as women who died in childbirth, but returned to plague the living by preying on young children and seducing men. They practice sorcery and can be killed by sunlight.

The Aztecs are infamous for practicing ritual human sacrifice. One rationale for immolating human beings—usually prisoners of war—was to feed the blood-drinking goddess, Cihuacoatl. She is also known as "the snake woman" and is traditionally represented as having two knives growing out of her forehead.

**Cold Fact**

The Mayans of Guatemala, just south of Mexico, recognized a god of the underworld known as Camazotz. Part man, part bat, Camazotz was said to live in caves like his little flying rodent cousins. He presided over the cycle of life and death, not only for humanity, but for crops as well.

# Getting Their Goat

Belief in vampiric creatures has resurfaced in Mexico in recent years, and in surrounding regions, including Puerto Rico and Miami. Many people in these areas have reported a vicious creature called a chupacabra, or "goatsucker," who preys on livestock by sucking its blood. Some reports have claimed that livestock was left bizarrely mutilated, and others that the goatsucker attacks humans as well.

Some reports describe the chupacabra as a three-foot-long rat with wings and enormous teeth. Others say it has long quills running down its spine instead of wings. Concern about the creature peaked in the mid-1990s and became so serious that police-style sketches of them, supposedly based on witnesses' descriptions, appeared in Mexican newspapers. Farmers went out and set bonfires in caves in which they were thought to have holed up. Puerto Rican officials organized public autopsies to show that animals thought to have been chupacabra victims were actually killed by dogs.

**Grave Mistake**

Don't assume that the chupacabra scare is mere nonsense. The creature itself may not exist, but the damage to livestock is real. The problem is reminiscent of another recent "vampire" scare in Puerto Rico, known as the Vampire of Moca, which preyed on pets and livestock. This creature turned out to be a group of renegade crocodiles!

Similarly, police in Mexico staked out the farm of one man who complained of chupacabra attacks on his livestock and said that dogs were to blame. The theory that chupacabras are just hungry dogs, however, has attracted less attention than alternative theories, namely:

1. They are pets or experimental test creatures belonging to an intelligent species from outer space.

2. They are experimental mutants that escaped from a lab in the United States, and their existence is being hushed by the U.S. and Mexican governments.

3. They are a species related to the dinosaur that has survived unnoticed since the Cetaceous period.

# Vampire Empire

Vampires have figured into political tension around the world stemming from colonialism—the process by which cultures with simple technologies and small economies are absorbed by other cultures with complicated and big ones. From the point of view of the culture being colonized, this process can be pretty scary. Vampires often provide a vivid representation of the fear involved.

## Hired Fangs

In the east and central African countries of Kenya, Uganda, Zambia, among others, working African men have been telling "vampire" stories about their fellow workers whom they suspect of conspiring with white men to drain the blood of other Africans. Especially suspect were those who drove cars or vans for Europeans or for the colonial government. Fire and medical trucks, in particular, were said to contain equipment for draining and transporting blood.

The vampires were said to work in secrecy, closely supervised by whites. Victims were kidnapped and either bled to death or their blood supplies were severely depleted. Their blood was transported to places where white people could drink it. Many people seem to have believed the stories. Local newspapers printed letters written by people claiming to have knowledge of blood-collecting activities. As you might imagine, widespread suspicion doomed more than one blood-giving drive to failure!

### Dead Giveaway

East and central African vampire stories have been exhaustively researched and discussed by Luise White, who has studied colonialism in Africa for over ten years. In her book, *Speaking With Vampires: Rumor and History in Colonial Africa* (2000), White shows that the stories express anxieties felt by many working Africans over the question of whether, and on what basis, one should work for white people. The stories were most commonly told by freelance day laborers about people with permanent jobs. In fact, the stories have a point. European colonialists may not literally have sucked African blood, but they did transform and undermine the traditional ways of life, often by paying one group of Africans to help them exploit the others.

## Scare Tactics

Here's a gruesome true story: A vampirelike creature known as the aswang played a role in a 1950 conflict in the Philippines between government troops aided by the American CIA and a group of guerilla insurgents known as the Hukbalahaps, or Huks. While seeking support for their cause among the peasants, the Huks posed a threat to the established government. Enter the aswang.

According to legend, the aswang lives by day as an attractive Filipina, leading an apparently normal life. At night, however, she turns into a birdlike menace with a long, pointy tongue. It flies off to prey on victims, usually children, by sticking its tongue into them and slurping out their blood.

Familiar with the aswang legend and aware that many Filipinos believed in it, CIA operatives spread rumors that an aswang had been preying on people in a village where Huks were active. After waiting a few days for the rumors to spread, government troops silently kidnapped a Huk foot soldier and killed him. Then they punctured his neck, hung him up by his feet, and bled him dry. Finally, they put the drained corpse on a busy pathway where it would be found and let fear do the rest.

The plan worked. The Huk soldiers cleared out right away. Unfortunately, so did many civilian villagers! Frightened by the aswang, no one wanted to live in the area anymore. The land was eventually bought up by large multinational corporations! How's that for vampiric?

# Entertaining Terrors

Fortunately, most vampires set about conquering the world through diabolical charm and popular appeal rather than by literally sucking the blood out of people. In fact, the old rule that says a vampire can only sleep in his native soil is plainly not true, since foreign soil has proven fertile for Western-style vampires of popular culture. Vampires have been well-received all over the world, wherever Western ways have found a foothold.

## Fangs Are Great for Nippon

Vampires have become easily recognizable within Japanese pop culture. Books, movies, and computer games feature vampires that are as Japanese as the car and the camera! And these Japanese vampires have many fans in the West as well.

A couple of Japanese computer games are "Castlevania," and "Countdown Vampires." Castlevania is based in part on the famous novel, *Dracula*, incorporating some of Stoker's plot into the game's storyline. In fact, play takes place in a number of different time frames, starting in the fifteenth century. "Countdown Vampires" is set in an American casino where something funny in the sprinkler system turns the crowd into a bloodsucking hoard. The game story line has been made into a comic book.

Two comic book and animated video productions featuring vampires are *Vampire Princess Miyu* and *Blood: The Last Vampire*. Miyu is a benevolent teenage vampire princess who helps mortals fulfill their dreams and patrols the human world for demons from the spirit world. She first appeared in a 1988 video and has been in comic books and videos ever since. A slightly darker vampire offering is *Blood: The Last Vampire*, in which a teenage female ninja warrior named Saya pursues vampires on a U.S. military base in Japan just before the Vietnam War. The story is likewise available in comic book and video form.

## Foreign Film

Vampires appear in great numbers, of course, in international cinema. Locally made vampire films have been popular in Mexico, Argentina,

Brazil, Malaysia, Hong Kong, Japan, and the countries of western Europe. Most of these places also have vampire books, comic books, and other pop culture stuff.

**Cold Fact** _____

Many vampire buffs know that one of the first vampire movies ever made came from Germany. This is *Nosferatu: eine Symphonie des Grauens* (1922), based on the novel *Dracula*. Less well known is that another vampire film, also based on *Dracula*, was made ten years previously in Russia, known in English as *The Secret of House #5* (1912). A more influential early vampire film is the American-made Spanish language version of Universal Pictures's *Dracula*, which came out in 1931, the same year as the Hollywood version.

This chapter has only scratched the surface of international vampiric lore. Many more cultures have creatures comparable to vampires in addition to those described here. But take a look at the next chapter before you go off feeling shortchanged. It describes a whole philosophical approach to seeing vampires as a multicultural phenomenon. The New Age vampire is a creature that knows no boundaries!

## The Least You Need to Know

- Vampirelike creatures can be found in folklore the world over.

- Multicultural vampire scares sometimes figure into tensions stemming from cultural and political conflicts.

- Vampires can be found in the popular culture of virtually every country where Western technology has taken hold.

Chapter **9**

# Blood Relations and Kindred Spirits

## In This Chapter

- Witches, werewolves, ghouls, and ghosts
- Similarities and connections to vampires
- Folklore and pop culture
- Goths and Theosophists

Intimately intertwined with the history of vampires are a few other creatures known for making mischief at night. These are the evil beings that loom largest in the dark imaginations of scare-prone people everywhere. Understanding them can help you understand vampires.

These creatures are interesting in their own right as well as in the ways they connect to vampires. In fact, there are some remarkable similarities between vampires and these other doers of dark deeds. Call me biased, but it almost seems like they took the coolest features of every spooky critter out there and gave them to vampires! Maybe vampires suck diabolical character as well as blood!

A subtext of this chapter concerns what happens when these evil beings emerge out of the murky mists of folklore and into the glare of popular culture. In general, they become much more sharply defined. But there's always room for ambiguity and uncertainty.

# Menaces of Distinction

Vampires in the modern West are often associated with witches, werewolves, ghouls, and ghosts. As defined in Western terms, all of these creatures are different, of course. Even little kids quickly learn to tell the difference between the wolfman and the vampire, the witch and the ghost. Everybody knows there are clear differences, not only in appearance, but also in the characteristics of the different creatures.

## Stereotypical Terrors

These distinctions are not absolute, but stem largely from the fact that certain ideas in folklore fall by the wayside while others are remembered and repeated. Then the ideas that are preserved get reinforced in modern times by popular stories and movies. Pretty soon, the distinct attributes of vampires, witches, ghouls, and ghosts become so familiar to everyone that it seems as if they were written in stone.

**Cold Fact** _____

In a survey prepared by Norine Dresser and administered to hundreds of high school and college students in America, 44 percent said they learned about vampires between age 5 and 8. Another 40 percent learned between age 8 and 12.

The differences among the various malevolent beings haven't always been so obvious. In folklore, factors that separate one creature from another are often found together in a single being. There are witches for example, who suck blood. There are spirits or ghosts who walk the earth as werewolves. Maybe someone should invent new categories like witchpire and woofergeist!

Suppose supernatural mischief was perpetrated on you. One of every pair of socks you own disappears, your car keys keep turning up in the silverware drawer, you have an unexplainable compulsion to eat ten

Egg McMuffins every day, and something keeps draining your mind so you can never remember birthdays or anniversaries! Could you finger the culprit in a lineup of unearthly beings?

## Real Compared to What

Think about the situation from the point of view of the old Slavic peasants who have never seen a movie, read a comic book, or played a computer game. If they had, they would all have the same ideas in mind whenever they thought about vampires. After all, in popular culture, huge numbers of people have access to the same set of ideas and information. In folk culture, in contrast, information spreads slowly and shifts and changes as it gets passed from one person to another.

And Slavic peasants never read or learned about the unearthly beings of other cultures either, but only heard stories and rumors about what might be out there. These stories and rumors are rooted in tradition, of course, but that tradition has always been fluid. It tends not to be written down but, instead, continues to be repeated in new ways.

Taken as a whole, folklore supplies a hazy and shifting picture of the supernatural menaces it describes. Each new menace must be taken more or less on its own terms, without preconceptions and categories. Labels like vampire, witch, and werewolf supply only rough guidelines for what the human world might be up against. The characteristics of the creatures these labels refer to have a way of bleeding together.

It takes a broad historical perspective, a popular tradition, and permanent record-keeping to build up the clear distinctions we recognize today. As writers, folklorists, and others latch on to specific characteristics as being especially significant, those characteristics become generally accepted and recognized. And they get reinforced again and again as

> **Grave Mistake**
>
> Don't rely too heavily on distinctions between vampires and other evil menaces. An oft-cited entry from Whitney's *Century Dictionary*, quoted by vampire scholar Montague Summers, defines the vampire in terms that connect it to other supernatural creatures: "A kind of spectral [ghostly] body ... Dead wizards, werewolves, heretics, and other outcasts become vampires."

people continue to refer to them. Even so, and despite the clear differences, people today recognize witches, vampires, ghouls, and ghosts as birds of a feather.

# Charming Companions

In Slavic folklore, vampires are often called witches, wizards, or sorcerers. In fact, many vampires have a lot in common with witches: evil intentions, magical powers, and knowledge of spells, for example. In addition, vampires, like witches, are often considered to have diabolical associations—to be fundamentally opposed to God and His Church.

## Common Ground

In some areas, namely Russia, vampire lore developed in the midst of anti-witch efforts taken by the Church. Witches in the Russian Middle Ages were considered heretical and were denied Christian burial. As outcasts from the Christian afterlife they were considered prime candidates to come back as vampires. Thus the concepts of witch and vampire were closely linked, at least in Russia, because both were seen in opposition to Christianity.

In Romania, a connection between vampires and witches can be traced etymologically (through language). The Romanian word *strigoi* is often used to refer to vampires. This word comes from a term that is closely akin to the Italian word *strega*, meaning witch. So again, Slavic witches and Slavic vampires are hard to distinguish.

Of course, witches have a long and rich history outside of Eastern Europe that helps people today see differences between witches and vampires. Vampires were not sought out and persecuted during the Spanish Inquisition anywhere near the extent that witches were. Vampires were not generally thought to be adept in occult philosophy in the Middle Ages as many witches and warlocks were said to be. And of course there were no infamous "Salem vampire trials" in old Massachusetts Bay Colony.

What's more, contemporary practitioners of Wicca don't ordinarily suck blood, and neither did the practitioners of the pre-Christian magic and ritual cults on which today's Wicca is reputedly based. All these things reinforce distinctions in people's minds between witches and vampires. These distinctions are further reinforced by movies, books, computer games, and even Halloween costumes.

### Grave Mistake

It's sad to say, but ardent vampire fans sometimes come down with cases of witch envy on account of the more prominent place witches occupy in history. This problem no doubt influenced Montague Summers to suggest that vampires were present in Salem, causing trouble around the time of the witch trials there in the early 1690s. He claims to detect evidence of vampires in the stories told by the girls who accused other townspeople of witchcraft!

## Shared Secrets

But witches and vampires have continued to hang out together in the modern world and witch and vampire lore can often be found in combination with one another. In the novel *Dracula*, for example, Dr. Van Helsing says that Count Dracula is an adept in occult learning and magic, and that he studied at a school run by the devil himself known as the Scholomance.

### Dead Giveaway

Witches are generally considered more scholarly and philosophical than vampires because witchcraft must be studied, learned, and practiced, whereas vampirism is something that simply gets into your blood. What's more, witches can get lots of forbidden knowledge from the devil, whereas traditional Slavic vampires only know what they knew in life as turnip farmers. Vampires seem to act on instinct while witches practice the black arts. Nevertheless, because they can remain in their undead state indefinitely and may walk the earth for centuries, vampires have a lot of time to catch up on their reading. Thus vampires like Stoker's Dracula and Rice's Lestat have become knowledgeable in occult lore and can vie with witches in their command of the black magic.

Very little is known of the Scholomance legend. Bram Stoker read about it in a book about Transylvania called *Land Beyond the Forest* (1888) by Emily Gerard. It is important because it associates Dracula, hence Slavic vampires, with witchcraft and Satan, as well as with occult philosophical learning. Vampire fans of today with an interest in the occult look to the Scholomance as a legendary precedent for the vampire/occult connection. Scholomance, incidentally, is also the name of a Goth techno-metal group.

Speaking of Goth, there's no hesitation among today's young gothic types to combine anything creepy with anything else creepy. Hence witch stuff and vampire stuff are often blended together in song lyrics, nightclubs, and websites, as well as in books and movies that appeal to Goths. For example, businesses that supply ritual and magic supplies for modern-day Wiccans, shamans, devil worshipers, etc. often sell vampire-related items as well. One reputable magic arts supply store, for example, sells vampire chalices, belt buckles, mirrors, ritual daggers, and wall plaques. You know what they say, whatever gets you through the night!

Popular vampire novels, most notably Anne Rice's *The Vampire Chronicles* often present vampires in the context of witchcraft and other occult doings. Anne Rice's vampires have occult links to the devil (who turns out not to be such a bad guy after all!) And comic books and movies such as *Blade, Vampire Hunter* present vampires in ritualistic groups that resemble witches' covens.

# Putting on the Dog

Vampires have a lot in common with werewolves as well as with witches. Both are fanged predators, both are shape-shifters, and both semi-human. Both are said to change their nature according to natural cycles—the werewolf becomes a wolf during a full moon while the vampire becomes a corpse during the day. These rules, however, don't necessarily apply in folklore. In Slavic folklore, in fact, it can be hard to tell werewolves and vampires apart. As you may remember from Chapter 6, the term "Vukodlak" can be used for vampires and werewolves interchangeably.

## Tale of Wolf

Romanians have a different term for werewolves, namely pricolici. (Actually, pricolici can change into a variety of animals, not just wolves.) One Romanian story tells of a pricolici, who kept up the appearance of normal life. One day he was riding in his carriage with his wife, who he kept ignorant of his dual nature. At that moment, however, he felt the change about to come over him, so he reined in the carriage and ran off into the bushes, where he was transformed into a dog.

The dog was in a vicious mood and ran out of the bushes, barking and snarling. Seeing the wife still sitting in the carriage waiting for her husband, the dog jumped up and attacked her, scratching her, biting her, and tearing her dress. But the woman managed to fend off the dog and drive the carriage back home, leaving the dog behind.

Eventually the dog turned into a man again and went home where his wife was waiting for him. Not realizing he had attacked her as a dog, he smiled to show her he was all right. But when he smiled, his wife saw that he had a shred of her dress caught in his teeth, so she figured out he was a pricolici!

### Grave Mistake

Don't assume all werewolf legends abide by the idea that werewolves change shape during a full moon. A Slovak tale tells of a creature called a vlkolak who doesn't actually turn into a wolf, but simply kills his own daughters in human form because he is tired of supporting them. The youngest daughter escapes, however, and marries a handsome prince who eventually kills him. Another story tells of a werewolf who went around for years in the form of a wolf until a hunter chopped off his head and he turned into a human being again.

## Mixed Breeds

Werewolf legends can be found outside of Eastern Europe as well. In fact, the term "werewolf" comes from Old English, although it may not have been used to describe any legendary wolf men until the nineteenth century when werewolves became popular in fiction. Since then, a number of werewolf novels have helped make the creature well known.

*Hughes the Wer-wolf* was a serialized novel by Sutherland Menzies published in the 1850s. It was followed by *Wagner the Wehrwolf* (1857) by W. M. Reynolds. In 1934, *The Werewolf of Paris* by Guy Endore was published. This was inspired in part by the actual case of Francois Bertrand, an officer in the French Army who was caught digging up dead bodies in graveyards. Endore's book was made into the Universal

Pictures movie, *The Werewolf of London* (1935). This was followed by *The Wolf Man* (1941), starring Lon Chaney Jr. in the title role. Werewolves have been popular in movies ever since.

Myth and folklore from around the world includes tales of wolflike men and people who change into wolves and other animals. Tribal healers known as *shamans* are often thought to have shape-shifting powers. The term shaman originally referred only to a sorcerer-healer-priest from Siberian tribal culture, but has since been applied to analogous figures in tribal cultures across Asia, Africa, and America. In these societies, much of the shaman's power is thought to stem from his experience with altered states of consciousness during which the shaman travels on spiritual journeys, communing with and learning from the spirits and demons of other worlds.

> **Stalk Talk** _____
>
> A **shaman** is a tribal healer and spiritual leader who often prepares for his vocation by exploring altered states of consciousness with the help of hallucinogenic drugs, sleep deprivation, or prolonged fasting. Having experienced these extreme states of being, he is thought to have privileged insight into the spirit world.

The shaman can send his spirit out into the world, sometimes in the form of an animal such as a wolf. Shape-shifting into animal form is closely connected with his experience with altered states of consciousness. Thus the animal world, the spirit world, and the inner world of the mind merge together in shamanic experience. Lore surrounding the shape-shifting shaman is part of the tangle of ideas lying behind the modern legend of the werewolf.

Tribal warriors have been known to identify with wolves and other vicious animals in order to get psyched up for battle. Notable examples are the legendary Scandinavian berserkers, warriors who went into such frenzied battle rages that they were thought to assume the form of bears. The phrase "going berserk" alludes to this legend. Interestingly, in the novel *Dracula*, "Bersicker" is the name of a wolf from the zoo in London who broke out of his cage and into Lucy Westenra's house at Dracula's command.

Men who kill innocent people are traditionally considered wolflike. The classic example is the Greek myth of Lycaon, the King of Arcadia, who had the god Zeus as a dinner guest and served him human flesh.

Zeus turned him into a wolf, which, in Greek, bears his name, "lykos." In fact, the word "lycanthrope" is another name for the wolfman based on the Greek words for wolf and man. Lycanthropy is the condition of being a werewolf or of believing that you are a wolf or can turn into one. It was once considered a form of demonic possession and has since been regarded as a psychiatric problem related to schizophrenia.

# Scavenger Hunt

As suave, sophisticated, and sexy as they may be, vampires are near kin to the grossest of the gross, the ghouls. Like ghouls, vampires hang around in graveyards, feel erotically and gastronomically attracted to dead people, and, despite their utter depravity, often like to pass themselves off as human beings. Ghouls have not made quite the splash in popular culture that vampires, witches, and werewolves have, but they have their own distinctive air about them that has rubbed off on vampires over the centuries.

## Unhealthy Eaters

Ghouls come from Arab folklore, where they are known as ghuls and ghulahs (guy-ghouls and gal-ghouls, respectively). They are demons who spend lots of time in graveyards because they like to eat human corpses. You might think they would be handy to have around as a way of disposing of dead bodies, but in the mind of the Arabs, eating dead human flesh is the ultimate evil.

**Grave Mistake**

An early, classic "ghoul" movie, *The Ghoul* (1933), starring Boris Karloff, failed to define the ghoul type with specific and compelling characteristics in the popular imagination. Maybe Karloff's character should have eaten some half-rotten corpses!

In fact, ghoul lore may have been imported into Eastern Europe where it influenced vampire legends way back when. Ghouls play into a dualistic religious view from the Middle East that took hold for a while in the Slavic countries. This view stems from Manicheanism, a Persian religion founded by the prophet Mani, who taught that existence was basically one big battle between good and evil. At death, the good aspect of human nature escapes the body, which, as a corpse, is evil and unclean. Only an evil being would want to touch a dead body without proper ritual cleansing, much less eat one.

Ghouls not only eat dead bodies, but lurk in thoroughfares trying to hook up with unsuspecting travelers and destroy them or simply do mischief. Ghouls can be destroyed if hit hard enough with a single blow. A second blow, however, can revive them. Many Arabian stories tell of ghouls who trick mortals into marrying them, apparently just for the sheer fun of grossing them out when they find what they are married to! The Slavic vampire tale retold at the end of Chapter 6 in this book has a trace of this feature of ghoul folklore.

## Twisted Image

Strangely, while vampires, witches, and werewolves have become more sharply defined in the process of emerging from folklore into popular culture, ghouls have lost some of their distinctiveness since moving west from the Middle East. Many people today think of ghouls as a kind of generic supernatural menace, like a ghost only uglier. Others equate ghouls with zombies—mindless corpses who rise from the grave in search of living human flesh.

Perhaps this is because Westerners don't think a creature who mainly attacks people who are already dead is that scary. It's gross, but it's almost like a victimless crime. As a result, the ghoul concept is somewhat lost on most Westerners.

**Dead Giveaway** _____

For a small handful of late-night TV watchers in northeast Ohio, the ghoul concept survives as an embodiment of silliness and bad taste. That's largely thanks to several generations of late-night TV horror movie hosts based in Cleveland, beginning with "Ghoulardie" in the 1960s, "The Ghoul" in the '70s, '80s, and '90s, and "Son of the Ghoul" in recent years. All three show really bad movies, wear fake goatees and mustaches, blow up toys with firecrackers, and carry on ritual celebrations of harmless bad taste, for example by doing strange things with white socks (made in nearby Parma, Ohio) and Cheese Whiz.

# Bad Spirits

And of course vampires have a lot in common with ghosts, too. Both are revenants—beings who return to the world of the living from the world of the dead—and both frequently menace family members and loved ones. Ghosts, like vampirelike beings, are found in the folklore of many cultures.

## Happy Haunting Grounds

Ghosts are not a prominent feature of Slavic folklore. Ghosts are disembodied spirits whereas vampires are undead reanimated corpses. Slavic vampires, however, sometimes carry on the same sort of house haunting that ghosts do in other places. In other words, Slavic vampires not only suck blood, but make a nuisance of themselves by rattling pots and pans, making scary moaning sounds, breaking things, and making a mess.

A vampire does these things not as a ghost would, but either as a moving body or else through magic. Ghosts and vampires out of folklore, in other words, typically follow different sets of rules. But almost as soon as vampires began to emerge into the modern West, starting around the mid-nineteenth century, people began bending the rules so that vampires and ghosts could occupy the same spheres. These people were American and European spiritualists, who were fascinated with ghosts and who became intrigued with vampires, too.

**Grave Mistake**

If your dead relatives aren't sending you messages that you can understand, chances are that's a good thing. Beware of people like the nineteenth-century spiritualists who want to be haunted on purpose or who offer to help others be haunted. When you look for trouble you almost always find it!

## Ghost Writers

Spiritualism was a popular hobby among many slightly eccentric, fairly well-off Europeans and Americans from the mid-nineteenth to early twentieth centuries. Spiritualists liked to get together in salons and hold séances in order to communicate with those who had passed over to "the other side"—ghosts, that is. There were many popular techniques for doing this:

- **Spirit mediums.** People, often hired for the purpose, could be taken over by the spirit of a dead person who would use their mouths to talk.

- **Table turning.** Participants put their hands on a small table while the spirit supposedly knocks it around and thereby sends messages.

- **Spirit writing.** This is a variation on the spirit medium, only instead of talking, the spirit uses someone's hand to write messages.

- **Planchette.** A planchette is a little piece of wood on wheels with a pencil or pen stuck into it. You put your fingers on it and get spirit writing.

- **Ouija board.** This is a board with letters and numbers for use with a planchette, invented in the 1880s and still in use today.

**Cold Fact** _____

The first makers of the ouija board claimed that they had to demonstrate its effectiveness at the patent office before they could secure a patent for the device. What question do you suppose they asked to test it out? "Will people pay good money for this thing?" If the answer was "yes," the spirits did not lie!

The idea behind all these techniques is that ghosts lack the physical wherewithal for communicating with the living by word of mouth, so they need mechanical help. And this goes to show that lots of people were getting excited about the possibility that spirits could exert at least some degree of force on physical reality. This force could be benign or predatory, and could even be vampiric. Anyway, some spiritualists believed that vampires could communicate as spirits before appearing as embodied individuals. Others believed in psychic vampirism, in which spirits of the living or the dead could prey on living people.

## Sappers and the Sapped

One of the major forces in the spiritualist movement during this time, both supplying theoretical ideas behind it and spreading these ideas around, was the Theosophical Society, founded by the infamous Helena Madame Blavatsky. Despite Blavatsky's reputation as a faker, Theosophy has been a major international influence on occult thought and practice ever since its founding. One Theosophist, Dr. Franz Hartmann, was particularly interested in psychic vampires.

> ### Dead Giveaway
>
> In one of his many inventive moods, Theosophist Hartmann tells of a miller's apprentice who became weak and sickly despite eating large quantities of food. He complained of an invisible force draining energy from his chest as he lay in bed at night. So the miller decided to spend the night in bed with him to try to figure out what was wrong. That night, when the apprentice began to feel the malevolent force, the miller reached over his chest and grabbed what felt like a gelatinous substance. As soon as he grabbed it, it struggled to get away. The miller threw the invisible thing into the fire. Soon afterward, the apprentice recovered and had no further difficulty. Hartmann described the thing as an "astral tumor."

Hartmann reported a number of psychic vampire incidents. He tells of a rich man who tried to prevent his heirs from inheriting his money by attacking their lawyer in spiritual form, ultimately killing him. He also tells of a woman who turned down a suitor who then killed himself. He returned to her in spirit, weakening her with his presence until she had the spirit exorcized.

In one of Hartmann's most elaborate stories, he claimed to be a first-hand witness. Learning of a suspected vampire who was killing children near a castle in the Carpathian Mountains, Hartmann went to investigate with some friends. Staying in the castle, the group conducted a séance using the method of table turning in an attempt to contact the vampire. They learned its identity in life was Countess Elga, a beautiful woman whose portrait was displayed in the castle.

Countess Elga indicated she would appear in bodily form to one of Hartmann's friends. That night, she appeared to the friend and made amorous advances, which he resisted. Hartmann later made some occult signs in front of her portrait and the portrait's expression became contorted. Unfortunately, Hartmann was never able to generate any concrete proof that any of this actually happened, but was suddenly called away on more pressing business!

## The Least You Need to Know

- ◆ Witches and vampires are similar, yet different.

- ◆ Werewolves and vampires are also similar, yet different, but for different reasons than witches and vampires.

- ◆ Ghouls and vampires are similar, yet different, but the similarities and differences are hard to compare to those linking witches and werewolves with vampires.

- ◆ Ghosts and vampires are similar, yet different, depending on who you talk to.

# Chapter 10

# Mania in Transylvania

## In This Chapter

- Slavic vampire scares
- Peter Plogojowitz
- Arnod Paole
- Reaction in the West

History shows that there is more to the Slavic vampire than mere legend. Flesh and blood enter into the picture as well. In fact, many of the vampires that haunted the imaginations of the old Slavic villagers were undead transformations of ordinary men and women from those same villages. The village vampire was often a former neighbor! They say that good fences make good neighbors. How about good vampire stakes?

As with many neighborhood spats before and since, neither side, living or undead, seemed willing to take offense lying down. When the Slavic villagers suspected their recently dead neighbors of attacking them as undead vampires, they did something about it. They dug up their corpses and staked them through the heart—or took any or all of a number of other vampire-destroying steps.

It's hard to say how long this went on in the isolated towns of Eastern Europe before the more citified Western Europeans found out about it. The beans were spilled by the middle of the eighteenth century when reports of vampire hysteria flooded West, touching off a brief but lively debate among clerics and philosophers about whether the dead could come back to life. But even after the debate blew over in Western Europe, corpse stakings continued in the Eastern countries for decades longer, up into the early years of the twentieth century.

# Unfinished Business

Two of the most famous vampire panics took place in villages in what is now Serbia. The region had been under the rule of the Ottoman (Turkish) Empire, but was taken over by the Austrian Empire late in the seventeenth century. At the time, Austrian military and government officials visited the region and reported on the strange doings in the new territories.

**Dead Giveaway**

Transylvania is a region of modern-day Romania. For centuries prior to the rise of the Soviet Union, it was under uneasy Hungarian control, subject to incursions by the Ottoman Turks. Transylvania has always contained several ethnic groups struggling for autonomy. It is only one of many Slavic regions whose people believe in vampires, and it became particularly associated with vampires as the native country of the fictional Dracula. Author Bram Stoker was evidently inspired by the book on Transylvania, *Land Beyond the Forest* (1888) by Emily Gerard. The name, Transylvania, by the way, is Latin for "land beyond the forest."

The many vampire scares throughout Eastern Europe tended to follow a pattern. When a member of one of the old Slavic peasant communities died unexpectedly and, one by one, his or her closest friends or family members died in a similarly mysterious fashion, supernatural forces appeared to be at work. The locals believed that the first to die was coming back from the grave to bring others with him.

This belief was strong within Slavic society. Locals organized vampire investigations in which dead bodies, suspected of rising by night in an undead state, were dug up and inspected for evidence of vampirism.

As often happens whenever people seek out the supernatural, they found what they were looking for! Here are some of the strange signs most frequently encountered in vampire hunts that were taken as evidence that an unburied corpse was actually a vampire:

- After several weeks or longer, bodies are suspiciously undecayed.

- Bodies appear plump and swollen, apparently bloated with blood.

- Bodies show reddish discoloration of the skin.

- Old skin and fingernails have fallen off and apparently replaced by new growth.

- Most significantly, large amounts of liquid blood may be found inside the corpse, sometimes even trickling out of the mouth and nose.

- And it was commonly said that, when staked, the vampire corpses let out a groan!

Corpses thought to be vampires were pronounced undead and "killed" a second time to prevent them from doing further mischief. A stake through the heart was a preferred method; or the head might be chopped off; or, as a last resort, the whole corpse might be burned. In some cases of vampire hunting, outsiders were present to witness and record the proceedings.

**Cold Fact** _____

Not every unburied corpse with blood trickling from its mouth is a vampire. In his study, *Vampires, Burial, and Death,* Paul Barber says that liquid blood gathering in the mouth is a normal phenomenon in the process of decomposition. Gasses may build up in the stomach, which can force any blood that has seeped into the digestive tract up into the mouth. Other characteristics typically found in "vampires" unearthed from their graves are also normal features of the decomposition process.

# Temporary Burial

Perhaps the most famous vampire case was that of a Serbian peasant and former soldier named Arnod Paole from the town of Medvegia.

Paole met an untimely death around the year 1725 by falling from a hay wagon and breaking his neck. They buried him in the village cemetery, but he was not forgotten!

## Domino Effect

The villagers said that Paole once complained of being harassed by a vampire during his life, while a soldier in Turkish-controlled Serbia. He is reported to have smeared himself with the vampire's blood and eaten earth from the vampire's grave in order to keep it away. You have to wonder where he got his information on vampire-prevention!

Anyway, about a month after his death, several people in Medvegia claimed they were being stalked by a vampire. Around that time, four more villages got sick and died. Suspecting Paole, the villagers exhumed his body. They said that fresh blood was flowing from his mouth, nose, ears, and eyes. They drove a stake through the heart. As they did so, the corpse let out a groan! After that they cut off the head. Finally the body was cremated. The four people thought to have been Paole's victims were dealt with in the same way.

And that was that, until years later, in 1732, when more villagers got sick and died. The living villagers again suspected vampires were responsible. It was said that before Paole was staked, he must have sucked the blood of some sheep, which were later eaten by some of the villagers, who subsequently died and became vampires. These new vampires were suspected of killing still more people. So the villagers wanted to start digging up more corpses.

**Grave Mistake**

You get the feeling that the hapless Arnod Paole actually sealed his own fate as a future vampire by smearing himself with vampire blood and eating earth from its grave in the attempt to repel the vampire who was stalking him. This, at any rate, seems to be the implication of the villagers who related his story. So don't try any risky vampire remedies! Stick with garlic if you want to play it safe!

# Expert Opinions

The Austrian authorities got wind of the situation and sent a military detail accompanied by medical officers to supervise. In charge was a military doctor named Johann Flückinger. Flückinger wrote a famous report of the incident known as *Visum et Repertum*, "Seen and Discovered," which sparked a great deal of interest in Western Europe. The report lent a degree of official credence to the problem of vampires.

Flückinger and his men were on hand to supervise the disinterment of some seventeen bodies. A few of the corpses were well on their way to complete decomposition. Others were only partially decayed while others were hardly decayed at all, despite having been buried for two or three months, according to the villagers. These undecayed and incompletely decayed corpses, said the villagers, were vampires. They got no argument from Flückinger.

The detail conducted crude autopsies of those suspected to be vampires. They found what Flückinger called "fresh"—by which he probably meant uncoagulated—liquid blood in all of the body cavities. Flückinger also noted that the old fingernails had fallen off and new ones had grown in and that, on some of the corpses, old skin had peeled off, leaving newer-looking skin underneath.

**Cold Fact**

Among the dead peasants suspected to be vampires were a soldier's daughter named Stanacka who became sick and, before she died, complained of being strangled by a vampire in the form of another soldier's son named Millo who had died recently. When her body was dug up, a blue mark in the shape of a finger could be seen on her neck.

One woman, sixty years old, was lean in life, but was found to be plump and ruddy in the grave, swollen with blood. She was thought to be the instigator of the new rash of vampires, after eating some sheep that had been vampirized by Paole. Among the other suspected vampires were several young children, as well as men and women who died in their prime. A local band of Gypsies was hired to cut off the heads and burn the bodies of the suspected vampires.

# Tell Me Another

Flückinger's report, signed as it was by officials with medical credentials, was read with keen interest all over Western Europe. Other reports of similar vampire scares emerged as well during the same time period. Another Austrian official, this one in the town of Kisilova, Serbia, recorded the story of a peasant named Peter Pogojowitz, whose dead body was causing trouble in 1725. A French botanist living in Greece had another story to tell.

**Cold Fact** _____

The cases of Arnod Paole and Peter Plogojowitz were largely responsible for the entry of the word "vampire" into the vocabularies of Western European languages. The official report on the Peter Plogojowitz case, written in German around 1726, contained the word, "vanpir," which is thought to be the first modern written use of the term. Flückinger's report was translated from German into French, introducing the word "vampyre," and into English, with "vampire."

## Peter, Peter Peasant Eater

The Austrian official in Serbia was reluctant to permit the corpse of Peter Plogojowitz to be dug up, but the villagers insisted on taking action. Since Plogojowitz's death, nine people got sick and died, claiming on their death beds that Plogojowitz had come to them in their sleep and nearly strangled them. So the official brought an Eastern Orthodox priest along and witnessed the proceedings.

The official was surprised to see fresh blood in the corpse's mouth. He did not try to stop the villagers as they sharpened a stake and drove it through the body. At the staking, blood flowed from the mouth and out of the ears. The official also refers mysteriously to another strange event, which he refuses to explain out of delicacy. Scholars have interpreted this to mean that the corpse appeared to be sexually aroused!

## Unlucky Stiff

In contrast to the cases of Arnod Paole and Peter Plogojowitz, a vampire scare on the Greek island of Mykonos in the year 1700 was reported by someone convinced that the dead could not come back from their graves. This was the French botanist, Pitton de Tournefort, who emphasizes the mob hysteria and what he takes to be an almost willful determination to believe in the impossible. To de Tournefort, the whole situation was disgusting and pathetic.

The suspected vampire—or vrykolakas, as it was called in Greece—was a peasant who was a troublemaker in life and was mysteriously murdered. Only two days after he was buried, the townspeople said that he was still causing trouble, entering people's houses and messing them up, as well as grabbing people from behind. No one was killed, but people were scared. The local priest was sympathetic and agreed to let the villagers unbury the body after nine days in the ground.

The priest said a Mass in the chapel where the body was buried, and then they dug it up. The village butcher was called in to take out the heart. He made a mess of the job, though, rummaging around in the guts first. He said the corpse's insides were still warm, which got everyone excited. Not surprisingly, the body smelled awful, so they burned lots of incense. There was so much smoke that some people claimed it was coming out of the body.

Everyone cried that the corpse was full of fresh blood. All de Tournefort, saw, however, was a pile of half-putrefied guts. Finally, the villagers took the heart down to the seashore and burned it. Then they reburied the body. It turned out, however, according to the villagers, that the vrykolakas was still capable of attacking people even without its heart!

The villagers said he broke into homes, destroyed property, and drank up people's wine. Many villagers were so afraid they couldn't sleep in their beds at night, but they took bedrolls into the public square where they felt safer. When their homes were pillaged by vagabonds in their absence, they were convinced the vrykolakas was responsible!

They unburied the corpse again and again—several times a day—just to look at it. They argued about what should be done and why the initial Mass and the burning of the heart didn't work. And they argued with de Tournefort about whether a vrykolakas can exist. Eventually, they dug up the body one last time and burned it to ashes. The local priest did not want to be involved, because he feared he would have to pay a fine to the Orthodox bishop.

**Dead Giveaway** _____

Some Greek superstition reflects tensions that existed between the Eastern Orthodox and Roman Catholic Churches. For example, some believed that the bodies of Roman Catholics buried in Greek soil could not decay. Hence Roman Catholics were especially likely to come back as vampires! The Greek vrykolakas was the first vampiric being to be discussed at length in a published book. The work was by a Greek priest named Leo Allatius, who spent a great deal of time in Italy working with Roman Catholics. Allatius sought reconciliation between the Eastern and Roman Catholic Churches, which split in the year 395 C.E.

# Dead Reckoning

These and other accounts of macabre undead doings filtered West where scholars and priests collected them and discussed them in treatises. These accounts in turn were eagerly read in salons and coffeehouses by everyone who had time to hang out with them. After all, major league baseball hadn't been invented yet, so people were thrilled to have something as fascinating as vampires to talk about!

## Tomb Tomes

Here are just a few of the better known of the early vampire authors and their works:

◆ **Leo Allatius** (Leone Allacci, 1586–1669). Greek priest who wrote what is apparently the first book on vampires ever published. The work describes the vrykolakas and indicates such beings may exist.

◆ **Philip Rohr** (seventeenth century). German author of *De Masticatione Mortuorum* (Of the Chewing Dead, [1679]), which describes the supposed ability of corpses to chew, and even eat their shrouds and parts of their own bodies.

◆ **Michael Ranft** (eighteenth century). German author whose work, *De Masticacione Mortuarum in Tumulus Liber* (Book of the Chewing Dead in Their Tombs, [1728]), refuted Rohr's position that the dead are capable of chewing.

> **Cold Fact** _____
>
> The issue of corpses chewing in their tombs was a subject of debate closely related to the subject of vampires in the late seventeenth and early eighteenth centuries. Questions concerned not just whether the dead can leave their graves, but whether they can even move their bodies and whether their doing so can have a supernatural influence on the living. Those who believed in the chewing dead attributed it to the influence of Satan.

◆ **Johann Christian Stock** (eighteenth century). German author of *Dissertatio Physico de Cadaveribus Sanguisugis* (Dissertation of the Physical Traits of Bloodsucking Cadavers, [1732]), claiming that belief in vampires stem from hallucinations sent by the devil.

◆ **Giuseppe Davanzati** (1665–1755). Italian archbishop author of *Dissertatione Sopra I Vampiri* (Dissertation on Vampires, [1744]) reinforcing the view that vampires are unreal and that belief in them may be inspired by the devil.

◆ **Dom Augustin Calmet** (1672–1757). French Benedictine monk and Bible scholar who wrote *Traité sur les Revenants en corps, les Excommunié, les Oupires ou Vampires, Broucolaques de Hongrie, de Boheme, de Moravie, et de Silésie* (Treatise on the Returned Dead, the Vampires and Vrykolakas of Hungary, Bohemia, Moravia, and Silesia, [1746]), the most exhaustive and widely read of all vampire books yet written.

## The Devil Makes You Do It

Dom Augustin Calmet's work became the most famous and influential, largely because he collected and repeated virtually all the known accounts of vampire attacks and stakings when he wrote in the late seventeenth and early eighteenth centuries. In general, he attributes the phenomenon to superstition and the influence of the devil on minds insufficiently fortified by religion. But he leaves room for doubt and often appears impressed by the evidence in support of vampires.

Calmet's work went through many editions and translations, including one in English called *The Phantom World,* published in 1759 and still available today. But the work attracted the most attention in Calmet's native France, where a group of philosophers commonly known as the French Philsophes were doing all they could to make the eighteenth century the Age of Reason. Two philosophers in particular, Denis Diderot and Francois Voltaire, denounced belief in vampires and implicitly blamed Calmet for not being more assertive in refuting their existence.

Many, including the Roman Catholic Pope himself, came to suspect priests of hypocritically encouraging belief in vampires in order to make extra money from conducting exorcisms and Masses. This view was supported by the personal physician of the Austrian Empress Maria Theresa, who was dispatched to report on a vampire scare in progress in Silesia, a region of what is now Poland.

In 1756, the Empress passed a statute prohibiting the digging up of corpses and prohibiting priests from exerting authority over the matter. Instead, vampire scares were to be handled by civil authorities. Interest in vampires among Western Europeans gradually shifted to focus on literary creations and the vampire scares were forgotten. Nevertheless, they continued in isolated regions of Eastern Europe into the twentieth century.

### Dead Giveaway

A number of suspected vampires were dug up in America—in Vermont, Connecticut, and Rhode Island at various times throughout the nineteenth century. These disinterments took place in response to outbreaks of consumption (tuberculosis) that were thought to have a supernatural dimension by some small-town New Englanders. People who were the first among several to die of the disease were dug up and had their hearts taken out and burned. A story on vampire unburials in Rhode Island was published in a newspaper called the *New York World* in 1896. This article came to the attention of Bram Stoker, who kept a clipping. It may have influenced him as he wrote *Dracula.*

## The Least You Need to Know

◆ Vampire scares took place throughout Eastern Europe and became a subject of interest in the West in the seventeenth and eighteenth centuries.

◆ Many corpses were dug up in search of vampires; those not sufficiently decayed were commonly staked, decapitated, and/or cremated.

◆ Two of the most famous of the Eastern European vampire cases were those of Arnod Paole and Peter Plogojowitz.

◆ Clerics and scholars collected and discussed accounts of vampire scares in a series of books that helped make vampires famous in the West.

# Chapter 11

# Bad Old Vlad

## In This Chapter

- ◆ Vlad the Impaler
- ◆ … and Bram Stoker's *Dracula*
- ◆ … in history and legend
- ◆ The Order of the Dragon
- ◆ Elizabeth Bathory

Yes, Virginia, there was a Dracula. He was Vlad Dracula Tepes ("the Impaler"), a Wallachian prince who lived from 1431 to 1476. He is famous today as one of the inspirations behind Bram Stoker's fictional Dracula, and as one of the cruelest rulers known to humanity. His story is not very pretty. It seems, for one thing, that he liked having people skewered on big long stakes. You might say he wasn't a very nice guy, even though he had his "fine points"!

As far as we know Vlad didn't have any supernatural powers like his fictional namesake. Even so, he was so sadistic that you'd be better off taking your chances with the undead count than crossing Prince Vlad's path on a bad day. After all, Count Dracula could only hold so much blood. Vlad's capacity for bloodshed was limitless.

Yet strangely, he has always commanded considerable respect from the Romanian descendants of those he ruled. He was hard as nails, a true warrior prince, and a staunch nationalist. All in all he was a complicated character, so it's no wonder that he has inspired many legends that reflect both good and evil aspects of his nature.

# Fact and Fiction

Vlad Tepes (which means Vlad "the Stake" in Romanian, usually translated "the Impaler") became legendary in his lifetime and has remained so ever since. For centuries however, he was remembered only in his native Romania. (Wallachia, where he ruled, is a region of Romania that borders Transylvania to the east.) That changed when Bram Stoker dug him up while researching background material for his famous book. Gradually, *Dracula* fans have grown interested in the historical figure behind the fictional vampire.

## Past Life

In the novel *Dracula*, Dr. Van Helsing figures out, and explains, that the mysterious count was once the infamous "voivode" (voivode, or voevod, is Slavic for prince). Van Helsing indicates that Prince Dracula was legendary, famed for his bravery, resourcefulness, and cunning, and that he won his reputation fighting against the Turks. All these things are basically true to historical fact.

**Cold Fact** _____

The fictional character Dr. Abraham Van Helsing not only identifies Count Dracula as the historical Voivode Dracula, but also cites a living historical scholar as the source of his information on Prince Vlad. This is Arminius Vambery (1832–1913), a Hungarian historian who immigrated to England where he became acquainted with Bram Stoker. Stoker evidently mentions Vambery in his novel as a way of thanking him for sharing his knowledge!

In addition, however, Van Helsing says that the prince studied with the devil at a school called the Scholomance and that he was referred to in an old manuscript as a "wampyr." Stoker invented these details—in fact, although vampires and Prince Vlad both come from Romania, there are no known legends or any other sources linking the fifteenth-century prince to vampires prior to the publication of *Dracula* in 1897.

## Turkey Sandwich

Early in the novel, prior to Van Helsing's explanation, Count Dracula himself says that he is connected to Prince Vlad. He tells Jonathan Harker that he is descended from the Voivode Dracula who fought courageously against the Turks. He also hints that Prince Vlad possessed supernatural powers when he claims that the prince was the only one of his whole army to return alive from the field of battle after one encounter with the enemy!

Count Dracula also mentions the prince's brother, not mentioned by name in the novel, but known to history as Radu the Handsome. The count complains that this brother was perfidious and sold his people into slavery by allying himself with the Turks. There's a kernel of truth to this claim, since Radu did take over the Wallachian throne from Vlad for a time, thanks in part to a peace agreement he had formed with the Turks. But making peace with the Turks back then was not nearly so unthinkable as Count Dracula makes it sound in the novel.

In fact, Wallachia was perched uneasily between the Turkish Ottoman Empire to the east and the Hungarian Empire to the west. Although the Wallachians, like the Hungarians, were nominally Christian while the Turks were Muslim, Wallachian autonomy depended on its rulers being capable of forging practical alliances with either side when the time came. Vlad Dracula and also his father, Vlad Dracul (Dracula actually means "son of Dracul") made agreements with the Turks when it suited them.

# Dragon's Brood

Vlad Dracul, Prince Vlad's father, took the name "Dracul" sometime after 1430, when he became a member of the Order of the Dragon. The order was a kind of fraternity, founded in 1418 by the King of Hungary. Members were expected to wear the insignia of the order at all times and to fight valiantly against the Turkish "infidels." No doubt they also had a secret handshake, passwords, and stuff like that as well!

**Dead Giveaway** _____

Dracul means "dragon," which stands for the devil in the minds of
many Christians, thanks to the Biblical Book of Revelation and such
legends as St. George and the Dragon. This view of dragon symbolism
has prompted speculation that Vlad Dracul and his son, Vlad Dracula,
have satanic affiliations, especially since this affiliation gets spelled out
in the novel, *Dracula*. It's likely, however, that the historical Order of the
Dragon refers not to the devil, but to heraldry (fantastic creatures such as
dragons, griffins, and unicorns were often used in coats of arms and
other insignias). After all, why would a society dedicated to fighting infidels (non-Christians) choose to do so in the name of the anti-Christian
devil? Even so, the dragon-devil connection is an intriguing coincidence,
and Stoker was clever to play it up in his book!

# Balance of Power

The Turk-fighting thing probably seemed like a good idea at the time.
Then again, Vlad Dracul may have been more or less forced to join the
order for political reasons—namely to keep the King of Hungary off his
back. In any case, if Vlad Dracul swore to fight the Turks, he backslid
on the oath within just a few years, when he found it necessary to forge
an alliance with Turkey.

Evidently, both the Hungarians and the Turks wanted to use Wallachia
as a layer of protection against one another. Each side wanted
Wallachian loyalty, and each side could exert considerable influence on
the ability of the Wallachian prince to remain in power. Obviously,
whoever wound up in charge of the little country was in a precarious
position. In fact, the job of Wallachian prince had a remarkably high
turnover rate!

As you may imagine, much of the precariousness Wallachian rulers had
to deal with stemmed from the fact that balances of power and alliances
could shift at any time. Under the circumstances, it could be pretty
tough to persuade anyone you sought an alliance with that you would be
loyal. Heck, you might have to promise them your own sons.

## Summer Death Camp

In fact, promising his sons was just what Vlad Dracul did. As a guarantee that he would abide by an agreement forged with Turkey, he left his sons, Vlad the future impaler and Radu the Handsome, in the care of the Turks. Vlad and his brother, in other words, were human collateral on a deal made by their father in an attempt to shore up his precarious power. The youngsters could expect to escape being killed by their Turkish hosts only so long as their father held up his end of the agreement.

Young Vlad lived in Turkey for four years, from 1444 when he was about 12 years old to 1448. Soon afterward, the intermittent Crusades against the Muslims built up a fresh head of steam, and Dracul was forced to send troops against the Turks. He fully expected that his sons would be killed as a result. The Turks, however, were merciful and let the young Romanian princes live, apparently in order to exert leverage over Dracul in the future.

Scholars have speculated that the years Dracula spent in Turkey helped to turn him into the hard, brutal leader he became. No one knows for certain, however, just how his character developed. It seems clear, though, that his own personal sense of loyalty must have been painfully divided and that he had to live his life under the constant threat of his own execution.

**Grave Mistake** _____

It's been misleadingly suggested that Prince Vlad staked people in order to compensate for sexual impotence. The impalings, in other words, were a form of phallic penetration he was unable to carry out in the usual way. Not only is there no evidence that Vlad was impotent (actually he kept mistresses and had three sons), there is no evidence that impotence makes guys want to stake people. Impalements per capita ratios have not gone down since they've come out with Viagra!

Meanwhile, the Hungarians felt that Vlad Dracul's support for their efforts was not strong enough, so they defeated and killed him in battle. Vlad Dracul's oldest son, Mircea, who was being groomed by his father to succeed to the throne, was murdered by the Romanian boyars—landholders who then held sway in national affairs. Soon afterward, the Turks released Vlad Dracula, allowing him to make his first bid for the Wallachian throne. He was unsuccessful, however, and did not become ruler until almost 10 years later, in 1456.

# A Prince of a Fiend

Actually, Vlad Dracula occupied the throne of Wallachia three separate times, which shows you how unstable things were. When he finally made it to the throne for the first time in 1448, he kept it only two months before being deposed. He returned eight years later, however, and maintained power for six years, until 1462. It was during this phase of his rule that he became known for cruelty.

## Public Works

His first notorious act of cruelty was to punish the boyars who had helped bring about the downfall and deaths of his father and older brother. He assembled them all together with their families on Easter Sunday when, presumably, they were all decked out in their elegant Easter clothes. The older ones he had staked, but the younger ones—including their wives and children—were sent on a forced march from the Wallachian capital, Tirgoviste, to the town of Peonari, where a crumbling fortress stood on the banks of the River Arges.

Across the river was the Arges Castle, which was also falling apart. The boyars—a ruling elite class unaccustomed to working—were put to work as slave labor, rebuilding the Arges Castle with brick and stone carried from the Peonari fortress. This castle was to be Vlad's headquarters.

Vlad's revenge against the boyars might seem, at first glance, like a more-or-less fitting punishment for a wealthy, coddled, ruling elite, a punishment motivated by a sense of social justice as well as personal revenge. Prince Vlad, however, was not a champion of the poor; he tormented the lower classes every bit as brutally as the upper. In fact, he waged a campaign to exterminate them entirely!

At one point, Vlad invited all the poor, sick, and elderly to a banquet. He provided a lavish feast for them. When it was over he stood up and asked them all if there was anything else they could desire. Satisfied for the moment, they said "no." Next, Vlad left the banquet hall and had the doors locked behind him, shutting in his guests. The hall was then set on fire and the banqueters all burned to death!

## Staking Out His Territory

And Vlad did not torture and massacre only his own subjects. He also invaded lands to the east and to the west, impaling men, women, and children wherever he went. When Vlad attacked the town of Brasov in Transylvania, he looted the local church and then surrounded it with thousands of staked victims. A German pamphlet that circulated in Western Europe in the decades following Vlad's death describes the event and depicts Vlad serenely enjoying a meal in the midst of the scene of torture.

Vlad's atrocities were described in illustrated fifteenth- and sixteenth-century accounts published in Germany and Russia. In some respects, these accounts have a lot in common with tabloid journalism today, sensationalizing the events they describe. Even so, the documentary evidence for the time of Vlad's life in the form of letters and government documents tends to support the claims made in these pamphlets about Vlad's cruelty. There is little doubt that Vlad did in fact have thousands of people put to slow, agonizing death by impaling. Victims were propped up to suffer in such numbers that they were described as "forests"!

**Cold Fact**

Vlad occasionally had thousands of victims tortured and killed at a time. Estimates of the total number throughout his life, including civilians of all faiths and nationalities, range from 40,000 to 100,000 people.

It is said that at the forest of staked victims at Brasov, one of Vlad's advisors expressed revulsion at the smell of the suffering victims, who must have been not only bleeding, but sweating and defecating in panic. Vlad commanded that the outspoken advisor be elevated above the stench of the multitude—on an especially high stake of his own! Obviously, Vlad was not particularly good at accepting constructive criticism. He is even said to have impaled the priest who served as his personal confessor!

## Hitting the Nail on the Head

Vlad was brutal not only toward his own officials, but to those of other leaders as well. It is said that emissaries of the sultan of Turkey visited him one day. It was the custom of these men not to remove their turbans while on official business, even while visiting foreign dignitaries. When Vlad asked them to bare their heads, they refused. So Vlad offered to help them uphold their tradition by having their turbans nailed to their heads with many small nails and sent them home bleeding.

As you might imagine, Vlad became a legend in his own time. Similar stories told about him then were later told about Ivan the Terrible (1530–1584), the notorious Russian czar. Some scholars have speculated that Ivan consciously adopted some of Vlad's torturing methods. Whether or not this is the case, both rulers were similarly nasty. Ivan the Terrible is famous, among other things, for killing his own son in a fit of anger. Vlad didn't kill his own son, but he did brutally torture and kill one of his mistresses, having her cut open from the genitals to the throat, apparently because she lied to him about being pregnant.

# Local Hero

Strangely, despite his astonishing cruelty, Vlad has been remembered with a surprising degree of respect in Romanian legend. Vlad appears in legend as stern and terrible, but also as wise and just. In fact, some tales imply that the brutality served the beneficial purpose of keeping everyone on their best behavior and promoting safety and fairness in the realm.

**Dead Giveaway**

The most prominent authorities on the life and legacy of Prince Vlad Dracula Tepes are Radu Florescu and Raymond T. McNally, joint authors of *In Search of Dracula* (1972) and *Dracula: A Biography of Vlad the Impaler* (1973). Florescu is a Romanian and claims descent from the infamous Wallachian prince. He is pictured on the back of the biography sporting a family heirloom walking stick with a carved head of Vlad the Impaler on the handle! Interestingly, both McNally and Florescu devoted considerable effort in searching for—and digging up— the grave of Prince Vlad, which is only fitting for the man who inspired the story of the most famous vampire!

## Tough on Crime

For example, one story tells of an Italian merchant visiting Romania carrying lots of money and merchandise. He asked Prince Vlad where he could store his valuables for safekeeping, but the prince responded that everyone in his kingdom was so trustworthy that there was no need to keep anything locked up. So the merchant left all his money and valuables out in the open in the public square.

And sure enough, no one touched anything—almost no one, that is. As it happened, a thief made off with 100 gold pieces in the night. When the merchant discovered that the money was missing, he notified the prince. "I'll look into it," said Prince Vlad, and he dismissed the merchant.

The prince sent word throughout the entire city that money had been stolen. He announced that if the thief and the money were not brought before him by sundown, the entire city would be burned to ashes. Knowing that their prince did not make idle threats, the citizens found the thief and turned him in, along with the money.

> **Cold Fact**
>
> According to one legend, Prince Vlad left a gold cup permanently standing by the fountain in the public square for public use. Anyone who was thirsty could drink from it. Despite its value, no one ever stole it. Obviously, people knew what would happen to them if they did!

## Keeping Strict Accounts

Meanwhile, however, Vlad decided to put the merchant's honesty to the test. Without telling the merchant, he had the missing gold pieces replaced out of his own treasury. In addition, he included an extra gold piece along with the rest. The merchant found the money and, at first, thought he had made a mistake in thinking it had been stolen. Acquainted with Prince Vlad's uncompromising reputation, he figured he had better leave town right away while he still could. But then, on counting the money a second time, he saw there was an extra gold piece and he knew something funny was going on.

He decided to tell the prince he had found the missing money and an extra gold piece besides. The prince said, "Yes, I put the money there.

If you hadn't come to tell me you had found it, I would have done *that* to you." And the prince pointed out a window into the courtyard where the thief was writhing on a stake.

## Wise Guy

Not all the stories told about Prince Vlad allude to his cruelty. In some, his wisdom alone keeps everything under control. For example, one story tells of another Italian merchant who lost a purse containing 1,000 gold pieces. The merchant offered a reward of 100 gold pieces to anyone who returned it.

A humble Romanian peasant found the purse. The peasant didn't know what was inside or that a reward had been offered for its return, but he could tell the purse was Italian and he knew that there was an Italian merchant in town. Being a firm believer in honesty and fair play, he brought the purse to the merchant and gave it to him. He waited by the merchant's side expecting only that the merchant would thank him.

But instead of offering thanks, the merchant began counting the money and, as he counted, concocted a scheme to avoid having to pay the reward. He decided to palm 100 gold pieces (he must have been a sleight-of-hand artist!) and he claimed that the peasant had taken it. "I see you've already taken your reward," he said, "so we have no further business."

The peasant felt he had been insulted. He argued with the merchant—not to get the reward money, but simply to get him to admit the truth. The merchant stuck by his story, however, and went on to accuse the peasant of trying to chisel him for more gold. Exasperated as well as insulted, the peasant decided to take the matter up before Prince Vlad.

The prince questioned both the merchant and the peasant and could tell just by judging their characters that the merchant was lying. So he asked the merchant, "You say you lost a purse with 1,000 gold pieces in it?" The merchant nodded yes and bowed. "And this purse was returned to you with 900 gold pieces?" The merchant nodded yes again.

"It's clear then," said the prince, "that this purse is not the one you lost. Since the true owner of this purse is unknown, it belongs to the peasant who found it. If anyone finds a purse with 1,000 gold pieces, we'll be sure to let you know." So, through Vlad's cleverness and penetrating wisdom, the peasant was rewarded for his honesty and the merchant was punished for his greed.

It is not known for certain how the historical Prince Vlad met his end. Some say he died in battle, others claim he was assassinated. Some say his own men accidentally killed him in battle, mistaking him for one of the enemy. All of these options seem a little too anticlimactic to be the death of such an incomparable scoundrel. So maybe it's a good thing that he has been revived in fiction and movies as Count Dracula, who suffers countless gruesome and, no doubt, excruciating deaths!

**Grave Mistake**

> There was no sure way to win when dealing with the legendary Prince Vlad. Two different stories about him tell how he questioned two monks in order to test their character, asking them what they thought about his rule. In each story, one monk gives an honest, disapproving answer while the other lies in order to flatter the prince. In one story, Vlad has the flattering monk impaled for lying. In the other, he has the honest monk impaled for insubordination!

# Bloodbath Beth

While we're on the subject of famous vampires of history, there are a few more worth mentioning, especially Elizabeth Bathory, the sixteenth-century Slovak/Hungarian countess with a sadistic streak wider than her hoop skirt. She is said to have made a practice of bathing in the blood of young virgins in the belief that this would keep her looking young. Her story has provided a kernel of truth behind a number of vampire films since the 1970s, as well as several novels.

## More than Skin Deep

Imagine Mary Poppins's worst nightmare: an employer whose idea of a jolly holiday is torturing the servant girls. That's what Elizabeth Bathory was like. For example, she liked sticking pins in them, especially underneath their fingernails. In wintertime, she would strip them naked and make them stand outside in the cold, then have water thrown on them until they froze to death.

Legend has it that Elizabeth developed her custom of bathing in blood when she hit a servant girl and drew blood, which then dripped onto the countess. As she wiped it away, it seemed to her that her skin looked fresher and younger where the blood had been. So she had the girl bled dry and took a warm bath.

Elizabeth had help from a few trusted accomplices, including a male servant named Thorko who dabbled in sorcery, an older nurse named Ilona Joo, and a woman named Darvula who is said to have been a witch. This little society of sadists had the run of the countess's Castle Csejthe in northwestern Hungary, where they drew on the local supply of Slovak peasant girls as subjects for their amusement. Hungarian authorities discovered the bodies of some 50 girls buried beneath the castle, although the countess left a diary in her own handwriting detailing her fiendish activities and indicating she killed over 600 victims.

> **Cold Fact**
>
> Scholars argue whether accounts of Elizabeth Bathory influenced Bram Stoker's novel, *Dracula*. Raymond T. McNally points out that Dracula appears to get younger as the novel progresses and suggests that Stoker got this idea from reading about the Hungarian countess.

The diary was eventually discovered during official maneuvering by which the Hungarian crown sought to confiscate lands Bathory inherited when her husband died. Bathory's accomplices were tortured and executed and she herself was shut in her room and fed through a crack under the door. She died after a few years, but lived on as a local legend.

> **Dead Giveaway**
>
> Another well-known fiend from history who has been likened to a vampire is the fifteenth-century French soldier, Gilles de Rais. Once an officer under Joan of Arc, he retired after her death and took up alchemy, the experimental mystic process of transmuting base metals into gold. De Rais apparently came to believe that the blood of children, together with the ritual torture of his victims, would help him achieve his alchemical purposes. He is said to have killed up to 300 youngsters. His story inspired the novel, *Là-bas* (1891) by Joris-Karl Huysmans. The title means "down there"—Hell, that is.

# B Girls

Here's a list of some of the lurid books and movies inspired by Bathory's life:

◆ *Countess Dracula* (1972)—a Hammer Films feature in which a countess discovers a fountain of youth in flowing blood.

◆ *Daughters of Darkness* (1971)—an artsy Belgian film set in the twentieth century at an empty seaside resort in which a bisexual lady vampire complicates an already complicated marriage of a vacationing couple.

◆ *Thirst* (1988)—Film in which a descendent of the Hungarian countess visits a scientific lab where human subjects are drained of blood.

◆ *Daughter of the Night* (1992)—a novel by Elaine Bergstrom based on you know who.

◆ *The Blood Countess*—a novel by Andrei Codrescu that weaves Bathory's story together with the story of a fictive modern-day descendent involved in a murder in Hungary.

There are many more historical human fiends who have been equated with vampires. If your thirst has been whetted for their stories, you can read about them in Chapter 14 which talks about blood-drinking as a criminal and psychiatric problem. Cheers!

# The Least You Need to Know

◆ Prince Vlad Dracula Tepes was a historical leader of Wallachia during the fifteenth century.

◆ Prince Vlad is woven into the plot of Bram Stoker's *Dracula* as the undead count in his early years.

◆ Prince Vlad was inhumanly cruel to tens of thousands, regardless of class, religion, or nationality.

◆ Prince Vlad is remembered with respect in many Romanian legends in which he appears wise and just.

◆ Countess Elizabeth Bathory is notorious for bathing in the blood of her servant girls.

# Part 3

# Out of the Coffin

Courageous individuals have always followed their dreams, but the vampires and vampirelike mortals of today are living their wildest nightmares. Fantasy and reality are merging in ever-changing ways, so that vampires are no longer merely figments of the imagination. In addition, they are part of an active, creative, and thriving counterculture that feeds deeply on the vampire mystique.

Today's Goth vampire scene is totally undead and crawling with dark souls of every description. There are role players, lifestylers, blood players, and weekenders, all in hot-and-cold pursuit of fellowship, fun, fashion, fetish, and flesh. Whatever gets you through the night is out there and waiting.

But watch out, for danger lurks around every corner, especially in the deep recesses of the heart, where bloodlust throbs as a spiritual truth or a clinical condition. Are you one of those who must reawaken your inner pain in order to feel alive? If you don't already know, you can take the newly developed Demonic Aptitude Test and find out!

# Chapter 12

# Honest to Goth

## In This Chapter

- ◆ A Goth overview
- ◆ Goth subculture
- ◆ Goth worldview
- ◆ Goth style

Creepy, sullen, alienated, strange, morbid, scary. Somehow all the personally traits that once would get you a trip to the nearest mental clinic have become *de rigeur* among the hippest trendsetters around. Goths have found the way to fit in by not fitting in, turning their inner darkness into outer cool. And it's worked so well that now lots of folks in mainstream culture are trying to fit in with *them!*

Goth is an informal movement based on many old and recent currents in music, fashion, lifestyle, and spirituality. It is dark yet dramatic, glum yet glamorous, tragic yet trendy. Goths flock together in nightclubs and on the Internet to socialize and make spectacles of themselves where and when more conventional souls will not bother them. They also splinter off into small, intimate groups to indulge in macabre fantasies and role-playing in an effort to transcend the sordid existence of ordinary people.

Today's human vampires are most at home in Goth circles. Not all
Goths are into vampires, but much of today's vampire activity feeds off
of Goth energy. And because so many vampire doings these days are
Goth, it's fitting that a chapter of this book is devoted to this larger
overarching movement.

# What's the Word

The term *Goth* has a long and peculiar history. It started out in ancient
times as the name of a "barbarian" tribe living chiefly in and around
Germany, known for marauding Rome and helping to bring about the
fall of the Roman Empire. Today we think of these Goths as a lot of
big, hairy guys in leather skirts and iron helmets, hacking away at
Roman legionnaires with battle axes and then tucking in to a big meal
of beef and pork eaten straight off the bone. Well hey, it's a living.

### Stalk Talk

The term **Goth** originally referred to an ancient European tribe
famous for sacking Rome. Many centuries later it was used to refer to
a style of medieval architecture. Then it designated a genre of novel written during the late eighteenth and early nineteenth centuries. Only during
the past two decades or so has the term been used to describe a fashionable subculture.

# Go Take a Flying Buttress

Ancient Roman civilization was a big deal, of course, and it had a profound influence on European civilization ever since. Roman influence
was so strong that historians of architecture could get away with using a
single word—gothic—to describe pretty much every kind of big
medieval building that wasn't constructed in the classical Roman style.
The famous gothic cathedrals of the Middle Ages were not actually
built by the Goths who sacked Rome. But since they weren't built
according to classical design concepts people came to call them gothic,
because the old Goths were famously unclassical, too. The logic was,
"If it's not this thing (classical), it must be the other (gothic)."

Gothic architecture was prevalent from the twelfth to the fifteenth centuries in Europe. It is strangely stark—unsubtle and yet ornate with lots of pointed arches, internal riblike supports, and yes, flying buttresses, which are basically big stands erected next to a big building for holding it up. And there were gargoyles, too. Gargoyles were way gothic, and still are.

## Denoting Darkness

From barbarian tribe and from medieval architecture, the term gothic shifted yet again when it was applied to a genre of literature that became semi-popular in the late eighteenth and early nineteenth centuries, especially in England. Gothic novels were scary stories, usually set in old castles and featuring ghosts and supernatural carryings on. It is from this scary aspect of the gothic novel that today's Goths derive their name.

Today, the term basically refers to anyone or anything that expresses creepiness on purpose, for artistic effect. Goths of today are not necessarily fans of old gothic literature, although many are. Some model their looks and behavior self-consciously on styles, ideas, and characters they have found in gothic novels. Most however, simply do their gothic thing in the context of today's world, without worrying too much about stylistic precedents.

# ... What Music They Make

The Goth movement began in the late 1970s and early '80s as part of the nightclub scene in the United Kingdom, where punk music was already burning itself out. Many punk-influenced music groups introduced a stylistic shift from rage and anarchy to despair and futility. Bands like Joy Division, Bauhaus, the Damned, and Siouxsie and the Banshees are sometimes referred to as first-generation Goth bands, even though, the term Goth had yet to be coined as a musical style at the time. But all the gothic elements were in place, and these bands even played in a London nightclub called the Bat Cave.

This new approach to music died out for several years before coming back to life starting in the late '80s, in the United Kingdom, the United States, and other countries, with bands like London After Midnight, Nosferatu, Mortal Coil, and Marilyn Manson. At this point, Goth was heralded as a bona fide musical style and soon became a lifestyle as well. And Goth has been going strong ever since, growing in size, scope, and variety. Goths can be found all over the world in nightclubs and other settings, too.

> **Cold Fact** _____
>
> Goths circulate in many of the same spheres occupied by "rivetheads"— fans of industrial music. In general, Goths tend to be more gentle and passive while rivetheads tend to be more rowdy and aggressive. Industrial bands of note include Throbbing Gristle, Pig, Leather Strip, and Einsturzende Neubauten.

Vampire imagery looms large in the band names and lyrics of Goth music. Vampiric names that Goth bands have selected for themselves include Vampire Rodents, Vampire Slave, Liquid Blood, Nosferatu, Astro Vamps, Type-O Negative, and Bloodflag. Names of albums include Cradle of Filth's *Vampire* (2000), Merciful Fate's *Return of the Vampire* (1992), and Paralysed Age's *Empire of the Vampire* (1999). Performers' names include Vlad of Nosferatu, Tony Lestat of Wreckage, and Eva Van Helsing of the Shroud. Bauhaus fans will remember the song, "Bela Lugosi's Dead," which can be heard in the soundtrack from the vampire film, *The Hunger* (1983).

> **Grave Mistake** _____
>
> Despite the Goth-like name, the band Black Sabbath is not a Goth group, but a groundbreaking heavy metal band that made a splash in the early 1970s before either Goth or punk music got started. Influential though they have been, few people today under age 35 think they are cool!

**Cold Fact** _____

Crossovers between Goth and industrial music are common, as are those between Goth and metal. Goth and alternative crossovers were once rare, but are becoming increasingly common. Goth-hip hop crossovers may happen someday in the future. So far, there's at least one Goth-leaning African-inflected techno group: Vampire Nation.

# Spreading Darkness

From music, Goth activities have spread to many other areas, especially fanzines and other publications and of course to the Internet, where the privacy of virtual space is every bit as effective a cover for macabre doings as traditional darkness. In addition to music, many Goths love stories, role-playing games, fashion, and the occult.

## Weird Scene

The success of the Goth movement beyond the music scene and into lifestyle and popular culture can be understood in different ways. For one thing, it suggests that lots of people are unhappy and dissatisfied for lots of reasons, and have found a measure of satisfaction in expressing their feelings stylistically, through music, fashion, fantasy, etc. Although everyone else may think Goths are weird and creepy, Goths understand one another. Not only do they relate to weirdness and creepiness, but they enjoy expressing these things and sharing them with like-minded souls.

But as Goth has increased in popularity, it has become increasingly difficult for Goths to tell who is one of them. Newcomers seeking entrance into the local Goth scene may be welcomed, scorned, laughed at, or ignored. Some Goth groups make a distinction between "weekenders" who visit the Goth scene occasionally, and "ultra-Goths," who live the lifestyle to the hilt every day. Sometimes there is intercommunication between these groups, and sometimes there isn't.

# Damned If You Do, Damned If You Don't

If they happen to be young, newcomers to the Goth scene are sometimes called *baby bats*. Baby bats may be evaluated and accepted depending on whether they are going gothic as an angst-ridden, desperate last resort or merely as a way to be cool. Don't ask how you tell which is which!

**Stalk Talk**

A **baby bat** is a young newcomer to the Goth scene. The term isn't necessarily a put-down, but it does imply a lightweight status.

At the same time, while many Goths and Goth wanna-bes worry about whether they are Goth enough, others are accused of being too proud of their gothic seriousness and intensity. Believe it or not, plenty of Goths out there are snobs about how thoroughly dissatisfied and alienated they are! The point is not that Goths are inherently snobbish or especially concerned with winning approval—they're not. But they do often walk a fine line between opposing conventional values and opposing one another.

This is especially the case since Goths have made such a mark in mainstream popular culture. Apart from Goth bands who get accused of "selling out" once they become successful, many Hollywood movies and TV shows have tapped into Goth appeal. *Buffy the Vampire Slayer* is only one outstanding example. Arguably, many of these shows bring a prettified version of the Goth subculture and worldview to mainstream society, where much of the intensity, desperation, and despair get lost.

You could say that Goths are involved in a continuing project of redefining themselves in relation to mainstream society. On the one hand, mainstream society has increasingly come to accept Goth style. Many Goths enjoy the public recognition that comes along with this acceptance, and find that the Goth scene benefits from greater variety and energy stemming from wide popular interest. On the other hand, many Goths find mainstream society shallow and feel that the Goth image is in danger of being sold out.

# Killer Fashion

Goths typically try to look scary in order to make a fashion statement. They wear black, including black lipstick and nail polish, tattoos depicting skulls and bats, and costume jewelry shaped like snakes and spiders. Some dress elegantly, some wear badly cut hair and torn clothes. Pierced body parts are fashionable, too, of course. Anything that looks bizarre is acceptable in Goth circles.

## Creep Show

In general, Goths are not as scary as they look. In part, they look this way because it's cool. In part, they do it to show they don't (can't or won't) fit in with non-Goth society where people are often much scarier than they look! Goths tend to suspect that non-Goths are either shallow, with little sensitivity or awareness of the deep and inescapable pitfalls of human existence, or phony, denying their real feelings about life in an attempt to seem "normal."

Although there is a real undercurrent of gloom that characterizes most Goth activity, Goths are generally more interested in finding outlets for their angst and despair than simply wallowing in them. Thus, when Goths go out for a night on the town, they can be extremely creative in expressing themselves, which they often do more or less theatrically, playing the parts of aggressors or victims, supernatural creatures, and other strange types as they interact with one another.

A retreat into fantasy is a familiar Goth response to the tedium and tragedy of existence. Though the fantasies are often spontaneous, they are just as often part of an ongoing thing. Goths may develop and cultivate fictive identities for themselves, endowed with macabre and unworldly traits. Equipped with a theatrical identity, they socialize among themselves in the characters they have invented.

Thus, when Goths flirt with one another, they are often flirting with danger. Sometimes Goth make-believe can be hard to separate from reality. Every once in a while, a real predator emerges on the scene in search of victims, willing or otherwise. In general, however, most Goths are clear on what they are doing and who they are doing it with.

# If the Collar Fits ...

Certain identifiable Goth types have emerged over the years. Three main looks and attitudes predominate:

- **Romantic.** These Goths are so cutting edge they're old-fashioned. They wear Renaissance, Edwardian, or Victorian outfits. They also cultivate lofty ideals about what life should be, thereby dooming themselves to eternal disappointment!

- **Grunge.** These Goths typically dress like assault or abuse victims: torn clothes and hatchet-job haircuts. It also helps to look starving, anemic, and deeply suspicious of others.

- **Fetish.** These Goths hang out dressed for sadomasochistic encounters: collars, chains, gags, skin-tight leather clothes, and pieces of metal through pierced body parts. The idea is that when you've lived in pain long enough, you start to think it's fun!

### Grave Mistake

Don't assume all Goths take their creepy fashion seriously. There are several Goth websites that poke fun at Goth fashion. One of these offers this tongue-in-cheek fashion tip: to combine fashion and convenience, why not put your key ring through your pierced nipple? You'll look like a fetishist and you'll always know where your keys are!

Of course, not all Goths fit perfectly into any single category. Combining different styles is not uncommon. In addition, there's plenty of room for variation within each of the three styles mentioned. This is especially true since different Goths have different backgrounds and different ways of looking at things.

Some take themselves very seriously; others take a campy or ironic interest in their own self-image. Some are heavily buffeted by painful life experiences and emotional baggage; others, though not exactly happy-go-lucky, are at least capable of having fun. Some are dirt poor, jobless, homeless, and uneducated. Others are sophisticated and resourceful, rich, and well-connected. Goth, in other words, is a movement including many currents, not a monolithic organization.

# Occult Cults of Counterculture

Goth subculture is not a religion or cult. Even so, it is often associated with cult activities, especially by people who are worried about the spread of violence and crime among young people. The fear is that Goth ideas may somehow be influencing kids to do terrible things— namely to kill themselves or others in the name of a far-out set of religious beliefs.

> **Dead Giveaway**
>
> The tragic massacre at Columbine High School in Littleton, Colorado, in 1999 left many people searching for answers to the question of why 2 students engineered the killing of 15 people at their own school. Some suggested Goth subculture was at least partly responsible, noting that the murderers were former members of a gang called the Black Trench Coat Mafia who flaunted creepiness and alienation. Evidence suggests, however, that the killers were more into guns than Goth lifestyle. Goths have denied the killers were fellow Goths and denounced the massacre. What's more, many authorities hold that cult or gang membership is more often a symptom of dissatisfaction than a cause of violent crime. So, although violent crimes are sometimes committed by Goths, there is little support for the view that Goth subculture contributes to violence.

## Mean Spirited

To an extent, Goth culture itself has deliberately played on this fear. Many Goth band names evoke cultism and cult-inspired violence. Marilyn Manson (named after Charles Manson, the cult leader and mass murderer) and My Life with the Thrill Kill Kult are obvious examples. Less decidedly violent, yet equally evocative of sinister cult doings, are such names as Ministry, Sex Gang Children, The Mission, Sisters of Mercy, and Christian Death.

Although some Goths are into cults, the fact is that most would rather just fantasize about cult membership. An invented cult is a great role-playing device for a Goth band, just as a supernatural identity is a role-playing device for a Goth individual. The idea of the cult adds drama and a certain romance, as well as conveying a countercultural attitude. Nothing says "we are not like most people" more clearly than the name of a cult.

Many Goths embrace Satanism—or say they do—as a similarly sinister role-playing device. Few are silly enough to believe they can truly gain supernatural powers by worshiping the Dark Lord. But heck, pretending to be evil can be fun, as every kid who has ever dressed up on Halloween knows. Goths simply pretend to be evil more often than most people. In fact, there's even a song, popular among Goths, called "Everyday is Halloween," performed by Ministry. The point of the song is that Goths dress up, not to attack people, but to defend themselves against others who don't understand the real traumas of existence.

## What the Devil

Satanism takes many forms and Gothic Satanism is only one of the most recent. Goths tap into older satanic traditions or invent new ones usually for the sake of dramatic self-expression, shock value, and spiritual experimentation. The most famous satanic cult predates the Goth movement. This is the Church of Satan, founded by Anton La Vey in 1966.

> **Cold Fact**
>
> Leading Satanist Anton La Vey conferred official recognition on the Goth movement when he met with Goth performer Marilyn Manson and ordained him a priest of the Church of Satan. It's pretty clear that La Vey was more impressed with Manson's success as an exponent of twisted feelings than with his (Marilyn's) spiritual connection with Satan.

By combining an interest in the occult with flair for theatrics, the Church of Satan anticipated many of the attitudes that later inspired the Goth movement. The Church staged kinky black Masses in which a naked woman served as the "altar," representing the pleasures of sex. La Vey became a minor celebrity and appeared on the *Tonight Show* with Johnny Carson and in the film *Rosemary's Baby* (1968), where he played the devil himself!

A group calling itself the Temple of Set split off from the Church of Satan in 1975. Its members denounced religious hypocrisy in mainstream religion and cultivated self-empowerment through the rejection of conventional morality. Among the highest honors the sect conferred on its members was fellowship in the Order of the Vampire. The vampire was held up as a model of enlightened and sophisticated self-interest.

As with the Temple of Set, Goth spirituality is usually more a form of expression than of devotion. Submitting yourself to a higher power is not what it's all about, but tapping into available spiritual currents in order to enrich your otherwise painful existence. Spiritual belief is not the important thing. Instead, what the spirituality means and how it feels are what matters. Plus, it's a rush to see how people respond when you tell them you're into Satanism and bloodsucking!

## Dark New Age

Some, but by no means all, Goths are into the occult, Wicca, and/or Paganism. These practices are not simply gothic, but aspects of a wider, larger, and slightly older spiritual trend, namely New Age. If you see "New Age" thinking not just as a fad carried on by an avid group of devotees, but rather as a general trend that has had a big influence on the cultural and spiritual values of our time, you might consider the Goth movement as essentially a dark outgrowth of New Age.

New Age represents a search for, and discovery of, new spiritual values to replace or supplement traditional religion. It draws on beliefs and practices from all over the world, both ancient and newly invented, and it makes use of these beliefs and practices chiefly as a means of self-expression, rather than devotion. Thus, like the Goth movement, New Age is largely about exploring and tapping the imagination. Style and spirit overlap in both Goth and New Age.

**Cold Fact**

New Age and Goth have economic ties in addition to philosophical ones. Goth-related fashion accessories and decorations are commonly available at stores that sell New Age supplies.

No doubt many Goths would reject the New Age label. For that matter, many New Agers reject the New Age label! But like New Agers in general, Goths are receptive to alternative lifestyles and nonmainstream spiritual attitudes. The main difference between typical Goths and typical New Agers is that New Agers tend to be optimistic about the power of human spirituality to bring about peace and harmony for themselves and for everybody. Goths, on the other hand, look to the darker side of spirituality in order to cope with evils in life, society, and human nature that they see as ingrained and unavoidable.

Vampires, by the way, fit in especially well with this Goth-as-dark-New-Age idea. They represent an ancient, supernatural, and powerful concept whose dark spirituality can be tapped for expressive purposes. A little vampire blood can augment and enrich any Goth personality, much as crystals can harmonize with, and enhance, a New Ager's astral energy. Thus, while actual bloodsucking is somewhat rare, a vampiric aura is practically everywhere in Goth subculture.

## The Least You Need to Know

◆ The word "Goth" originally referred to an ancient Germanic tribe, then to a style of medieval architecture, and then a genre of novel before it was applied to today's subculture.

◆ The Goth scene got its start in British nightclubs during the waning years of the punk movement.

◆ Goths elevate despair to an art form, converting dissatisfaction with ordinary life to creative self-expression.

◆ Goth spiritual practices emphasize self-expression over devotion and is akin to New Age in embracing variety and experimentation.

# Chapter 13

# Cutting Edge

## In This Chapter

- ◆ Real vampires and blood-play enthusiasts
- ◆ Blood-play awareness
- ◆ Blood play as fetish and ritual
- ◆ Blood play as creative expression

Let's see here ... this is going to require some delicacy, sensitivity, clarity, control, and understanding. There's going to be some pain involved but, if we're careful, we should be able to avoid serious injury. In fact, you just might enjoy this. At any rate it should certainly get your juices flowing! So just relax, empty your mind, and live in the moment. Allow the experience to play itself out and who knows, you might learn to be more accepting of yourself.

Some might say this thing is distasteful, but it really isn't about taste. If you're offended, just move on; no one's forcing you to get involved in this. If you're not sure how you feel but you're curious, that's fine, but try to reserve judgement until it's over. We need to trust each other, so let's not make a lot of demands or harbor a lot of expectations. We'll take things slowly, step by step.

God knows, this isn't for everybody. I certainly never imagined I'd ever be doing this. But hey, live and learn. Deal. Cope. Come to terms. This is how it is. That's right folks, the moment you've been waiting for, dreading, longing for. I can hardly believe it myself. It's *The Complete Idiot's Guide to Sucking Blood!*

# Tapping the Source

The Goth vampire scene and the general current fascination with vampires has helped raise awareness for people who are into blood play—eroticism, fetish, and ritual based on blood. Those for whom blood play includes drinking blood are often referred to as real vampires or blood vampires, as opposed to lifestyle vampires and psychic vampires. Real vampires enjoy drinking blood for recreational, sexual, spiritual, and artistic purposes.

> **Dead Giveaway**
>
> Fiona Corealis is a blood player who has worked to focus public attention on blood play since the age of 19. She started the Blood Play Awareness Campaign in 1997 with two goals in mind: to counter the widespread perception that blood play is freakish and to encourage people to recognize the distinction between compulsive self-mutilation as an expression of self-hatred and blood play that can be creative and beautiful. She explains she once mutilated herself out of despair and self-hatred before she came to appreciate blood play as a creative and fulfilling activity. She says she loves how she looks when she is bleeding and loves the feel of a metal blade cutting her flesh.

## Blood Network

Blood play is not exactly a megatrend like stock car racing, pro wrestling, or reality-based TV. Even so, there are enough real vampires and blood donors to support many websites, including portals, personal pages, and message boards. In some major cities like San Francisco, it's sometimes possible to see blood-play rituals performed in public. There are a few artsy photography books that document blood play in action and a few videos as well. An artist in New York City even paints with his own blood. Roll over Jackson Pollack!

Blood play is unusual, but it's growing in popularity, especially since it is becoming more widely recognized and accepted among vampire lifestylers and other Goths who may not be into blood play themselves. In addition, there's a growing body of vampire literature and movies that romanticize blood rituals. So even though there aren't exactly enough real vampires out there to support a chain of fresh blood franchises, there is a small, thriving community of people more or less openly interested in the gushy stuff.

## Obey Your Thirst

In general, the motivation for blood play seems deep-seated and complex. It can satisfy a desire for adventure, drama, and excitement. It can make people feel strong or feel a special sense of belonging and intimacy. And if you happen to be someone who likes inflicting or receiving pain, blood play offers both. For many, blood play supplies a preferable alternative to self-loathing.

Up until fairly recently, few people recognized the desire to cut or be cut as anything but pathological. Those who obeyed a compulsion to cut themselves did so largely in secret and, if discovered, were often made to feel ashamed of their behavior. They might be institutionalized, regardless of how well they were able to deal with life when they weren't playing with needles and knives. Take a look at the next chapter for more on compulsive blood play as a clinical problem.

Today, people increasingly regard blood play as a more-or-less healthy outlet for deep-seated emotional trauma. Blood play can take the place of the emotional pain, guilt, or despair people might otherwise feel in response to wrenching life experiences, such as child abuse or neglect. Ritual bleeding can be a symbolic way of standing up to all the unkind cuts life has to offer. Cutting and blood drinking can also be an intimate way of understanding, and sharing in, another's emotional pain.

And, let's face it, blood play is becoming increasingly trendy and fashionable. In addition to the fetishistic satisfaction derived from the actual cutting, some blood-play enthusiasts are also into scarring as an aspect of skin and body art. In this sense, scarring from blood-play rituals is akin to tattoos and body piercing. It's hard to think of a more radical fashion statement! Regardless of their reasons, for all who do it there's a

**Cold Fact**

Many real vampires say that the AIDS crisis has actually brought about an increase in blood drinking because it has heightened the symbolic significance of blood as a taboo substance. Many feel that drinking blood in the age of AIDS constitutes either a statement of death defiance or an expression of profound trust of the person whose blood they drink.

growing awareness that what they do, though unusual, is not sick. Those who are most actively involved in promoting awareness of blood play stress the need for a safe, reasonable, and respectful approach. They say blood play must be strictly consensual among willing participants—no victims! Sharp, sterile equipment should be used: scalpels, syringes, razors, and lancets—teeth are not a good idea—and when blood drinking is involved, prior and rigorous blood testing is appropriate to avoid the spread of AIDS.

# Blood Is Thicker

Some blood players are ambivalent about calling themselves vampires and about gaining recognition among people who don't engage in blood play. Not many of them are out there encouraging the rest of the world to be more like them! Some even recommend avoiding it unless you feel a deep-seated urge you cannot satisfy in any other way. But many say that for them it's exciting, even beautiful, and that it helps them feel better about themselves.

## Different Strokes

Because people who practice blood play do so for various reasons, the way they go about it varies from case to case. For many, blood play and real vampirism are extensions of *sadomasochist* activity. Some like cutting, others like being cut, some like both. Some like the sight of blood, some like the taste, some like the feeling of sucking it from another person or having it sucked from them. Many just want the experience of doing something bizarre. There are no rules or standardized procedures for becoming a real vampire or donor or for engaging in blood play.

**Stalk Talk** _____

Although **sadomasochism** is very real, the term comes from the names of two novelists whose fiction describes inflicting and receiving pain, respectively, in erotic terms. The work of the French Marquis de Sade (1740–1814) emphasizes the joy of inflicting pain while that of Austrian Leopold von Sacher-Masoch (1836–1895) dwells on the pleasures of being hurt.

There are, however, many things one must know about blood and human anatomy to perform blood play without causing sickness, permanent injury, or death. (And no, actually, this book is *not* going to teach you how to do it!) Dangers include infection, damage to nerves and tendons, tetanus, and hepatitis—not to mention loss of blood! And of course there's AIDS, which can be contracted by using unclean implements and by drinking any bodily fluid of an infected person.

Some blood players are discrete and lead ordinary lives apart from their blood-play episodes. Others make a radical show of their fetishistic interests and flaunt visible scars or wear scalpels or razor blades as jewelry. Some people cut only themselves, some cut only others, some are only donors, some only blood drinkers, others swing both ways.

## Trickle-Down Effect

Many blood players say they are responding to bad childhood experiences. Physical and/or psychological abuse has made them deeply unhappy with themselves. Fantasies about being cut are not an uncommon response to such unhappiness. Some people even feel a compulsive urge to cut themselves and, in fact, do so.

But it seems that cutting and being cut is more meaningful and satisfying when other people are involved. So people who find solace in cutting and blood often look for partners. The stereotype of the aggressive, magnetic vampire seeking donors through seductive means doesn't always hold true. More often, it's the blood donor who initiates a blood-play relationship. In these situations, the blood vampire is not a predator, but a friend doing a friend an intimate personal favor!

# Cases in Point

Today, there are web postings where blood players can get in touch with one another. And, of course, there's the Goth and vampire scene where strange doings are becoming increasingly common. In many nightclubs these days, Bela Lugosi's famous pick-up line, "I vant to suck your bloood" might actually work! Or, for you donors out there, you can always use the old standby: "wanna neck?"

> **Dead Giveaway** _____
>
> Blood-letting was a common and popular Western medical practice for most of the past two millennia, thanks largely to the medical theories of the second-century Greek physician, Galen, a doctor who is second in historical importance only to Hippocrates. Galen espoused the view that many illnesses stem from "bad blood" and may be cured simply by letting out this bad blood. Blood-letting persisted as a medical practice well into the nineteenth century. Patients' veins or arteries would be cut with knives and bled over a bowl, or else live leeches would be applied to do the work. For many years, "leech" was a common term for a medical practitioner.

But it wasn't long ago that blood play was not so widely recognized and accepted. In her book, *American Vampires* (1989), Norine Dresser tells of a blood-play partnership that formed by chance in the 1980s between two people attending a fan club meeting of the hit TV vampire soap opera, *Dark Shadows*. The two vampire enthusiasts, a man and a woman, confided their fantasies to one another and decided to act on them. He said he wanted to be bitten and she said she wanted to bite, so there you go!

The only problem was that biting turned out to be inefficient and unbearably painful, so she started pricking his fingertips with needles instead. Slowly, the partnership expanded into a feeding circle, as more donors became involved. For this particular group, blood play was a private, personal thing, not at all messy, and with virtually no repercussions on the public lives of the participants.

In the book, *Piercing the Darkness: Undercover with Vampires in America Today* (Harper Collins, 1998) Katherine Ramsland tells of a slightly messier firsthand encounter with blood playing. While investigating the vampire scene, she met a real vampire who called himself Diogenes. He invited her to attend a blood-fetish ritual in a somewhat squalid New York City apartment.

When she arrived, she saw a woman leaning forward while sitting on a bed. Behind her was another woman making long, shallow cuts in her back with a surgical knife while a man stood and watched. As blood oozed down her back, the woman being cut claimed that she did not feel any pain at all, since her system was producing endorphins (natural, pain-relieving body chemicals). After a few more minutes, however, Ramsland reported that the woman started whimpering.

Evidently there was more on tap for this particular get-together than the cutting and bleeding that Ramsland witnessed. There were rubber tubes and big syringes on hand for later. Ramsland had seen enough, however, and left the apartment before things got any wilder.

### Cold Fact

Katherine Ramsland originally made her mark in the world of vampires as an Anne Rice scholar and author of *Prism of the Night: A Biography of Anne Rice* (Dutton, 1992) and *The Vampire Companion: The Official Guide to Anne Rice's Vampire Chronicles* (Ballantine, 1993). Since then she has become interested in real vampires and, more generally, the current fascination with the vampire myth.

# Looking Sharp

Many real vampires are writers and artists, and many others would like to be! As a result, many accounts of blood play are woven into fiction. Although blood play is graphically real, it often goes along with a rich fantasy life and a vivid imagination, so that it's often tricky to tell where reality leaves off and fantasy enters in.

## Graphic Designs

The award-winning vampire writer, Poppy Z. Brite, author of *Lost Souls* (1992) and *Love in Vein* (1994), is rumored to be a blood drinker.

Her work combines realistic accounts of the Goth underground with supernatural accounts of vampires. Another writer who is highly active in the blood-play scene is David Aaron Clark, who writes erotic Goth novels.

Clark says he became a blood donor and blood drinker after being traumatized by the suicide of his girlfriend in an apartment they shared. As if coping with his friend's death wasn't enough, he found himself stuck with the job of cleaning up the bloody mess caused by her death! He felt a sense of guilt over the fact that she had died while he remained alive and he wanted to bleed the way she did. He sought to deal with his feelings by flagellating himself.

With the help of friends, Clark transformed his private flagellation sessions into group blood-play rituals. Clark feels empowered and revitalized by bleeding, drinking blood, and identifying with vampires. Clark has performed as a blood donor in the artsy Soho district of New York City where a girlfriend cut him on the chest and palms and drank his blood as it flowed down his body.

Clark wrote text accompanying a book of photographs by Charles Gatewood called *True Blood* (1997). The photos document blood-play activities in a graphic, yet artistic manner. Gatewood, incidentally, has also put out videos for people interested in vicarious blood-play experiences. Some viewers of Gatewood's work have found it exhilarating, although most people find it disturbing.

**Dead Giveaway**

Many blood donors and drinkers say that blood ritual can lead to a deeper understanding of one's self. This view suggests a parallel between blood play and shamanic rituals in which an initiate or an adept is deliberately exposed to intense pain or physical hardship in order to bring about an altered mental state. A fairly well-documented example of this kind of ritual is the Sun Dance, traditionally practiced by Sioux medicine men, most notably Sitting Bull. The "dancer" is pierced through the chest with leather thongs that are attached to the top of a pole. Dancing around the pole, he stretches out the thongs, which pull at his pierced flesh. The ritual is intended to produce visionary ecstasy.

## Going With the Flow

Blood play is a big part of today's vampire mystique. It figures heavily into vampire role-playing and fantasy that, as you may have figured out by now, can sometimes be extremely difficult to distinguish from reality. If you steep yourself in the blood media long enough, you begin to suspect that many stories about blood play are fabricated.

Some vampire lifestylers enjoy talking about themselves and their experiences as vampires and many embellish their stories with supernatural details stemming from vampire myths as well as with attention-getting accounts of blood-play episodes. Many vampire lifestylers not only claim to be into blood play, but claim that drinking blood satisfies not simply an emotional urge, but a physiological and/or supernatural hunger as well.

Such vampire narratives often re-create the provocative premise of Anne Rice's best-selling novel, *Interview with the Vampire*, in which a vampire recounts his life—and undeath— story to a spellbound reporter. Real journalists who go out into the night in search of information on the vampire scene have found willing vampire informants, ready to divulge the chilling and paranormal details of their personal histories. As grisly as some of the tales often are, there's no need for garlic for protection. A grain of salt may be in order, though!

> **Grave Mistake**
>
> Don't get sucked into the supernatural claims many role players and lifestylers make for blood drinking. Though it can be a powerful and moving ritualistic or erotic practice as well as an intriguing romantic fantasy, it isn't magic!

Katherine Ramsland is a vampire reporter who has recorded numerous "interviews with vampires," registering on the credibility meter from astonishing-though-plausible to more-far-fetched-than-postcards-from-Pluto! According to Ramsland, many of her informants derive a peculiar satisfaction from imagining dark fantasies so vividly that they almost seem real to the person who dreams them up. In her book, *Piercing the Darkness*, Ramsland talks to a centuries-old vampire from the lost city of Atlantis, another with a 300-year-old vampire mentor from Copenhagen, and several who claim to possess an uncanny ability to fill others with sexual passion by cutting them and licking their blood.

# Blood Ties

A variation on the "interview with a vampire" spontaneous role-playing scenario is the vampire-as-teacher. Ramsland encountered a number of vampires who offered both supernatural and practical instruction on how to become a vampire. The instruction some claimed to offer combined erotic awareness, spirituality, and blood play.

One interesting example of the vampire-as-teacher is Viola Johnson, vampire lifestyler and author of *Dhampir: Child of the Blood* (1996), subtitled *A Vampyre's Babybook*. The book is supposedly intended to provide instruction in how to get along as a vampire to Johnson's surrogate "daughter" and blood-play partner. It combines supernatural vampire mythology with insight into the Goth scene.

Johnson says she became a vampire at age 17 when her vampire "father" offered her some of his blood to drink from his cut wrist. She claimed she drank a large quantity of his blood and then fell asleep in his arms. When she woke up, she felt ravenously hungry and found that nothing except more blood could satisfy the hunger.

Johnson says that her hunger was caused by a virus that got into her system when she drank her "father's" blood. She has passed this virus along to her "daughter," who also claims to feel a physical need that blood alone can satisfy. In addition to the virus, Johnson says that some vampires have a genetic drive to drink blood.

## Dead Giveaway

Many people into blood play begin through childhood experimentation and continue into later life, often after hooking up with likeminded companions. Not sure if blood drinking is right for you but curious to try it out? Be careful you don't bite off more than you can chew or get swept up in a dangerous social situation! Next time you cut yourself shaving or chopping vegetables, try a little of your own blood. Does it give you a supernatural thrill? Do you fill energized and more alive than usual? Or do you get a sense of inner calm, or perhaps a heightened understanding of who you are? If not, you should probably stick with your usual beverages!

In addition to bringing "children" of her own into vampire life, Johnson partnered up with a vampire "husband" and a "wife" (both of whom are women) from whom she drinks blood regularly. You know what they say, "the family that bleeds together …!" According to Johnson, her vampire family provides a nurturing environment for its members. The nurturing is not only physical but moral and spiritual, too, since vampires need to learn how to live in a way that's suited to their unusual condition.

## The Least You Need to Know

♦ Fascination with vampires in recent years has raised awareness for people into blood play.

♦ Blood-play enthusiasts cut themselves for emotional, spiritual, erotic, and artistic purposes.

♦ For many, blood play is a healthy expression of emotional hardships stemming from childhood traumas.

♦ Blood play is dangerous and participants require trust and experience to do it safely.

# Chapter 14

# Blood Clinic

## In This Chapter

- ◆ Clinical vampirism
- ◆ Psychological theories
- ◆ Freud and Jung
- ◆ Clinical and criminal cases
- ◆ Sexual psychopaths and vampire copycats

Vampires tell us a lot about human nature in symbolic, supernatural terms. Psychologists and psychiatrists tell us a lot about human nature using theoretical and scientific terms. Interesting things happen when vampires and psychoanalysts come together.

In many ways, bloodsuckers and headshrinkers have grown up side by side. The novel *Dracula* was published right around the time that Sigmund Freud and Carl Jung were laying the foundations of modern psychoanalysis. Many clinical cases of blood drinking and blood play came to light—before, during, and since that time—that bear striking similarities to vampires out of legend and fiction. While the vampire concept helped make these cases seem more familiar, psychological theories helped make them understandable.

So, thanks to decades of clinical theory and practice, we can develop a pretty good idea about why vampires are so batty! And in the process, psychologists have paved the way to helping troubled souls come to terms with their inner demons—even their bloodsucking ones. After all, the first step in making progress is to recognize the problem.

# Blood Rushes to the Head

Before Freud and Jung developed their influential theories of human psychology, most people were forced to rely on romantic or supernatural explanations for deviant behavior. Behavior that we might call psychopathic today would once have been considered demonic or diabolical, or simply depraved. Bizarre acts that once passed for the influence of evil spirits have since come to pass for the influence of psychosis. Gradually analysts and therapists have taken over from inquisitors and exorcists.

An important pioneer in the field of psychopathology was the German doctor Richard von Krafft-Ebing, who noticed that many of the most bizarre and disturbing acts perpetrated by psychopaths were sexual in nature. He explained his view and compiled massive amounts of evidence to support it in a work called *Psychopathia Sexualis* (1886). Many of the cases he described are concerned with subjects whose erotic impulses became heightened in connection with blood, violence, or death.

**Cold Fact**

Although Krafft-Ebing's work provided an important point of departure for Sigmund Freud, Krafft-Ebing did not look favorably on Freud's new ideas. Similarly, although Jung began studying psychotherapy as a Freudian, Freud was not receptive to Jung's innovations.

We know Krafft-Ebing's work had an important impact on the thinking of Sigmund Freud. Some scholars believe, in addition, that his work influenced Bram Stoker as well. In any case, the novel *Dracula* closely links sexuality and blood lust, as have many vampire stories ever since. In fact, many literary scholars have picked up on this element in *Dracula* and other vampire tales and link the blood lust they describe and the appeal they hold for readers to these psychoanalytic theories.

Meanwhile, some psychoanalysts have been using ideas borrowed from vampire stories to characterize actual clinical cases. "Clinical vampirism," "Dracula syndrome," and "Renfield's syndrome" (Renfield is the bug-eating lunatic in the novel, *Dracula*) are terms that have been used to describe actual mental patients. Similarly, certain psychopathic killers have been referred to as vampires in the news media, including Peter Kurten, "the Dusseldorf vampire," and Ali Kordiyeh, "the Tehran Vampire."

# Psyched Out

Most psychoanalytic accounts of vampires and vampirism draw on Freudian or Jungian theories of the psyche, or both. Actually, neither Freud nor Jung had much to say about vampires or vampirism *per se*, but their ideas have been applied to vampirism by other thinkers. So, as in other areas of psychology, it makes sense to talk about Freudian and Jungian views of vampirism.

### Dead Giveaway

The classic Freudian interpretation of the psychological significance of vampires and vampirism is the chapter titled "The Vampire" from the book, *On the Nightmare* (Liveright Publishing, 1931) by Ernest Jones. Jones links the vampire legend to infantile regressive oral fixation, and to feelings of guilt and hate, especially in relation to incestuous desires. Jones points out that when vampires return from the grave in legend, they typically attack their own relatives. Jones says such activity amounts to a displaced violation of the incest taboo made famous by Freud in his discussion of the Oedipus complex. In other words, when people feel a combination of hatred and erotic desire for members of their own family, those feelings can find expression in the fantasy, nightmare, or belief that those family members are vampires returned from the grave.

## Sex on the Brain

One of Freud's most important contributions to his field has to do with recognizing that sexual desires are shaped in early childhood. As a result, many psychological problems are both sexual and stem from childhood traumas. Freud developed a useful theory explaining how childhood development can influence adult sexuality. It's a complicated theory involving many steps and stages, but the basic idea is that we all learn to regulate our sexual drives in ways that will help us minimize negative repercussions. Each of us forms our own personal sense of what these negative repercussions are all about during childhood.

According to Freud, if you are taught as a child that sexual desire is bad, you will come to feel anxious and guilty about your sexual urges. In addition, you will develop what he called "defense mechanisms" to protect yourself from your guilt and anxiety. These defense mechanisms don't exactly solve the problem, but rather serve to disguise it.

## Desires in Disguise

Freud says everyone develops defense mechanisms on the road to becoming a functioning adult in a civilized society. It's all a part of being human. Freudian defense mechanisms include:

- **Denial.** "No, I don't have any sexual urges!"

- **Repression.** "What's an urge? I have no idea what you're talking about!"

- **Regression.** "It's time for beddy-bye and I want my blankie!"

- **Projection.** "*You* have the hots for *me*, don't you?"

- **Sublimation.** "Cathedrals and art museums make me feel all tingly inside!"

- **Reaction formation.** "No, I hate sex! I hate it, I hate it, I hate it! No, don't! Please, no sex! Please, please, please! I'll do anything!"

- **Displacement.** "My potted fern understands me, don't you fern? Yes, beautiful fern."

**Grave Mistake**

Don't develop a superiority complex just because you're not aware of having any defense mechanisms in your own psyche. According to Freud, everyone has them. He says we are all born "polymorphously perverse" (sexually attracted to everything) before we learn to channel our desires along socially acceptable lines. This means the difference between "normal" and "perverse" is purely conventional.

## Seeing Through the Cape

Equipped with the concept of defense mechanisms, it isn't hard to figure out how an ordinary, reasonably innocent baby could develop into
a bloodsucking fiend just by going through enough rotten experiences
as a child. Reaction formation and displacement are especially useful
ideas. Reaction formation helps explain why some people want to do
harm to those they are attracted to while displacement helps explain
why someone might feel sexually aroused by things most people find
repulsive, including blood and dead bodies.

> **Dead Giveaway** _____
>
> Psychoanalysts have described many characteristics that their clinical
> subjects share with vampires, even if they don't actually suck blood.
> For example, it's common for people who have been wounded emotion-
> ally to retreat into themselves and look down on everyone, much as a
> vampire who lives alone in a castle. Another connection concerns the
> addictive nature of the thrill of breaking taboos that can be compared to
> blood thirst. What's more, psychologists have noted that some schizo-
> phrenics are unable to recognize themselves in the mirror and have com-
> pared this peculiarity to Dracula's supernatural inability to cast a reflection.

Regression may also be a factor if you regard bloodsucking as an oral
fixation stemming from issues that arise during breast-feeding and
weaning. So from the Freudian perspective you could say that vampires
are big babies who:

1. Like to suck jugular veins instead of their thumbs (or their
   mother's breast).

2. Like blood because they're afraid of sex.

3. Want to hurt those they find attractive to punish them for arous-
   ing their desires.

So much for the vampire mystique!

## Drawing Blood from the Well

Jungian theory has a somewhat different take on vampires. Jung and Freud were once colleagues, but Jung broke with Freud partly for placing too much emphasis on sexuality. Freud understood pretty much everything in sexual terms, whereas Jung believed that the dreams and fantasies of his patients drew on an ancient and universal symbolism that represent the common heritage of humanity. In Jung's view, it's not just sex we're all after, but self-realization within an archetypal, collective unconscious.

### Grave Mistake

Jung points out that psychoanalytic diagnoses (a Freudian specialty) don't really help the people being diagnosed, regardless of how accurate and insightful they may be. In contrast, Jung encouraged people to think about their problems in a more positive light in terms of their deep, psychic connections with humanity. He found that this approach helped them feel better about themselves.

Jungians regard vampires as a symbolic expression of primal instincts. Blood represents life and power, so drinking blood can be seen as a symbolic expression of the need for power. Those who harbor a deep, psychological need for power may dream of drinking blood or, in extreme and rare cases, actually do it. Such dreams and compulsive actions represent the collective unconscious asserting itself, often in defiance of polite social conventions.

## Bloody Archives

Few psychoanalysts come into contact with actual cases of clinical vampirism—cases in which mental patients feel a psychic compulsion to act in some way like a vampire. But enough such cases have occurred to make a dent in the psychoanalytic literature. Most notably, a number of them have been described in the book, *Vampires, Werewolves, and Demons: Twentieth Century Reports in the Psychiatric Literature* (Brunner/Mazel Publishers, 1992) edited by Richard Noll.

## Coming to Terms

Many of us are blessed with supportive (or sarcastic) friends who, when we do something crazy, nod their heads and say, "yes, there's a word for that!" So it's nice to know there are words for people who do things that are so bizarre and morbid that they make most people queasy just to think about them. And for some of these words, we have vampire stories to thank.

Clinical vampirism, sometimes called Renfield's syndrome, has been applied to people compelled to drink other people's blood or their own blood (auto-vampirism). In addition, it is sometimes applied to necrophilia (sexual attraction to dead bodies) and necro-sadism (pleasure derived from mutilating dead bodies). Fortunately these problems aren't as common as, say, video game addiction or business-presentation-phobia, but a handful of cases stand out nonetheless.

One of the early cases was that of Antoine Leger, a nineteenth-century French vineyard worker described by Krafft-Ebing, who classified him as a "lust-murderer." Leger had a hard time fitting in with society, so he spent most of his time wandering around in the forest. There he encountered a twelve-year-old girl, whom he raped, killed, and muti-lated. He tore out her heart and ate some of it and drank some of her blood. Although Leger was hardly the first lust-murderer, he was among the first to be treated as a mental patient. Instead of being exe-cuted or sent to prison he was confined in an insane asylum.

## Self-Absorbed

Many more recent cases have been studied more thoroughly. One is that of an "auto-vampiric" young man described by R. S. McCully in the *Journal of Nervous and Mental Disease* (1964) and reprinted in Noll's book. This subject was examined and underwent mental tests while hospitalized for his condition.

As an adolescent, this young man learned to open arteries in his neck while looking at himself in the mirror. He sometimes saved the blood in a cup and drank it. Later he took to cutting a vein in his arm and drinking from that. He found that cutting himself and drinking his blood excited him sexually. He said sometimes it made him feel peaceful and other times victorious, as if he had defeated an opponent. He sometimes fantasized about taking blood from other boys, although he never did.

The patient underwent a Rorschach (ink blot) test and was asked to make a series of drawings. The examination indicated he was depressed, lonely, and emotionally underdeveloped, though he was well-developed intellectually. He was not at all delusional, and was aware of how unusual his blood-drinking behavior was. Interestingly, had he started his habit thirty years later, it wouldn't have been quite so unusual. He might have been right at home in a lifestyle vampire-feeding circle of today!

**Dead Giveaway**

R. S. McCully, who described a well-known case of auto-vampirism in the 1960s, drew on Jungian psychology in explaining the case by relating it to ancient myths concerned with blood drinking. He pointed out that Tibetan Buddhists recognize blood-drinking Gods that serve to assist those who meditate on their images in their efforts to take control of their emotions. His patient drank his own blood apparently as a way of compensating for his underdeveloped emotional responses. In both cases, blood drinking is, in effect, the opposite side of the coin of intense emotional restraint.

# Bloody Murder

A number of strange and gruesome criminal cases of vampire killings took place in the twentieth century, some of which are well-known. Disturbingly, despite the bizarre and compulsive nature of many of the killings, many of the murderers have maintained a normal appearance in other respects. Psycho killers are every bit as capable of disguising their crimes and concealing the evidence as those who murder for money or revenge.

## Vat of Horrors

John George Haigh, "the acid bath murderer" of London, killed eight people during the 1940s and successfully escaped detection before finally being apprehended for his ninth murder. He typically shot or bludgeoned his victims in the head, cut open a vein in their necks, and drank a cup of their blood. Then he immersed the bodies in a vat of acid, effectively destroying the evidence.

Although he took possession of the property of some of his victims—former friends of his!—through fraud, his primary motive for the killings was blood thirst. He reported having bloody dreams that prompted him to kill. In one recurring dream, he found himself in a forest of crucifixes. The crosses turned into green trees that had blood dripping from the leaves. He drank the blood in his dream and then awoke with a desire to drink more blood.

After killing eight victims in a span of five years, he became careless with his ninth. He killed a woman and sold her jewelry soon afterward. He also sent her blood-covered coat to the cleaners! It wasn't hard for the police to track him down. He confessed to the nine killings, then was convicted and hanged. His likeness was sculpted in wax and put on display in London's famous Madame Tussaud's House of Horrors.

> **Grave Mistake**
>
> Don't kid yourself into believing that "true crime" stories are educational. They tend to be long on sensational appeal and short on useful and intelligent analysis. Maybe that's why true crime books are often shelved in the "fiction" section of many bookstores!

## On the Fritz

Another notorious blood-drinking killer was Fritz Haarmann, "the Vampire of Hanover," who operated in Germany in the 1920s. He lured men to his home, raped them, bit them in the neck, and drank their blood. He was charged with committing over 20 murders, but suspected of killing over 50 victims.

Haarmann spent time in jail at various times during his life for petty crime, including sex offenses, before his arrest for murder after several friends disappeared. The police searched his place and found the remains of twenty victims. At that time he confessed and claimed to have worked together with an accomplice, his lover Hans Grans.

At one point during his killing spree, Haarmann worked as a butcher. He claimed to have sold the flesh of several of his victims in the butcher shop where he worked. Haarmann was convicted and beheaded. Grans was imprisoned for life. Upon his death, his brain was preserved and examined at Gottingen University.

# Copycat Bats

While most vampire killers are sexual psychopaths who are largely unaware or uninterested in their own resemblance to vampires, some vampire killers are self-consciously vampiric. Part of their profile as murderers concerns their self-image as vampires and part of their motive in killing is to reinforce this sense of themselves.

## Playing Rough

A famous case of recent years involved what has been called a vampire "cult." The killers were a group of teenagers from Kentucky who apparently got carried away with the excitement of pretending to be vampires in the role-playing game, *Vampire: The Masquerade.* So they stopped role-playing and took up vampire imitation in earnest. They were kicked out of the game, but that didn't stop them living like vampires.

The group was led by a seventeen-year-old named Roderick Ferrell, who went by the vampire name of Vessago. He and his followers dressed up as vampires, slept during the day, and held clan meetings and initiation rituals involving cutting each other with razors and drinking blood. Reportedly as many as 30 young people took part in the cult meetings.

In 1996, Ferrell and three friends went to Florida to visit Ferrell's girlfriend, Heather Wendorf. She was initiated into the cult with a blood-drinking ritual and later claimed that she had found it to be a spiritual experience for her. At some point after the proceedings, Ferrell attacked Wendorf's parents and bludgeoned them to death. They were found with "V's" branded into their bodies, along with other marks.

The teenagers fled to Louisiana where they were apprehended. Found with them were works of vampire fiction and the occult. Ferrell eventually pleaded guilty, but only after Wendorf testified against him. He was sentenced to die in the electric chair.

**Dead Giveaway**

The so-called vampire cult killings have fueled debate over the question of whether role-playing vampire games and lifestyle vampire culture are inciting young people to acts of violence. In the wake of the trial, articles and editorials about this issue ran in the press. Most concluded Ferrell was capable of killing whether or not he was involved in *Vampire: The Masquerade.* Speaking of vampire culture in general, vampirism psychologist Richard Noll has stated that he believes its influence on young people is mostly positive in providing an avenue through which to channel and even reverse negative feelings.

Another, much earlier teenage killer and vampire imitator was Salvatore Agron from New York City. He murdered several people while dressed in a cape à la Bela Lugosi. At his trial in 1959 he said he was a vampire. Another self-identified vampire was Tracy Wigginton of Brisbane, Australia. In addition to harvesting blood from willing donors, she murdered a man, stabbing him and drinking his blood.

On the other side of the coin, at least one murder was perpetrated by a vampire hunter. In the mid-1990s, a man from California suspected his girlfriend of being a vampire. After stabbing her to death, he was sentenced to 16 years in prison.

## Hit List

Sadly, there is no shortage of cases in which killers kill apparently for the sake of doing violence and drinking blood. Here are a few more of the more famous and unusual ones:

- Peter Kurten, "The Vampire of Dusseldorf," was an infamous serial killer of the late 1920s who delighted in the blood of his victims, mostly young women.

**Cold Fact**

The name Peter Kurten was signed to a note as an alias used by the psycho-killer in the Hollywood movie, *Copycat* (1995), starring Sigourney Weaver as the detective who tracks him down after figuring out his imitative M.O.

◆ Baron Roman von Sternberg-Ungern of Russia drank blood in the 1920s, apparently in the belief that he was Genghis Kahn.

◆ Stanislav Modzieliewski of Poland killed and drank his victims' blood. He was convicted with the help of testimony of a woman who pretended to be dead while he drank her blood.

◆ James Riva shot his grandmother and drank her blood in 1980. He later claimed he was instructed to kill by a vampire whose voice he heard in his head.

◆ Ali Kordiyeh, "the Tehran Vampire," was a serial killer in Iran who was publicly executed by hanging in 1997. Before being hanged he was flogged by relatives of his victims.

## The Least You Need to Know

◆ Neither Freud nor Jung had much to say about vampires or vampirism, but their ideas have strongly influenced those who are interested in vampires from a psychological perspective.

◆ Clinical vampirism is a term describing the compulsion to draw or drink blood.

◆ Those who suffer from clinical vampirism may be normal and healthy in other respects—or they may be psychopathic killers.

◆ Vampire copycat killings may or may not be sexual in nature.

# Chapter 15

# Inner Vamps, Inner Victims

## In This Chapter

- Demonic aptitude test
- Predators and victims
- Shifting and binding
- Annihilating and infecting
- Seducing and repulsing

It's here at last! The "please understand me" personality test for vampires, demons, witches, ghosts, werewolves, and their victims: the Demonality Assessment Test. Take this test to get a razor-sharp understanding of your inner demons or your need to be victimized.

Find out whether you're really a shape-shifting predator trapped in the body of a mere mortal. Learn whether you have a hidden death wish, subconsciously driving you to destruction. Decide whether you should quit your day job and take up witchcraft full time. See whether your current victim-predator relationships have a promising future.

Modeled after the famous Meyers-Briggs personality test, the Demonality Assessment Test can measure the personal characteristics of your inner demons to help you come to terms with your own demonic style. Assessing your demonality may help your inner demon function better in daily life. Or it may prove conclusively that everything is hopeless! Either way you'll have fun.

# Demon Scheme

The Demonality Assessment Test divides demonic personalities into sixteen different types put together from eight distinct demonic characteristics. These eight characteristics are organized into four pairs of opposites. Find where you stand in relation to these four pairs of opposing types, put them together and *voilà!* Your inner demon will be revealed!

**Dead Giveaway** _____

This Demonality Assessment Test is modeled after the Meyers-Briggs Type Indicator Test which, as you may know, has become a popular tool for categorizing personality types. The Meyers-Briggs test measures character in these terms:

| | |
|---|---|
| **E** Extroversion | **I** Introversion |
| **N** Intuition | **S** Sensing |
| **F** Feeling | **T** Thinking |
| **P** Perceiving | **J** Judging |

The Meyers-Briggs test is intended to promote awareness of how personality types differ to make it easier for people to get along despite the differences.

The eight demonality characteristics are paired because, in theory, everyone tends to exhibit either one paired term or the other. It's possible, however, to be more or less neutral or to exhibit a little of both characteristics to some degree. The four pairs of opposing demonic characteristics are:

**P** predator                     **V** victim

**Sh** shifting                    **B** binding

**A** annihilating                 **I** infecting

**S** seducing                     **R** repulsing

**Cold Fact** _____

The vampire myth and the self-help industry seem made for each other, don't they? Two self-help books that describe interpersonal problems in vampiric terms are *Unholy Hungers: Encountering the Psychic Vampire in Ourselves and Others,* by Barbara E. Hort (1996), and *Vampires: Emotional Predators Who Want to Suck the Life Out of You,* by Daniel Rhodes and Kathleen Rhodes (1998).

# Blood Test

Ready for the test? Below are four sections with four questions each for each of the four pairs of opposites. For each question score yourself on a scale of 1 to 5 according to how much either option applies to you. A score of 5 or 1 means you fall into one or the other extreme. Scores of 2 and 4 are more moderate and 3 is right in the middle. If you cannot decide, don't understand the question, or feel that the question doesn't apply to you either way, score your answer 3. Add up your total score for each section to see which characteristic most applies to you.

**Predator or Victim**

1. If you came across a dangerous wild animal caught in a trap, would you be more likely to set it free (1) or kill it? (5) _____

2. Do you spend more time thinking about how you can acquire more nice things (5) or worrying about losing the things you already have? (1) _____

3. Are you more likely to hurt yourself a little to help others a lot (1), or to hurt others a lot to help yourself a little? (5) _____

4. If you were shipwrecked with a fellow castaway who rescued you from drowning, would you be more likely to share your last loaf of bread (1) or have cannibal sandwiches? (5) _____

Add up your total for the first section and mark it in the space provided below. Any score from 4 to 11 indicates victim (**V**). 12 is neutral. 13–20 indicates predator (**P**). A score of 18–20 means you're way lethal. A score of 4–6 means you're a sitting duck.

Total _____     Characteristic _____

**Shifting or Binding**

5. When others are foolish does it make you happy (1) or angry? (5)

    _____

6. Would you rather be superior (5) or seem superior? (1) _____

7. Do you have more fun when you're in control (5) or when you lose control? (1) _____

8. Suppose you booked an economy class flight on an airplane and they were moving passengers to fill empty seats in first class. If someone else's name were called ahead of yours would you be more likely to claim your name should have been called first (5) or pretend to be that person whose name was called? (1) _____

Add up your total for the second section. Any score between 4 and 11 indicates a shifting personality type (**Sh**). 12 is neutral. 13–20 indicates binding (**B**). A score of 4–6 means you could slide off of flypaper. A score of 18–20 means you could nail Jell-O to the ceiling.

Total _____     Characteristic _____

**Annihilating or Infecting**

9. Are you more likely to act on the spur of the moment (5) or to bide your time and wait for the right opportunity? (1) _____

10. Would you rather make others be more like you (1) or make yourself less like others? (5) _____

11. If you wanted to get through a locked door would you be more likely to pick the lock (1) or break down the door? (5) _____

12. Would you rather humiliate your enemies (5) or weaken them without their noticing? (1) _____

Add up your total for the third section. Any score between 4 and 11 indicates an infecting personality type (**I**). 12 is neutral. 13–20 indicates annihilating (**A**). A score of 18–20 means you're a walking time-bomb. A score of 4–6 means you're probably cheating on this test, just like on all the others!

Total _____    Characteristic _____

**Seducing or Repulsing**

13. Would you rather be envied (5) or feared? (1) _____

14. Would you like for people to understand how you really feel inside (1) or would you prefer that they didn't? (5) _____

15. Would you rather have the power to become invisible (1) or the power to hypnotize? (5) _____

16. Are you more likely to love yourself for hating others (5) or to hate yourself for loving others? (1) _____

Add up your total for the fourth section. Any score between 4 and 11 indicates a repulsing personality type (**R**). 12 is neutral. 13–20 indicates seducing (**S**). A score of 18–20 means you're a born heartbreaker. A score of 4–6 means you freak people out without even trying.

Total _____    Characteristic _____

Now combine the results from each section in order and match your traits with the descriptions below to see what kind of inner demon you have. Your demonic profile should conform to one of the following types: **PBAS, PBAR, PBIS, PBIR, PShAS, PShAR, PShIS, PShIR, VBAS, VBAR, VBIS, VBIR, VShAS, VShAR, VShIS, VShIR.** Each type is described below.

# PBAS, PBAR, PBIS, and PBIR

The PBs strive for absolute power. They are intense, keenly intelligent, and charismatic. They tend to be rather high strung, but they always play by the rules, even when they make up their own. They make excellent witches, cult leaders, terrorists, and lawyers.

## PBAS: Predator Binding Annihilating Seducing

No one inspires fear and respect at the same time like PBASs. They are clean, efficient, insistent, uncompromising, and brutal, though they can be charming to the point of inspiring awe. They never show fear or remorse, although they often have a deep spiritual side and sometimes even a good sense of humor.

Famous PBASs include the Angel of Death, the Hindu God Shiva, the Norse Valkyries, Salome from the Bible, Vlad the Impaler, and Lestat.

> **Dead Giveaway** _____
>
> Salome's story is told in the Gospel of Matthew 14:3-12. It seems that John the Baptist had the moral fortitude to criticize Herod Antipas for shacking up with Herodias, the wife of his own brother. Herod didn't like for commoners to tell him how to behave, so he had John thrown into prison. He was reluctant to put the prophet to death, however, for fear of causing an uproar among his followers.
>
> One day, Herodias's daughter Salome danced before Herod. He liked her dancing so much that he promised to grant her any request. She demanded the head of John the Baptist on a platter. She got it. The PBAS personality is evident in Salome's drive for power for her mother (P), in her ability to bind Herod into an agreement (B), in her ruthless wish to destroy John the Baptist (A), and in her seductive dancing (S).

## PBAR: Predator Binding Annihilating Repulsing

PBARs are shock specialists and masters of intimidation. Though they are commonly misunderstood and carry chips on their shoulders as a result, they can be surprisingly unselfish and are never happier as when they are destroying themselves right along with everyone else. They make good professional wrestlers and torturers.

Among the more notable PBARs are the Grim Reaper, the giant Goliath, the gorgon Medusa and the Harpies from Greek mythology, Frankenstein, the Creature from the Black Lagoon, and Freddy Kruger.

## PBIS: Predator Binding Infecting Seducing

PBISs are as suave as a well-oiled knife. They have refined and polished temperaments, though they can be flamboyantly quirky. They don't like to take no for an answer and rarely have to, since they can find or persuade willing accomplices and victims almost wherever they turn. They are dependable, responsible, and make excellent ringleaders in conspiracies.

PBISs who have made their mark include Lilith, Mephistopheles, Lord Ruthven, Vampirella, Charles Manson, and superior, highly evolved aliens from outer space who want to control our minds.

## PBIR: Predator Binding Infecting Repulsing

PBIRs are highly imaginative and creative and they love their work. They are the perfect evil geniuses. They are unpredictable, but not flighty or flaky as is commonly supposed of them. Instead they are difficult to figure out, inhabiting realms known to few ordinary mortals. They make excellent zombies, mad scientists, sadistic nurses, and bioterrorists.

PBIRs include every character ever played by Vincent Price, as well as Dr. Demento, Dr. Mabuse, Dr. Cyclops, Dr. Caligari, Dr. Morbius, Dr. No, Dr. Evil, and the Unabomber.

**Grave Mistake**

The fictional character often thought of as the classic original mad scientist, Dr. Frankenstein, was actually not fiendishly evil in Mary Shelley's famous novel where he first appeared, but a well-meaning scientist intending to conquer death as a boon to humankind. Only in later Hollywood movie versions of the tale did he become a demented switch-throwing maniac.

# PShAS, PShAR, PShIS, and PShIR

The PShs are wily and elusive. They thrive in the midst of mystery, have a flair for drama and suspense, and are often hopeless romantics. They tend to be private and secretive, but they love to seek people out for their own nefarious purposes. They are first-rate vampire material, and also make excellent werewolves and politicians. They can also make good spies, traitors, and psycho killers.

## PShAS: Predator Shifting Annihilating Seducing

PShASs are charming and perverse. They love nothing better than an impetuous crime spree and they take delight in evading capture despite their audacity. As allies, they can betray you and make you believe it's your own fault. As killers, their victims suffer exquisitely from a wrenching sense of heartbreak combined with their death throes.

Famous PShASs include Marcus Junius Brutus, Judas Iscariot, Benedict Arnold, Bonnie and Clyde, Hannibal Lecter, and Danny Glick (from *Salem's Lot*).

## PShAR: Predator Shifting Annihilating Repulsing

PShARs always make their own rules and usually change them whenever it suits them. They relish their own unpredictability, the better to confuse and torment those in their power. Self-centered, ruthless, and unreasonable, the PShARs march to their own beat. They see themselves as superior to everyone else and only they know or care why. They make effective though untrustworthy hit men and mercenaries, as well as excellent werewolves, dragons, and barbarian warlords.

Some notable PShARs are Genghis Kahn, the Headless Horseman, the Grinch that stole Christmas, Ebenezer Scrooge, and Monty Burns.

## PShIS: Predator Shifting Infecting Seducing

PShISs are quintessential romantic vampires. Sensitive, dashing, devious, sophisticated, and secretive, they select their victims carefully based on characteristics that complement their own. They relish and cultivate the special, intimate bond between predator and victim. They make fine sirens, incubae, succubae, brain washers, hypnotists, and secret agents. And they are especially well cut-out to be someone's evil twin.

Famous PShISs include Lamia, Iago, Dracula, Carmilla, Sabella, and Mata Hari.

**Cold Fact** _____

Iago, the villain in Shakespeare's tragedy, *Othello*, subtly and deviously deceives Othello into thinking his wife, Desdemona, was unfaithful to him. Othello becomes so enraged that he strangles her even though he loves her more than life itself. He then kills himself. At the conclusion, Iago is taken away to be tortured for his villainy, but he was a great PShIS while he was at it.

## PShIR: Predator Shifting Infecting Repulsing

PShIRs are gross, icky, and disgusting. They like crawling out from under rocks and getting slime all over everything. They are also extremely needy and love to be pitied, often selecting those who pity them as their primary victims. They make excellent plague-carrying rats, parasitic aliens, pod people, drug dealers, and tobacco company executives.

Well-known PShIRs are Nosferatu, Varney, and the Toxic Avenger.

# VBAS, VBAR, VBIS, and VBIR

On to the victims! The victim binding types are intelligent, serious, and principled, invariably getting into trouble because they will not or cannot settle for ordinary ways of doing things. Though generally somewhat proud, they are often generous, even while they are careless of their own well-being.

## VBAS: Victim Binding Annihilating Seducing

VBASs are faithful, trusting, and sincere. They care about only one thing more than love and that's dying for love. Only love comes close to meeting their lofty expectations for existence and even then it's a stretch. They are loyal to those they truly love unto the death, which usually isn't far away. They make first-rate suicidal lovers, martyrs, and sacrificial virgins.

VBASs of note include Helen of Troy, Lucretia, Guinevere, Romeo and Juliet, and Thelma and Louise.

## VBAR: Victim Binding Annihilating Repulsing

VBARs are impetuous but serious and uncompromising. They love throwing babies out with the bath water and cutting off their own noses to spite their faces. They often have lofty spiritual or intellectual ideals, which they use to make themselves miserable. They make excellent religious flagellants and frustrated, failed inventors.

Well-known VBARs include people whom no one has ever heard of because they died so ignominiously.

**Cold Fact** _____

Elizabeth Bishop's ingenious poem, "One Art" makes an excellent VBAR manifesto. It describes "the art of losing" as a skill you can get really good at with only a little practice! "The art of losing isn't hard to master ... Then practice losing farther, losing faster ..."

## VBIS: Victim Binding Infecting Seducing

VBISs are strong, intelligent, and even chic, but tend to be too jaded or hopeless to make full use of their talents. They often walk with their eyes wide open into disaster simply because they don't care enough to avoid it. They make excellent Goths and really good supermodels who become heroin addicts.

Famous VBISs include Hamlet and the Marlboro Man.

## VBIR: Victim Binding Infecting Repulsing

VBIRs are fatalistic, down-to-earth, and accepting. They are also highly insightful, though they share their insights with others only rarely. If they live past the age of 13, VBIRs become clear about who they are and comfortable with themselves and with the life of abject misery to which they are doomed. Meanwhile they remain enigmas and sources of vexation to everyone else. They are masters of pathos and are often objects of fascination, though they themselves appear somewhat bored with life. They make top-notch toad eaters, poison food tasters, and circus geeks.

Famous VBIRs include Franz Kafka and all the main characters in stories by Franz Kafka.

# VShAS, VShAR, VShIS, and VShIR

VShs are sensitive yet receptive, eagerly seeking out new experiences that cause their undoing. They often have a tough time fitting in and make magnificent scapegoats. After they die, they almost invariably leave unfinished business behind them and are forced to haunt their old environs as ghosts, unable to find peace.

## VShAS: Victim Shifting Annihilating Seducing

VShASs are dynamic, energetic, and destined to be blackmailed. They always seem to end up getting forced to do bad things against their own will, or for a good, but impossible purpose. Thus they manage to be perfectly innocent and guilty as sin at the same time. They make charmingly inept secret agents and easy-to-spot perpetrators of fraud for good causes.

Famous VShASs include Delilah and all those beautiful spies on the side of evil in James Bond films.

## VShAR: Victim Shifting Annihilating Repulsing

VShARs are philosophical, as well as astonishingly tolerant and forbearing, and they need to be, because they get the short end of just about every stick there is. They are misunderstood, and are commonly feared and hated without good reason, especially by themselves! Through it all they tend to keep an open mind, which only makes them even more misunderstood. They make excellent scapegoats and toilers in thankless obscurity.

Famous VShARs include the Elephant Man and the guy at the office who does all the most unpleasant work and gets no appreciation for it.

> **Grave Mistake**
>
> Don't underestimate VShARs. They may be the single most powerful force in history, having built the Egyptian pyramids, dug the Panama Canal, and put on all those little stickers you find on pieces of fruit.

## VShIS: Victim Shifting Infecting Seducing

VShISs are highly inquisitive and experimental but charmingly tragically naive, somehow managing to put their delicate fingers right on—and through—the weakest and most tender aspects of human nature. They hold romantic ideals, and are constantly in search of what they can never hope to find. They make good explorers who get eaten by cannibals and emissaries sent to hostile countries on the brink of war.

Well-known VShISs include Eve, Pandora, Persephone, Oedipus, Orpheus, and Edgar Allen Poe.

## VShIR: Victim Shifting Infecting Repulsing

VShIRs are big-hearted, generous, would-be do-gooders who become so fascinated with the evil and sorrow of the world that they are overcome by it. They make great doctors who experiment on themselves, missionaries who contract malaria or leprosy, and peacemakers who get caught in the crossfire.

Famous VShIRs include Dr. Jekyll and the Fly.

That's it for the test. Hope it has given you a measure of respite from your miserable life of internal torment!

## The Least You Need to Know

♦ The **PB**s strive for absolute power.

♦ The **PSh**s are wily and elusive.

♦ The **VB**s are serious and intelligent.

♦ The **VSh**s are sensitive and receptive.

# Part 4

# Classic Vampires We Love to Hate

It's no surprise that novels and literature are the lifeblood of the ongoing vampire legend. Not only have they made vampires what they are today, but they show that vampires are truly immortal. And reading novels is a whole lot safer than looking for vampires in person!

Vampires have also made a great showing on the silver screen, dating back to the silent classic *Nosferatu*. In this part, you'll discover how these early offerings from page and stage contributed to our ongoing fascination with the undead.

# Chapter 16

# Written in Blood

## In This Chapter

- ◆ Vampires in literature overview
- ◆ Then and now
- ◆ Gothic, *sturm und drang* decadence, *fin de siècle*
- ◆ Romanticism and the Victorian period

Vampire fiction is a hot phenomenon of recent years, thanks to books by Anne Rice and other big-selling authors. But, as you may know, literary vampires go way back. The fact that vampires in fiction are so popular now can make it harder to understand what they were like 200 years ago, but heck, it's hard to understand what anything was like 200 years ago!

No doubt, one of these days Masterpiece Theater will come out with a miniseries dramatization of John Polidori's *The Vampyre* for public television. Why? Because it's a distinguished representative of a proud tradition of great English books. And having a vampire show in the line-up probably wouldn't hurt the network's ratings any!

Until that day comes, however, you'll just have to make do with this chapter to find out the basics about how the literary vampire emerged and developed in England and the rest of Europe. Even though readers of the eighteenth and nineteenth centuries found vampires *tellibly, tellibly ahwful,* they still recognized star quality even back then and made a place for vampires in their busy reading schedules.

# What Are We, Barbarians?

Vampires in literature can be dug up from the crossroads of many trends. The largest and most widely encompassing of these trends is gothic fiction. Gothic literature emerged on the world literary scene in a small way in England during the second half of the eighteenth century—100 years before the Victorians came along. Writers like Horace Walpole and Ann Radcliffe started creating stories fraught with macabre and supernatural thrills about haunted medieval castles, corrupt priests, and decayed aristocrats.

Gothic fiction is known by dark and sinister tendencies such as these:

- ◆ **Fantastic**—filled with supernatural and other wonders

- ◆ **Archaic**—set during times of long ago, especially the Middle Ages, but sometimes even farther back

- ◆ **Creepy characters**—concerned with depravity, social decay, and all kinds of human and supernatural evil

- ◆ **Creepy settings**—macabre atmosphere with musty castles, bleak landscapes, graveyards, and lots of storms

- ◆ **Mysterious**—suspense, intrigue, and plot reversals help make some gothic novels the prototypes of modern mystery novels

**Grave Mistake** _____

Don't assume literary vampires are as old as literary ghosts and other supernatural menaces of gothic fiction. Somehow the first gothic novels managed to get written in England before anyone there had heard of vampires. Literary vampires became incorporated into gothic literature many years later, when the gothic style had already become well developed.

## Gothic Gets Respect

At the time, these first gothic novels were generally considered pretty cheesy—all right for the sake of entertainment if you didn't have anything better to occupy your time (like a life), but not great literature. Instead, gothic was considered somewhat weird, barbaric, and extravagant—as opposed to the other novels of the time in which everyone practiced really good manners, even the bad guys. Even so, gothic style spread from England to the rest of Europe—especially to Germany—and to the United States.

As it spread, gothic eventually got swept up into what then was a much larger and more important literary trend known as Romanticism, which emerged right at the end of the eighteenth century and lasted most of the way into the nineteenth. It was at this time that vampires first emerged onto the literary scene and established themselves as gothic characters. Romanticism in England is most strongly associated with nature poetry, especially that of Wordsworth, Coleridge, Keats, and Shelley, but it had its creepy side, too.

The Romantic movement was largely concerned with attempts to discover heightened and deepened conceptions and experiences through art and literature— conceptions and experiences that science could not define or explain. Most Romanticism has to do with emotional freedom and the love of nature. Convention for its own sake was considered stultifying. And above all, Romantics hate to be stultified!

**Cold Fact**

Much as you could say today's Goth movement represents the dark side of New Age sensibility, early nineteenth-century gothic represents the dark side of Romanticism. Fear and other morbid feelings counterbalanced the Romantic quest for freedom and renewing experiences.

The Romantics looked at gothic style as a free and natural one, so it came to be seen not simply as cheesy entertainment, but as a valuable approach to pushing the experiential envelope. It's weirdness, extravagance, and barbaric qualities became assets. Many believed that the supernatural and scary elements of gothic literature could enrich, refine, and elevate the human spirit by taking it places that a more rational approach could not.

So gothic literature gained new respect in its Romantic incarnation. Writers such as the Brontë sisters, William Godwin, Charles Maturin, Mary Shelley, and Lord Byron in England, and Nathaniel Hawthorn and Edgar Allan Poe in America dished out serious creepiness for readers prepared to take creepiness seriously. Meanwhile, in Germany and France, dark literary movements within Romanticism took hold that paralleled English and American gothic.

## Euro-Chic

In Germany, a dark mood within Romanticism fueled a literary approach known as *sturm und drang* (storm and stress). *Sturm und drang* was in vogue during the late eighteenth century and included the works of Goethe, Schiller, and Klinger. The style inflates tragic and dramatic elements to the point of hysteria as fictional characters and narrators became angst-filled sounding boards for all the hardship, pain, and misfortune that fill the world.

In nineteenth-century France, a group of poets known as the Decadents rose to prominence. They included Rimbaud, Verlaine, and Baudelaire. Their work revels in depravity, conveying feelings of torment and disgust through rich and sensuous imagery, often in celebration of death, decay, and debauchery. The English writer Oscar Wilde was heavily influenced by the French Decadents.

**Dead Giveaway** _____

Charles Baudelaire's book of poetry, *Le Fleurs du Mal* (The Flowers of Evil) was published in 1857 only after six of the poems intended for publication in the book were banned by censors who found them obscene and immoral. One censored poem was "Les Metamorphoses du Vampire," which depicted the demoralization a man experiences when he satisfies his lust for a woman. At night she seems dangerous and more powerful than the angels. After they have sex, she seems like a sort of wineskin, bloated with pus. But the next morning, she is like a lifeless rusty sign, rattling in the winter wind!

# A Place in the Dark

Vampires did not figure into any of the first generation of gothic novels, but instead they came on the literary scene late in the eighteenth century and have stuck around ever since. Thus, although they are not responsible for the rise of the gothic novel, they are partly responsible for gothic's success and longevity. Thanks in part to vampires, gothic fiction has spanned many literary periods.

## Adaptable Characters

Not all of gothic literature fixated on vampires, but vampires were quite well represented in gothic writings throughout the nineteenth century. They figure into the poetry and fiction of the time in three ways:

1. As supernatural creatures actually referred to as "vampires," exhibiting at least some of the characteristics of legendary vampires. These include Polidori's Lord Ruthven, Le Fanu's Carmilla, Rymer's Varney the Vampire, and, of course, Stoker's Dracula.

2. As supernatural creatures *not* referred to as vampires, but nevertheless exhibiting characteristics of legendary vampires. These include Coleridge's Cristable, Keats's Lamia, and Poe's Bernice, Morella, and Ligeia.

3. As mortal, realistic human beings referred to as vampires metaphorically because of their predatory or parasitic tendencies. These include characters from Charlotte Brontë's *Jane Eyre*, Emily Brontë's *Wuthering Heights*, Charles Dickens's *Bleak House*, and George Eliot's *Middlemarch*.

**Cold Fact**

Literary scholar Carol Senf discusses the vampire myth as a metaphor in some realist English novels of the nineteenth century in her book, *The Vampire in 19th Century English Literature* (1988). She suggests that for many readers of the period, reality was strange enough even without supernatural revamping!

## A Link to Reality

Because of the continued importance of the literary and social themes represented by vampires, the ability of vampires to accommodate themselves to gothic literature in different ways enabled them to remain vital and believable as gothic novels changed. Vampires, after all, are interesting for their human qualities as well as for their supernatural ones. Similarly, gothic fiction is interesting for both its fantastic aspects and its realistic ones, both of which are capable of reflecting troubling features of society. You could say gothic fiction bridges the gap between impossible, imaginary wonders, and realistic, believable issues and events. Vampires help it do this.

In fact, although gothic fiction was originally quite fantastic, populated by lots of ghosts and supernatural wonders, it went through periods in which it was quite realistic. Obviously, vampires were right at home in stories filled with fantastic things, but they also fit pretty well into the realistic stories. And they were perfect for stories that were basically realistic except for a few subtle touches of supernaturalism.

This is true, for example, of Polidori's *The Vampyre*, in which the vampire Lord Ruthven appears completely human, despite his many faults and vices. Only after we've already gotten to know him as a human character do we learn that he is actually a supernatural one. Vampires in gothic fiction ever since have been more or less realistic or supernatural depending on the book.

## End of an Era

Not only the vampire figure, but also the gothic elements of mystery, creepiness, dreaminess, the supernatural, the archaic, and the horrid were well established in European literature as the nineteenth century came to a close. This time in the history of arts and letters is often referred to as *fin de siècle*, which is French for "end of the century." The phrase has come to imply extravagance and excess, thanks to its association with the decadent attitudes evident in the literature of the period.

Romanticism, as you may remember, involved the search for moving experiences wherever these could be found. By the time the *fin de siècle* rolled around, people were becoming pretty jaded with the Romantic spirit. The Romantic hope that new experience could bring renewal had given way to a lot of fashionable wallowing in anything risqué. This was when *Dracula*—an especially risqué book—was published.

> ### Stalk Talk
>
> *Fin de siècle,* is French for "end of the century"—the end of the nineteenth century, that is, when arts and letters were decadent, artists and writers were jaded, and pretty much everyone else who could afford to was hunkering down into bourgeois respectability. The phrase is usually used to refer to the arts and literature of the time.

## Prim and Proper

Although *fin de siècle* literature, including late nineteenth-century gothic fiction, tended to be risqué, and although many writers and artists of the time had a reputation for leading wild and decadent lifestyles, most people were basically reconciled to leading boring, ordinary, conventional lives. They were dubbed the *bourgeoisie*, the "middle class," the people who bought and read the books written by the *fin de siècle* artists.

In *fin de siècle* England, readers were not only predominantly bourgeois, but Victorian as well. In fact, the Victorian era marked a high point of staid, conventional bourgeois culture. Bourgeois Victorians practically considered it a point of honor to be normal in every respect. For this reason, it's fun to imagine them reading *Dracula*. You can just picture them swallowing hard with their eyes bugging out and their palms getting all sweaty!

> ### Stalk Talk
>
> The **bourgeoisie** were the middle class, originally distinguished from the aristocracy on one hand, and the peasant class on the other. Many artists of the nineteenth century, as well as social critics of recent years, have expressed contempt for bourgeois complacency, conformity, and materialism.

Anyway, the industrial revolution was making rich people really rich, middle-class people really comfortable, and poor people overworked. On the surface of it, it's hard to see why the comfortable ones who bought the books would care much about vampires. Fortunately, there are plenty of literary scholars around to tell us why they did!

# Nice Meets Vice

Vampires are a juicy literary subject. Literary scholars find a lot to talk about when they consider vampires as literary symbols. They're so complex and intriguing, loathsome yet irresistible, powerful yet needy, believable yet bizarre, that they practically cry out to be explained. And the explanations scholars use the most say more about the people who are fascinated by vampires than they say about vampires themselves.

## Reading the Readers

When literary scholars read books, they generally start with the idea that literature reflects and transforms issues that matter to the people who read and write the books. So what issues do literary vampires deal with? It's a long story, since vampires have been characters in works of fiction for over 200 years, ranging from the Romantic period, through the Victorian era, to today. But to give a short answer, vampires are two thrills in one. They represent both what people fear most and what they would most like to be.

Of course, this is something of a paradox. Few people would admit to fearing qualities in others that they would like to possess themselves. Fortunately, thanks to the power of fantasy and literary imagination, no one has to. When you read books, you can have it both ways. You can be horrified and disgusted and excited and enthralled all at the same time. You can tell your chums down at the club that you think that the Dracula character is one dastardly scalawag. Then you can go home and read all his lines while sneering into the mirror! Doing so doesn't mean that you're a phoney, but rather that you (appropriately) keep your fantasy life separate from daily reality.

> **Cold Fact**
>
> The Victorian period is named for Queen Victoria, who ruled England for the impressively long stretch from 1837 to 1901. "Victorian England" is often remembered for sexual prudery and social conformity. These traits rose to the surface in response to a rising current of sexual licentiousness that many feared would undermine society.

In fact, literary scholarship on vampires suggests that this divided, self-contradictory attitude is pretty much the way the reading public as a whole has responded to vampires in fiction all along—and this is a big reason for the literary vampires' appeal. On the one hand, they resonate with readers' deepest paranoia about other people while giving them something despicable to feel morally superior to. At the same time, they hold out the appealing fantasy of having special powers and freedoms. And best of all, vampires somehow manage to handle this illogical, paradoxical job in a way that seems to make sense. At any rate, vampires are pretty compelling once you're ready to go along with their supernatural aspects.

## Stiff Upper Lips

But of course, the story of vampires in literature is a little more complicated than this, for two simple reasons: first, society has changed a lot over the past 100 to 200 years and second, so have literary vampires. The vampire Lestat is a good deal different from Dracula, just as hanging out at the mall these days is a lot different from strolling through the marketplace in Victorian England.

And of course, people have changed, too. Take people in Victorian England when *Dracula* was first published. Many of them—especially the ones who read novels—were staid, conventional and bourgeois. The bourgeoisie were the middle class, known for their preoccupation with material comforts, conformity, and respectability. (Well, maybe people haven't changed that much!)

One reason the Victorian bourgeois were so staid and conventional was because Victorian society was kind of new, and people wanted to make sure it would work, despite all the nonbourgeois elements out there. They were successful and prosperous and afraid of foreigners and deviants coming in and messing up their good thing. Vampires symbolized these fears, so bourgeois Victorians liked to read about them both because the vampires usually died horrible deaths in the end and because the Victorians felt morally superior in comparison.

## Traits to Hate

Here are some of the bad things literary vampires represented that helped bourgeois Victorians feel morally superior in comparison:

- Moral and social decay
- Alienation, deviance, strangeness, foreignness
- Foulness, sickness, and death
- Parasitism and exploitation, especially of women
- Evil and brutality
- Deviousness; secrecy; a plotting, grasping, greedy nature

> **Grave Mistake**
>
> Not everyone agrees on who's a vampire and who isn't. In his famous work, *Das Kapital*, Karl Marx likens the bourgeoisie to vampires for the way they exploit the working class, saying "Capital is dead labor which, vampire-like, lives only by sucking living labor, and lives the more the more labor it sucks."

At the same time, bourgeois Victorians identified with vampires to some extent because they represented what they themselves wanted to be.

## Finer Qualities

Here are some of the things about vampires that may have reminded Victorian readers of themselves and what they wanted to be:

- Aristocratic, wealthy, and powerful
- Able to exist beyond sex and (merely) sexual desire
- Able to gain power from others and to make others more like them
- Equipped with superior abilities
- Able to attract others and bend others to their will through charisma and/or force

You might say that the Victorians were a little conflicted about themselves and that literary vampires helped them deal psychologically with the conflict.

# The Romance Is Back

Since Victorian times, of course, the reasons behind the interest in vampires have changed. Some of what Victorians found horrible now seems pretty cool. For example, where they once seemed creepily strange and deviant, they now seem freethinking and uninhibited. The supernatural aspects of Victorian vampires made them sinister and threatening to conventional society. In contrast, the supernatural aspects of today's vampires tend to make them more complicated and deeper as individual characters—their personalities are more interesting.

At the same time, many vampire stories of recent times have toned down the more disgusting characteristics of vampires. Vampires of today rarely hang out in graveyards. And though they still suck blood, they usually have other things going on in their lives as well. In addition, many readers of today relate to vampires because they must adapt to unusual lifestyles. So although vampires of today remain creepy to some extent, there are new things to add to the plus side.

For example, today's literary vampires are:

**Cold Fact** _____

Unlike vampire fiction of the nineteenth century, it's not unusual to find recent vampire stories presented from the vampire's point of view, which makes them seem less like inhuman monsters to be feared and more like interesting individuals to be understood. The most obvious case is Anne Rice's *Interview with the Vampire* (1979) in which Louis relates his own story.

- Able to cope with and maintain a radical lifestyle.

- Able to satisfy peculiar desires with style and dignity.

- Able to look past conventional morality to a profounder understanding of life.

- Able to be true to their own natures despite being misunderstood and disliked by others.

So vampires have become more likable, less despicably fiendish, and hence, easier to identify with. And like today's literary vampires, more people these days have unusual lifestyles and peculiar ways of conducting intimate relationships. There's less of a general sense that personal behavior should conform to established rules of decency, as at the time when *Dracula* was written. In general, these changes reflect a greater appreciation for individuality in readers of today than in Victorian readers.

You could say that it's taken vampires so long to become more likeable because it's taken readers this long to start admitting they like them more. But the shift is more than simply a matter of moving past Victorian social hang-ups. The process through which vampires have become more likeable is also a process of discovering new things about vampires to like and relate to. Vampires still combine elements of terror and attraction. But some of the things people like and hate about vampires today are different from the things people liked and hated about vampires 100 and 200 years ago.

### Dead Giveaway

On August 14 to 17, 1997, *Dracula '97: A Centennial Celebration* took place in Los Angeles in honor of the one-hundredth anniversary of the publication of *Dracula*. On hand were fans, scholars from diverse vampire-related fields, writers, actors, and others, including an impressive array of people well known for a wide range of reasons having to do with vampires. For example, there was Bela Lugosi Jr., writers Chelsea Quinn Yarbro and Fred Saberhagen, stage personalities Elvira and Ingrid Pitt (star of several Hammer Films productions), psychiatrist Richard Knoll, and Jeanne Youngson, founder of the Count Dracula Fan Club. Awards were awarded, lectures delivered, performances performed, in addition to assorted festivities and a whole lot of vampiric schmoozing. Yeah *Dracula!*

Gradually, many writers figured out that bourgeois readers were not that choosy about their fiction, so they stopped trying so hard to be creative and original. Thus, pulp fiction was born, and has thrived ever since. Vampires, of course, have been featured in pulp fiction throughout the twentieth century and into the twenty-first, but you can read about that later. For now, cued up in the next chapter, are all the gory details on the literary vampires of the Romantic and Victorian periods.

## The Least You Need to Know

♦ Vampires in literature have a history of combining attractive and repulsive traits.

♦ Vampire fiction emerged largely out of the English gothic literary tradition during the Romantic period.

♦ German and French traditions that encouraged the growth of vampire fiction are *sturm und drang* and the Decadent School, respectively.

♦ Vampires in fiction have tended to become more likable over the years.

# Chapter 17

# Romantic and Victorian Vampires

## In This Chapter

- ◆ Vampires in nineteenth-century literature
- ◆ Polidori's *The Vampyre*
- ◆ Gautier's *La Morte Amoureuse*
- ◆ Prest's *Varney the Vampire*
- ◆ Le Fanu's "Carmilla"

Vampire stories of the nineteenth century established the three basic vampire varieties that have become mainstays of vampire fiction ever since: the suave, polished, seductive type first exemplified by Lord Ruthven and later by Clarimonde; the brutal, repulsive, forceful type, who first shocked readers as Sir Francis Varney; and the subtle, alluring *femme fatale*, of whom Carmilla is the original.

All are aristocrats, all feed on human blood, all combine attractive and evil elements, and all reflect the moral preoccupations of their times in supernatural terms. In addition, all are intriguing characters that have been largely ignored and forgotten by posterity as a result of having been overshadowed by that other nineteenth-century vampire, Dracula (whom you can read about in the next chapter).

Yet despite the relative obscurity today of these pre-Dracula vampires, they remain the great originals of literature. They first made the transition from folklore to fiction, showed how the vampire myth could be applied to modern settings, and set the variations in mood from shocking to sensuous. And they really put some teeth into the idea of romance!

# Drawing First Blood

One of the most important and least recognized vampire stories ever written is John Polidori's *The Vampyre* (1819). It's the first work of prose fiction to explicitly identify its main character as a vampire. In so doing, it opens up the rich vein of symbolic correspondences between vampires from Slavic folklore and the social customs and literary traditions of Western Europe. And while the story is a pretty good yarn in its own right, there's a story behind the story that makes it even more interesting. This true story might not compare to the novel, but would at least make for a good soap opera!

## Odd Couple

Polidori was trained as a medical doctor in England, but was preoccupied with the imagination and literature. He fell in with the famous Romantic poet George Gordon, Lord Byron, who was planning to leave the country in the wake of sexual scandal stemming from Byron's infidelity to his wife. Byron invited the younger Polidori to join him on a trip to the continent (Europe, that is) and the two set off together.

**Cold Fact** _____

Before leaving England for Europe, Byron had already written and published a poem about a vampire called "The Giaour" (the infidel) about a soldier who is cursed by a Muslim to return from the grave as a vampire and prey on those closest to him in life. This poem, published in 1813, marks the first explicit appearance of the vampire into English literature.

In Switzerland, they were joined by some of Byron's friends, including fellow poet Percy Shelley and his second wife, Mary Godwin Shelley. There, at the rented Villa Diodati, the group engaged in a gothic tale-telling contest, for which Mary Shelley came up with the story that later became the novel *Frankenstein*. Byron's story, which he never finished, concerned two traveling companions who bore clear resemblances to Byron himself and his companion Polidori.

Byron lost interest in his story, but Polidori later reworked it into a short novel, which he called *The Vampyre* and published under Byron's name. The tale was published together with an introduction by Polidori explaining what vampires were and citing cases of Slavic vampirism, including Arnod Paole and others known to many European readers through the writings of the French scholar Dom Augustin Calmet. (You can read, or reread, about these cases in Chapter 10.)

The point is, Polidori had been doing his vampire homework as, no doubt, Lord Byron had also done, and both noticed parallels between folkloric vampires and parasitic human relationships. Interestingly, Polidori's and Byron's relationship was somewhat parasitic. Byron was a famous, wealthy aristocrat who evidently enjoyed having Polidori around for laughs. Polidori enjoyed basking in the aura of the famous poet, but seems to have felt disrespected. Some tensions resulting from this situation apparently served as partial inspiration both for Byron's tale and for Polidori's reworking of it.

**Dead Giveaway**

Polidori adapted his novel, *The Vampyre*, from a tale told by Lord Byron and originally published it under Byron's name. Byron immediately wrote the publisher and denied writing the book and asked that his name be retracted. But of course, since it was attributed to such a famous writer, *The Vampyre* received a great deal more attention than it otherwise would have, so the publisher continued to sell the book as Byron's. Fortunately for Byron, the work did no harm to his literary reputation. In fact, Byron's German contemporary and fellow famous Romantic poet, Johann Wolfgang von Goethe, hailed *The Vampyre* as Byron's greatest work!

## Return of the Rake

*The Vampyre*, however, is not simply an account of Polidori's and Byron's relationship in literary code. In fact, it picks up on current and traditional literary approaches to the age-old problem of good and evil and focuses them through the concept of the vampire. The vampire concept, as you may have gathered by now, has a lot to do with mixing good and evil together in a single appealing, bloodsucking package. Vampires are evil yet likable. By the time Polidori's *The Vampyre* was published, evil-yet-likable characters were already a mainstay of English fiction. Polidori simply gave these characters a new, supernatural twist.

One well-known type of evil-yet-likeable character familiar from Restoration (late seventeenth-century) plays and from eighteenth- and nineteenth-century fiction is the *rake*. The rake is a charismatic, aristocratic, self-interested, devilish, seductive young rapscallion who charms young women out of their pants (thus ruining their lives), swindles greedy old codgers out of their money, and generally has a good time drinking, gambling, dueling, adventuring, and flaunting a devil-may-care attitude.

Famous rakes from literature include Dorimant from the play *The Man of Mode* (1676) by Sir George Etherege and the title character from Henry Fielding's novel, *Tom Jones* (1749), which was made into an Oscar-winning film starring Albert Finney in 1963. Interestingly, Lord Byron was himself quite a rakish character. Not only did Byron lead a rakish lifestyle, but he wrote poetry about rakish characters, most notably *Don Juan* (unfinished at his death in 1824).

Byron's rakes, however, were not so fun-loving and frivolous as the typical rakes of yore. His were more gloomy and gothic, like Byron himself. Because of their distinctiveness, they are often referred to as "Byronic heroes." Lord Ruthven, the title character of Polidori's story, is a case in point, as Polidori himself was well aware. The name alludes to a rakish character modeled after Byron in a novel by one of Byron's former lovers, Carolyn Lamb's *Glenarvon*.

**Cold Fact** _____

> Lord Byron continues to appear as a character in fiction—and vampire fiction at that. The novel, *Lord of the Dead: The Secret History of Lord Byron* (Simon & Schuster, 1995) by Tom Holland tells of a fictionalized account of Byron's life as a vampire. The book has been quite popular, especially in England.

# Road to Ruin

While Lord Ruthven is a rakish character from Polidori's novel who corresponds to Lord Byron in real life, the well-meaning but naive Aubrey is Ruthven's companion who resembles Polidori himself. Throughout the first half of the novel, Aubrey witnesses the disastrous and mysterious effects that Lord Ruthven has on those who get close to him. Then, about halfway through, Aubrey learns Ruthven's secret.

## Sworn to Secrecy

Unfortunately for Ruthven's victims, his vampire identity must remain secret because Ruthven makes Aubrey swear an oath not to reveal it for a year and a day. Unable to warn Ruthven's victims, he can only follow Ruthven around trying to minimize the damage he does. Despite Aubrey's efforts, however, Ruthven drags all those around him into ruin. Women fall in love with him and become disgraced when he refuses to marry them. Then they die from mysterious causes.

Men become addicted to gambling and dissolution. They borrow money from Ruthven only to get sucked further into vice and debauchery. Then they, too, die from mysterious causes. Thus Ruthven's evil is infectious and Aubrey powerless to stop him. As Polidori himself suggests in his introduction to the story, the supernatural aspect of the vampire isn't strictly necessary for the plot. Much of the evil that unfolds makes sense in purely human terms. But the vampire supplies compelling symbolism for that evil. For example, Lord Ruthven's deathlike pallor and undead status symbolizes his lack of humanity in a moral sense. He doesn't care about others, even when they are close to him.

**Cold Fact** _____

According to Polidori's *The Vampyre*, moonlight has the power to reanimate the dead corpse of a vampire, who must prey on those who become closest to it. Although these traits eventually disappeared from vampire literature, *Varney the Vampire* (1847) preserved the notion that moonlight brings the vampire to life.

## A Rash of Acts

*The Vampyre*, though influential, did not immediately touch off a rash of more vampire publications. It may be that other fiction writers didn't want to impinge on the vampire territory Polidori established. There were, however, a number of stage productions featuring vampires in France and Germany as well as England, some of which were explicitly based on Polidori's tale, while others were merely chiming in with the vampire vogue. These included serious melodramas, farces, and even operas.

The most successful of these productions was *Le Vampire*, written by the French dramatist Charles Nodier. This play was adapted into an English version by James Planche, who also designed a special trap door through which the vampire could mysteriously disappear. This special-effects technique was known as "the vampire trap."

Planche's version of Nodier's play in turn inspired a German opera, *Der Vampyr*, by Heinrich August Marchner. Throughout the rest of the nineteenth century, the vampire figured into melodramas, reviews, and spoofs. The best-known musical vampire spoof is *Ruddigore*, by the famous Victorian operetta-writing duo, Gilbert and Sullivan.

**Grave Mistake** _____

Don't assume that literary fame necessarily goes along with literary greatness. The famous Lord Byron did not write the great original vampire novel, *The Vampyre*, but only a rarely remembered vampire poem, "The Giaour." Similarly, the equally famous French novelist, Alexander Dumas, author of *The Three Musketeers* (1844) and *The Count of Monte Cristo* (1844), wrote an unremarkable reworking of Charles Nodier's more famous play, *Le Vampire*.

# Toujour L'amour

*The Vampyre* and nineteenth-century British vampire stories in general tend to make it pretty clear how the reader is supposed to feel about things. Vampires may have attractive qualities, but they do evil deeds. So even in the midst of juicy sex scenes, for example, you get a running moral commentary reminding you that, however much fun sex may seem to be, it is actually not good. The English were sometimes a little stuffy about these things, even though they enjoyed a lurid tale as much as anybody else.

The French, however, were another story, and the difference is evident in their approach to writing vampire tales. In *La Morte Amoureuse* ("the dead woman lover") (1836) by Theophile Gautier, there's a striking contrast between what you might suppose to be the world of "good" including religious devotion and self-restraint, and the world of "evil" including sex and other forms of sensuality. In this story, however, when "good" triumphs over "evil," it seems like a rotten shame! But once you get past having to worry about good and evil, *La Morte Amoureuse* is just a good old-fashioned love story of boy meets vampire, boy gets vampire, boy loses vampire.

## Death Becomes Her

*La Morte Amoureuse* is the story of a young priest named Romuald. Just as he is about to be ordained, he sees the most beautiful woman he's ever encountered and instantly falls madly in love with her ("bad, bad!"). Torn between taking his priestly vows and running away with this beautiful woman, he ends up getting ordained ("good, good!"). Yet he immediately senses he made a bad choice, especially when the woman comes up to him afterward and gives him a piece of paper with her name and address written on it ("bad, bad!").

Haunted by the memory of this beautiful woman, he is unable to concentrate on his religious duties. Wracked with desire ("bad!") and guilt ("good!"), he is miserable until one day he's called in to perform the last rites for a beautiful courtesan named Clarimonde who had just died. He arrives at her death bed and finds she was the woman he had fallen in love with. Dead though she is, she appears enchantingly beautiful and Romuald can't resist pulling back the shroud and kissing her on the lips.

Just then—shades of Snow White!—she comes alive for a moment and promises to return to him. Sure enough, a few days later after Clarimonde has been laid in her tomb, she appears to the priest and takes him away with her. In fact, she appears every night and sweeps him away to a lush, exciting, sensual world where he is known as Lord Romualdo. Lord Romualdo enjoys a free and happy existence full of feasting, drinking, dancing, and love-making with the ravishing undead Clarimonde.

---

**Cold Fact** _____

In many respects, Gautier's tale, *La Morte Amoureuse* looks ahead to the writing of the French Decadents of the late nineteenth century who were preoccupied with achieving heightened experiences through art. Some scholars have suggested that Clarimonde represents a kind of muse for the decadent artist—a source of inspiration who leads him down the path of sensuality.

---

## Holy Horror

All Clarimonde wants is for him to be happy. Well, that, and to suck his blood. But actually, the bloodsucking isn't gross. She pricks him gently with a little pin and drinks only a few drops. The blood keeps her alive, young, and beautiful, so it doesn't seem like a major problem to Lord Romualdo.

Meanwhile, by day, the unhappy young priest Romuald struggles along with his bleak life, confused and torn by spiritual anxiety. His superior, Father Serapion, figures out the whole situation and leads the young priest to Clarimonde's tomb where they do the only "good" thing possible. There they splashed holy water on her corpse and she immediately crumbles into dust. But as you might imagine (unless you have a medieval religious fixation), Romuald is miserable. He regrets the loss of Clarimonde for the rest of his life.

## Serial Killer

In England at mid-century, a new, rawer sort of vampire fiction emerged with the publication of *Varney the Vampire, or the Feast of Blood*, a serialized tale that eventually swelled into an 800-plus page monstrosity.

*Varney* had a certain gut-level shock appeal, thanks to the graphic quality of the descriptions of the seemingly endless succession of the vampire's feedings. The gruesome formula worked. *Varney* was quite popular in its day, especially among working-class readers.

## Budget Brutality

*Varney the Vampire* literally supplied cheap thrills. Installments were sold for a penny a piece. That's why it, and other low-budget horror tales like it, were affectionately called *penny dreadfuls* by the British book-sellers. Of all the penny dreadfuls, *Varney* was among the most popular. The first episode went on sale in the mid-1840s and the story continued for another 108 weekly installments over the course of 2 years, before its eventual publication in a single volume.

It seems, however, that few people wanted to read *Varney* more than once. Most people threw their copies away when they were finished and, as a result, it is quite a rare book today. There is some doubt as to who actually wrote it. The candidates are Thomas Packett Prest and James Malcolm Rymer.

> **Stalk Talk**
>
> **Penny dreadfuls** were serialized horror stories that sold for a penny each in nineteenth-century England. They often included an illustration or two so, in a way, you could say they were an ancestor of the twentieth-century comic book.

Though you wouldn't call it uplifting literature, the first chapter is at least vivid, featuring an attack by Varney on the beautiful and virtuous Flora Bannerworth. Though he is an aristocrat, the title vampire, Sir Francis Varney, has none of the dash or subtlety of Lord Ruthven. He is ugly, brutal, and not very complex. He simply grabs his victim by the hair, pins her down against her bed, bites her neck, and starts sucking.

> With a strange howling cry that was enough to awaken terror in every breast, the figure seized the long tresses of her hair, and twining them round his boney hands he held her onto the bed .... The glassy, horrible eyes of the figure ran over that angelic form with a hideous satisfaction—horrible profanation. He drags her head to the bed's edge. He forces it back by the long hair still entwined in his grasp. With a plunge he seizes her neck in his

fang-like teeth—a gush of blood, and a hideous sucking noise follows. The girl has swooned, and the vampire is at his hideous repast!

As you can tell from the excerpt, the writer uses the word "hideous" a lot—three times in the space of about 55 words, but who's counting? That should give you a clue that a) Varney is not particularly subtle or attractive and b) whoever did the writing didn't have a lot of time to waste thinking up richly evocative adjectives to flesh out his vampires character!

Anyway, fortunately for young Flora, her father, Henry Bannerworth, arrives on the scene and wounds Varney with a pistol. The wounded vampire escapes and quickly recovers, thanks to the supernatural healing powers of the full moon. (Varney habitually feeds when the moon is full, in case of just such an emergency.)

## Shifting More Than Shape

In subsequent installments, the brutal Varney's character changes again and again, not because his character develops, but because whoever wrote it seems to have changed his mind! Varney's old enemies the Bannerworths come to appreciate his nobler qualities and later take his side and protect him from an angry mob.

The series also provides, at different points, conflicting versions of Varney's life story. Readers could choose their own favorite from these options:

- ◆ Varney was a Royalist during the Puritan Revolt in seventeenth-century England who was shot by some of Oliver Cromwell's men. He came back to life as a vampire as a curse for having struck and killed his own son in a fit of anger.

**Cold Fact** _____

Killing your son, though not a good thing, is not usually recognized as a way to become a vampire. However a famous son-killer out of Greek myth, Lycaon the King of Arcadia, was turned into a wolf for his crime. In contrast, Ivan the Terrible, the tyrannical czar of sixteenth-century Russia, killed his son with no apparent metamorphic results.

- Varney had mysterious and supernatural origins sometime around the fourteenth century.

- He was actually not immortal, but a criminal who was sentenced to hang but survived the hanging.

Although Varney sometimes had his good points, episode after episode recounted his attempts to hunt victims—usually young women—and suck their blood. Interestingly, he wasn't particularly good at it and usually failed. The locals quickly became wise to him and he was forced to move on. Varney eventually became disgusted with his wretched existence and killed himself for good by leaping into the volcano of Mt. Vesuvius. His suicide brought the series to a conclusion.

# Girls' Night Out

Next to Dracula, the best-known Victorian vampire is Carmilla, the creation of the Irish writer of short stories, Joseph Thomas Sheridan Le Fanu. "Carmilla," the short story published in 1872, is unashamedly gothic. It's set in an old castle in the Austrian province of Styria, the ancestral home of the Karnstein family. The story unfolds from the perspective of a Karnstein descendent named Laura, whose father has purchased the castle, where he brings his daughter to live.

## The Face Is the Same

Carmilla shows up at the castle one day after her carriage breaks down. She takes an intense liking to the 19-year-old Laura and proceeds to cultivate intimacy between the two. Carmilla says that she had an aristocratic background, but gives evasive replies to Laura's questions. There is, however, a portrait hanging in the castle dating from 1698 that looks exactly like Carmilla. It is a likeness of Countess Mircalla Karnstein.

You guessed it, Carmilla is the undead Mircalla. It seems that according to Le Fanu's rules of vampiric order, vampires must assume names that are anagrams—made from rearranged letters—of the names they had when living. We learn later that Carmilla/Mircalla had previously attacked a different young woman going under the name of Millarca. Lucky for her she had such an adaptable name!

**Grave Mistake**

No, contrary to what you might think, although Carmilla is a super-naturally undead vampire, there's nothing supernatural about her portrait. Ghostly portraits, however, have been stock features of gothic literature at least since Horace Walpole's *Castle of Otranto* (1764) in which the sinister Manfred has conversations with the portrait of his grandfather.

## Made for Each Other

Fortunately for Dracula, Lestat, and Angel, who might otherwise be known as Larduca, Estalt, and Nagel, the anagram tradition didn't catch on in subsequent vampire fiction. "Carmilla" did, however, introduce from folklore into literature the shape-shifting power of the vampire. Carmilla stalks her prey in the form of a cat. Another nifty folkloric touch that became a standard feature of the vampire is that Carmilla sleeps in her coffin. We tend to take these things for granted today, but at the time it may have seemed like a brilliantly creepy innovation!

**Cold Fact**

Feminist readers of Carmilla have pointed out that while Carmilla may be biologically dead, her victim, Laura is legally dead, having virtually no rights of her own, but legally subject to her father. Hence it is not surprising that someone with so few options in life would respond favorably, if hesitantly, to Carmilla's advances.

Carmilla is also the first seductive vampire who chooses same-sex victims. As you may imagine, this aspect has made the story an exploitation film favorite. A number of racy costume-drama films have been based on "Carmilla," including the Hammer Films offering, *The Vampire Lovers* (1970) and sequels, *Lust for a Vampire* (1970) and *Twins of Evil* (1971). A made-for-cable-TV *Carmilla* aired in 1989. Carmilla has also been featured in more than one comic book series.

Anyway, back to our story: the Karnsteins eventually learn that Carmilla is their ancestor, transformed into a vampire when bitten by another vampire. But in the meantime, Laura's relationship with Carmilla blossoms into a pretty weird-yet-believable neurotic inter-dependency that showcases two complementary monstrosities of

Victorian femininity. Laura is basically your typical daddy's girl who has no life of her own and never will, even if she survives having blood periodically sucked out of her.

Carmilla is a mistress of indirection: coy and seductive, attempting to manipulate others through her feminine wiles. The two of them seem to be flip sides of the same repressed coin. One lesson to be drawn from the tale is that if women back then had more fulfilling lives they wouldn't need to be vampires or victims. Give Le Fanu credit for conveying some insight into the Victorian female predicament even while sensationalizing it into a steamy and dreamy gothic fantasy.

## The Least You Need to Know

◆ Polidori's *The Vampyre* (1819) is the first piece of prose fiction to identify one of its main characters as a vampire.

◆ Gautier's *La Morte Amoureuse* (1831) makes "evil" seem more attractive than "good."

◆ Prest's *Varney the Vampire* (1840s) was sold in weekly installments for a penny each.

◆ Le Fanu's "Carmilla" (1872) is often hailed as the first lesbian vampire.

# Chapter 18

# The Count

## In This Chapter

- ◆ Bram Stoker's novel *Dracula*
- ◆ Influence and reputation
- ◆ The main characters
- ◆ Scholarship and sexual suggestiveness

And now, a vampire who needs no introduction, together with the book that didn't exactly make him famous, but which inspired the movies that did.

## A Cut Above the Rest

More films have been based on *Dracula* than on any other book. *Dracula* may be the only great novel ever written that has become great because of the films based on it. More people have known the vampire Dracula from the movies than from Stoker's book. And Dracula the "literary" vampire was never really that famous until he became a notorious movie villain.

## Seen Through a Filmy Shroud

Many of the Dracula movies are only loosely based on the novel. They often treat the story more like a legend to be explored and played around with than like a literary classic to be brought to the screen. As well-known as *Dracula* has become, few people have a clear idea of what happens in its pages.

> **Cold Fact**
>
> Dracula is featured in an episode of TV's *Buffy the Vampire Slayer*. The episode suggests that his mystique as a vampire stems largely from his fame, which is a big part of his hypnotic power over mere mortals.

But it's safe to say that author Bram Stoker is not exactly turning over in his grave because so few people appreciate his book as a literary creation. In fact, Stoker brought to the writing of *Dracula* years of experience in show business. For many years he was the manager of the Lyceum theater in London, so he understood spectacle and melodrama the way a baker understands flour and yeast. It's possible that to some extent, the novel *Dracula* was written with show business in mind, even though the film industry was in its earliest infancy at the time.

Even so, *Dracula* remains a decent read. At the time it was written, the supernatural notions and the graphic violence struck reviewers as a bit much. Today, the high-toned yet middle-brow moralizing about good and evil can strike readers as a bit much. But no one says it's dull or stupid or a waste of time. In fact, lots of people think it's the greatest. And with good reason.

Most of the book's biggest fans love the work not simply as a work of fiction, but as the beginning of something that grew far beyond the book. Chances are that if you love *Dracula* you love not only the book, but also the movies based on it and vampires in general. You can see Dracula as a seed that has grown into a tree of many branches.

## Undead Yet True to Life

And just as *Dracula* has laid the foundation for the growth of the vampire myth in books and movies ever since, it has also drawn on the vampire legends that came before it and used them in especially compelling ways. It's surprising how seriously Bram Stoker took notions that most people of his day regarded as mere superstition—not that he believed them himself, but he treated them as though they were true by combining them with true-to-life historical and scientific trimmings.

---

**Dead Giveaway** _____

For the most part, so far, *Dracula* has evoked serious critical response only from a select few literary scholars—people whose business it is to study, interpret, and teach what literature means. Compared to say, Edgar Allen Poe or Charles Dickens, Bram Stoker is a lightweight as a literary figure, despite the fact that *Dracula* is only one of many novels Stoker wrote. Nevertheless, the modest vampiric fascination *Dracula* has held for scholars and critics has gained momentum in recent years, thanks to both a greater readiness among them to focus on popular culture and to the growing importance of vampires to readers of fiction today.

---

Stoker did some careful research in writing the novel. He not only put plenty of blood in the pages, but also lots of sweat in the details! And because the historical background is carefully worked out, it's easy to forget how impossibly far out and fantastic so many of the supernatural elements are.

For example, Dracula himself has a specific and detailed pedigree. He says that he comes from the Szekler tribe of Romanians and is descended from Attila the Hun. He suggests he's a descendent of Vlad Tepes as well, although we learn later that he *is* the undead Wallachian prince himself. In addition, many of the details of Harker's journey through Transylvania come from recent traveler's accounts Stoker read. The details in the book are so consistent with real places, it's possible to take "Dracula tours" in both England and Romania.

---

**Cold Fact** _____

The vault in which Arthur Holmwood stakes the vampire Lucy Westera appears to be modeled after a vault in St. Mary's churchyard in Hendon, a village in Stoker's day that has since been swallowed up as London expanded. The churchyard was a favorite spot of Stoker's friend, Tommy (Hommy-Beg) Hall Caine, a fellow writer to whom Stoker dedicated *Dracula*.

---

Details about Dracula's homeland and background help bolster the ideas about vampires Stoker borrowed from legend. Stoker combines legend, history, and fiction in ways other vampire stories have often done since, but none had done so extensively prior to *Dracula*. Stoker made the vampire myth both more believable and more accessible to the modern imagination.

To take another example, the novel is basically accurate about the information it provides regarding Lucy's symptoms after she gets her blood sucked by Dracula—not that medical science has anything to say about vampire victims, but loss of blood is certainly a familiar medical problem. Accordingly, Lucy is exhausted, has a rapid heartbeat, and breathes heavily, just as a doctor might expect of anyone who was low on blood.

# Fleshing Out the Skeleton

Stoker researched not only Slavic legend and "superstition,"(folk beliefs were often called superstition in Stoker's time), but he also read books on American Indian superstition, popular superstition, medical superstition, and superstitions of sailors. Of course, he incorporated some of his reading on Slavic folklore into his account of the nature of Dracula. In addition, he made up a few details of his own.

## Curriculum Mortua

Many of Dracula's vampiric characteristics are so well-known they've become clichés. You probably already know Dracula doesn't like garlic, crosses, or stakes to the heart. Here are some less-widely known particularities (although you probably know at least a few of these already):

- Dracula can influence the weather and he likes storms.
- He can telepathically influence animals as well as his own undead victims.
- He sleeps without breathing and with no pulse.
- He can see in the dark.
- He cannot enter someone's home unless he's invited.
- He can sail in or out of port only at high or low tide, not in between.

- He must sleep near his native soil.

- He casts no shadow and no reflection.

- He can crawl face downward down the side of his castle.

**Grave Mistake** _____

Contrary to popular belief, Dracula can survive and even function perfectly well in daylight, although his shape-shifting and hypnotic powers are diminished there. The notion that Dracula crumbles into dust when struck by sunlight is a movie invention. Another misconception is that Dracula gets staked through the heart. He doesn't. He gets stabbed with a knife and then decapitated.

## One of a Kind

In addition to the supernatural traits, Dracula exhibits a number of other quirks that help make him a distinctive character. For one thing, although he is a count and lives in a castle, he doesn't have any servants. For this reason, when Jonathan Harker comes to stay with him, Dracula himself acts as chauffeur, cook, and butler. (According to Harker, the food was good. Dracula lost points with his housekeeping, though. The place was pretty dusty.)

Interestingly, much as Stoker boned up on Transylvania before writing his novel, Dracula reads up on England before he makes his trip there. As he explains to Harker, he wants to fit in. (He probably should have gone to Los Angeles instead!)

Anyway, he didn't exactly succeed in fitting into the scheme of things in England. In fact, a sea captain reported having seen him dressed inappropriately in a straw hat. Drac's attempt at jauntiness didn't go over. In Dr. Van Helsing's words, the hat "suit not him or the time." So now you know, even the notoriously elegant Dracula is capable of a fashion *faux pas*.

**Grave Mistake** _____

Just because Dracula casts no reflection in the mirror doesn't mean he was unconcerned about his appearance. After all, those 50 crates full of Transylvanian soil for his beauty rest weren't the only grooming supplies he brought with him to England. He also had a comb and a hairbrush.

# Choosing Sides

The novel *Dracula* is often regarded as depicting a classic confrontation between good and evil. In fact, most of the characters definitely fall into one or the other category. Dracula has his qualities, but there's no doubt in anyone's mind that he's a bad egg. And as for the good guys, they never so much as think bad thoughts or talk with their mouths full.

## Bat-ing Order

*Dracula* doesn't exactly have a cast of thousands, but it has enough characters so that the action can be hard to follow if you don't have a program. So here's the starting line-up for team Good and team Evil, together with vital (as well as fatal) statistics for each one. First, the good guys:

- **Jonathan Harker.** A real estate agent who goes to Transylvania in order to arrange the sale of an old mansion in England to Dracula. As soon as the papers are signed, he is taken prisoner in Castle Dracula and narrowly escapes with his life and sanity.

- **Arthur Holmwood.** Stock two-dimensional good-guy character who becomes Lord Godalming when his father dies and then Lucy's fiancé. (No, really, she didn't just intend to marry him for his money and title!) He does the honors of staking Lucy the vampire on what would have been their wedding night.

- **Quincey Morris.** A real honest-to-Pete American cowboy type. He's a real good sport when his offer of marriage to Lucy is rejected in favor of his adventuring buddy Arthur—so much so that he sticks around to help with the Dracula hunt and ends up dying a right noble death for a Yank!

**Cold Fact** _____

The American (Texan, in fact), Quincey Morris, has the honor of being possibly the least important to the plot of the novel of all the main characters. As a result, his character gets left out of virtually all the Dracula movies. (*Bram Stoker's Dracula*, 1992, directed by Francis Ford Coppola, is an exception.) Nevertheless, his name lives on. At the end of the book, Mina and Jonathan have a son and name him Quincey. As a grown-up, this Quincey was one of the main characters in Marvel Comics' *Tomb of Dracula* series of the 1970s.

- **Dr. John Seward.** He's in charge of the friendly neighborhood lunatic asylum and is always on hand when a scientific mind and medical expert is needed to express bafflement at the supernatural goings-on that are taking place.

- **Dr. Abraham Van Helsing.** Dr. Seward's mentor with the thick Dutch accent called in to help with the Dracula case. Only he has the wisdom and experience to throw the laws of science out the window despite a lifetime of medical training in order to fight Dracula with techniques out of folk-superstition.

- **Mina Murray.** A whiz at shorthand, typing, and other clerical skills useful for conducting an organized vampire hunt. What a gal! She marries Jonathan Harker, despite the fact that he was no longer all there since escaping from Castle Dracula and then barely gets saved from turning into a vampire, despite getting bitten by Dracula and being forced to drink his blood.

- **Lucy Westenra.** Mina's slightly-more-attractive, less-businesslike friend who plays Barbie to Arthur's Ken and serves as Dracula's most clueless supplier of blood. An occasional sleepwalker, you get the feeling she's not that much sharper when awake. She receives blood transfusions from Arthur, Quincey, and Dr. Seward to keep her going, but dies anyway and becomes a vampire.

And now the bad guys …

- **Count What's His Name.** For some unexplained reason he wants to get at the men through the women they love. At least this makes more sense than visiting England for the food!

- **Those three sexy, unnamed female vampires in the castle.** They come on to Jonathan Harker and almost put the bite on him, but Dracula shows up and gives them a stolen baby to suck on instead. Talk about teething pains! Still, it beats the heck out of what happened to the kid's mother, who was devoured alive by wolves.

- **The wolves.** "Ah, the children of the night." They obeyed telepathic messages from Dracula. They all lived in Transylvania except for the one that escaped from the zoo in England.

♦ **R. N. Renfield.** The mental patient in Dr. Seward's asylum who worships Dracula as his "Master." He's "*zoophagous.*" A compulsive visitor of zoos? No, he eats bugs.

### Stalk Talk

**Zoophagia,** or "life-eating," was not recognized as a psychological condition before *Dracula* was written (not that it is now, but at least the word exists, thanks to Stoker). Renfield's compulsion to eat bugs is mysteriously related to Dracula's need to suck blood. Renfield hopes Dracula will turn him into a vampire some day, so he can move a few steps up on the food chain.

♦ **Undead Lucy Westenra.** Far more interesting than the living version. It's kind of a shame her staking didn't get saved for closer to the end of the book.

## Right Makes Might

Notice that the bad guys are outnumbered, especially after Dracula sails for England, land of all that is Good and True. Some Dracula fans point out that he's the underdog, trying to make it on his own in a strange country. But the good guys face the risk of turning into bad guys, so at least he has a fighting chance.

And of course, the good guys can't replenish their ranks. They can't let others know what they're up to because they don't want to spread panic. So Dracula, as threatening and contagious as he is, poses a rather intimate problem that must be dealt with discretely, like an embarrassing pregnancy or a case of syphilis. Those involved must put aside their differences and pull together for the common good to do what must be done. So the fate of the world is resting on their shoulders. But hey, that's what being a vampire-hunting team is all about.

While the good-guy group is intimate—sharing blood and personal information as needed—they are also well-organized, efficient, and up-to-date. They make full use of such cutting-edge Victorian technology as the typewriter, the telegram, and the Dictaphone. You've got to admire that British efficiency!

In fact, the whole novel is presented as a kind of casebook, made up of a series of letters, written communiqués, diary entries, and other documents shared among the whole crew so every one of them can keep abreast of the developments. In the novel, this process is Mina's idea. She collects, compiles, and copies all the information for everyone. Anyone who has ever worked as part of a team in an office can relate to this aspect of the novel. Finally, administrators and clerks come into their own as world-saving heroes!

> **Cold Fact** _____
>
> In its time, *Dracula* was unusual as a gothic novel set in modern England with modern characters using modern technology. At least one nineteenth-century reviewer of *Dracula* expressed the view that, since it concerned the supernatural, it should have been set during the Middle Ages, like so many other gothic novels had been.

# Lit Crit Gets Bit

Dracula is buried in his grave for good at the end of Stoker's novel, and he took whatever secret memories of whatever experiences he may have had with him. We'll never know whether he preferred the taste of Lucy's blood or Mina's, or whether he secretly craved the bulging neck vein of Arthur or Jonathan. But rumors of some certain secrets have been coming out in recent years, thanks to the efforts of literary scholars who make it their business to get to the bottom of whatever dirt goes on in the books they read.

## Dirty Secrets

As you might imagine, the aspect of *Dracula* that literary scholars find most intriguing is the way it deals with sex. Although there is hardly any plain-and-simple sex in the novel (three men propose to Lucy and she accepts Arthur, but they never marry; Mina and Jonathan marry and conceive a child) there are all kinds of kinky doings that appear a lot like sex. It's hard to ignore the fact that something peculiar is going on in the sphere of interpersonal "relations." And scholars are leaking the gossip to a spellbound academic community.

It's not news that the "good" characters in *Dracula* are staunchly opposed to the emerging Victorian women's liberation movement and the so-called "New Woman" who represents what many regarded as a dangerous degree of sexual freedom. But how about the notion that Lucy *becomes* a New Woman after Dracula vamps her? No, she doesn't exactly carry a "vampire suffrage" sign, but she *is* a whole lot more obvious about her sexuality.

And speaking of sexy, just who are those three alluring vampire women who almost have Jonathan Harker for lunch in a secret room of Dracula's castle? It's been rumored that they are Dracula's sisters, his daughters, his brides, or some kinky combination of all of the above. Or try this observation on for size: the three women vampires are sexual surrogates for a homosexual liaison Stoker wanted to describe but couldn't between Dracula and Harker. They're not exactly same-sex partners for Jonathan, but they are unusual as women with the power to *penetrate* their partners!

## Dirtier Secrets

When Jonathan was imprisoned in Dracula's castle, was he actually being used as Dracula's love slave? If not, why didn't Dracula simply vamp him? Why do the two have so much in common and why does Stoker devote most of the first half of the book to their time together in the castle?

Why are John Seward, Arthur Holmwood, and Quincey Morris all falling over themselves in a rush to donate blood to the depleted Lucy? Could it be a covert expression of their lustful feelings? Arthur himself says that he felt that giving Lucy his blood meant they were already married in the sight of God. If he had realized he'd just entered into a group marriage with two other men, would he have opened *another* vein?

Could Jonathan Harker, that mere shadow of his former self, really be the father of Mina's baby, or was little Quincey really named after his *true* father, Quincey Morris? Or, more likely still, was little Quincey the love child of Mina's former late vamping partner, Dracula? Certainly toward the end, Mina and Drac had a close affinity for one another.

**Dead Giveaway**

*Dracula* scholar Talia Schaffer has argued that the novel is Stoker's sublimated response to feelings of guilt and disgust stemming from the prison term served by his friend, fellow Irishman, fellow writer, and— according to Schaffer—fellow homosexual Oscar Wilde. Wilde was convicted of sodomy in a notorious trial in British court and sentenced to two years of hard labor. In Schaffer's view, Stoker was unable to speak out in defense of Wilde and homosexuality and equally unable to remain silent about his own homosexual feelings, so he wrote a novel representing, in subconscious symbolic terms, his dread of the social threat of homosexuality (represented by Dracula), his desire for homosexual union (represented by the simultaneous threat and promise of vampiric bloodsucking), and his sympathy for the punishment of Oscar Wilde (represented by Jonathan Harker's imprisonment in Dracula's castle).

—"A Wilde [sic] Desire Took Me": The Homoerotic History of *Dracula*," *English Literary History* 61(2), 1994, reprinted in *Dracula: A Norton Critical Edition* Nina Aurbach and David Skal, eds., 1997.

## The Least You Need to Know

◆ *Dracula* is perhaps the only novel, with the possible exception of *Frankenstein*, to become extremely famous largely as a result of the movies based on it.

◆ Stoker's novel incorporates extensive research on Eastern Europe and is remarkably consistent with known history.

◆ *Dracula* can be read as a tale of good vs. evil, despite the fact that the evil has it's appealing side while the good are often too good to be believable.

◆ *Dracula* scholarship commonly focuses on the sexual implications of the strange relationships depicted.

# Chapter 19

# Cooking with Rice

## In This Chapter

- ◆ Anne Rice's *The Vampire Chronicles*
- ◆ The vampire Lestat
- ◆ Breaking vampire rules
- ◆ The origin of Rice's vampires

Most vampires have the power to change mortals. Anne Rice is one of the few mortals who has been able to change vampires. She's made them easier to identify with for millions of readers by presenting their unique condition as an intriguing, steamy, and supernatural version of the human condition with all its pain and possibility. Thanks to Rice, the world has come to feel that there's at least a little vampire blood in everyone, and that this isn't necessarily such a bad thing.

Rice has written the most influential vampire fiction since *Dracula*. Her work draws on a supernatural vision that goes far beyond the Slavic and Hollywood vampire legends of earlier times, interweaving religion, philosophy, fantasy, and human experience to create vampires who are both larger-than-life icons and flesh-and-blood individuals. And underneath the flesh and blood, some of them even have soul.

Rice has been writing and publishing vampire stories for 25 years so far. To the delight of her many fans, she is one of the most prolific writers going, serving up a blood feast of vampire novel after novel. And that's in addition to her many other books featuring such things as witches, mummies, and kinky sex!

# Dark Times

Anne Rice introduced an important shift in the vampire myth by creating the hugely popular *The Vampire Chronicles* in which the supernatural condition of vampires is both a curse and a blessing—a *dark gift*. The good part is that becoming a vampire is a profound and indescribable experience that opens up thrilling new possibilities to gain power, have adventures, and feel the beauty and drama of existence in new ways. The bad thing is that "turning" can cut vampires off from their humanity and leave them struggling to find ways to compensate for this painful and disorienting loss.

> **Stalk Talk** _____
>
> The **dark gift** is everything that goes along with being a vampire in *The Vampire Chronicles*, including indefinite existence, heightened perceptions, the power to turn others into vampires, and blood thirst. As you might imagine, it's a mixed blessing at best.

## Cutting Both Ways

Rice's vampires have keener senses, so they are better able to appreciate beauty than mortals. They also live indefinitely in close-to-indestructible, perpetually young-looking bodies. Both of these attributes make them perfect party animals, ready to savor the nightlife and mingle with human beings who become their playthings and victims and, at times, their friends and lovers.

On the down side, they can't eat ordinary food but must drink blood to live. This makes it next-to-impossible to have ordinary relationships with human beings. But they may strive to retain a sense of their own humanity and can feel wracked with guilt about killing others to survive. Meanwhile, their connections with one another are somewhat tenuous. Vampire-vampire ties are continually breaking off as new ones develop.

Despite their power, they can be spiritually and emotionally needy and struggle to come to terms with their situation.

*The Vampire Chronicles* recount the struggles of a select number of especially interesting vampires throughout virtually all of human and vampire history. The first five books focus on the charismatic and defiantly tormented vampire Lestat. But there are other vampires also seeking out their own personal solutions to help them cope with their condition. This means the *Chronicles* can continue indefinitely.

### Grave Mistake

If you're just starting on *The Vampire Chronicles* for the first time, you probably don't want to begin with any of the later books in the series, since they draw on background laid out in the earlier books. It helps to begin with the first or the second one. You're definitely in for a challenge if you start with the third or fifth book, which are more complicated and potentially confusing.

## Off the Shelf

Here, in order, are the first seven volumes that make up *The Vampire Chronicles*.

- *Interview with the Vampire* (1976). The interviewed vampire is Louis, who tells his story of how he was turned into a vampire by Lestat and of their relationship with one another as well as with Claudia, the little girl vampire they create.

- *The Vampire Lestat* (1985). Lestat writes his own account of his astonishing experiences, including how he became a vampire, and how he was taken, for a brief period, under the wing of the wise and kind vampire, Marius, who teaches him about the origins of vampires in ancient Egypt. Lestat later audaciously drinks the blood of the mother of all vampires and has to lay low for a generation before re-emerging in the 1980s as a rock star.

- *The Queen of the Damned* (1988). Queen Akasha, the first vampire revivified at last by Lestat's music and bent on securing control of the world with her newfound lover, Lestat. Her evil scheme to rule the vampires and destroy 99 percent of the male population on Earth nearly works, but is foiled in the end by the twins, Mekare and Maharet, who had a score to settle with her from way back.

♦ *The Tale of the Body Thief* (1992). The body-snatcher is Raglan James, a mortal who offers Lestat a chance to be human again for a short time, but tries to make the exchange permanent. Lestat gets his vampire body back with the help of his mortal friend, David Talbot, an older man, who winds up with a younger body before Lestat vamps him.

♦ *Memnoch the Devil* (1995). Memnoch is the King of the Under-world who wants Lestat to join him to help souls in Hell repent so they can get into heaven. (It seems the Devil is actually a good guy.) He takes Lestat to Heaven and to Hell and explains how morality fits in with God's cosmic plan. Lestat also travels back in time and meets Christ on his way to his crucifixion. The savior gives Lestat the legendary *Veronica's Veil* with an image of his face on it. Later, in Hell, Lestat rushes to escape, but has an eye poked out by Memnoch as he leaves. Back on Earth, Lestat gives Veronica's Veil to the host of a religious cable TV show who uses it to win souls for Christ. Lestat comes to realize this was all part of Memnoch's plan.

### Stalk Talk

**Veronica's Veil** is named after the true image, or "vera icon" of Christ, which was said to have been imprinted on a veil or handkerchief after Christ wiped his face with it on his way to Calvary. He borrowed it from a woman known to legend as St. Veronica.

♦ *The Vampire Armand* (1998). With Lestat literally put to rest in a coma, the *Chronicles* recount the tale of Armand, who was born in Kiev in the sixteenth century, but is sold into slavery in Istanbul before being acquired as a sex slave in Venice by the vampire Marius, who eventually vamps Armand. But Marius's whole set-up is destroyed by the Children of Darkness, who capture Armand and eventually make him their leader. By the end he faces a choice between remaining immortal and saving his soul.

◆ *Merrick* (2000). In this tie-in with Rice's Mayfair witches books, Louis the vampire is still grieving for Claudia, who was destroyed in the first book of the series. David Talbot calls on his one-time pupil, Merrick the voodoo witch, to raise Claudia's ghost. But Talbot falls under Merrick's spell himself as he learns her story, including her swashbuckling adventures in South America.

# Venal Vampire

The bloody heart of *The Vampire Chronicles* and a major source of the series' appeal is the irrepressible vampire Lestat. He is selfish and arrogant, but also a troubled and searching soul. Although he is often contemptuous of others' feelings and plans, and though his impulses often seem destructive, he succeeds in uncovering new and enriching possibilities for vampire existence. What's more, he is not fundamentally evil, but rather committed to being true to himself and to finding his place in the world.

> **Cold Fact** _____
>
> Much of the action of *The Vampire Chronicles* takes place in New Orleans and in San Francisco, cities in which Rice has lived herself. Rice fans have put together tours of places in these cities that figure into the books.

## Hard-Luck Hero

Lestat had it rough as a mortal back in eighteenth-century France. His father was a tyrant who kept Lestat on a tight leash. When Lestat tried to leave home to live and study with some monks, his father brought him back. When Lestat left home again to join an acting troupe, his father brought him back again.

So Lestat was denied the chance to gain knowledge and to develop his talents. As a result, he grew up resentful, restless, and impetuous. Finally Lestat runs away a third time with his friend Nicolas. They join a theater and are happy until a new father figure comes into Lestat's life. This is the vampire Magnus.

Magnus kidnaps Lestat and turns him into a vampire. Soon afterward, before Lestat has had a chance to come to terms with his situation, Magnus kills himself by walking into a fire, leaving Lestat alone and confused. He confides in his friend Nicolas, who agrees to let Lestat turn him into a vampire, but they soon find they don't get along nearly as well as vampires as they did when they were mortal. Wouldn't you just know it?

### Dead Giveaway

*Interview with the Vampire*, the first Anne Rice novel published, was made into a movie in 1994 starring Brad Pitt as Louis and Tom Cruise as Lestat. Rice created a media stir while the movie was being filmed when she objected to the casting of Cruise as Lestat. Rice said that she envisioned Lestat as an androgynous character and suggested that Cruise was too stereotypically male to play the part well. She changed her mind, however, after she saw the completed film. In a statement printed in *Variety* that she paid for herself, she praised the film and all of the actors, including Cruise's performance, which she hailed as "courageous." In fact, Cruise does not come off as particularly macho, especially since he's wearing a long-haired wig throughout the movie.

## More Than He Can Chew

Lestat has a chance to join with other vampires known as the Children of Darkness, but their leader, Armand, is too controlling. After that, Lestat is so depressed he buries himself in the ground and goes to sleep, planning to remain underground indefinitely. Fortunately for Lestat, not to mention the many fans reading his story, the wise and kind Marius, who has been a vampire since ancient times, wakens him. Marius cares for and admires Lestat, so he digs him up and teaches him about vampire kind. From Marius, Lestat learns about the very first two vampires, "they who must be kept."

These are Akasha and Enkil, who created all the other vampires and have since become petrified. They are still alive, however, and must be preserved since the well-being of all vampires depends on them. Taking care of them is Marius's job. Lestat puts himself and all of vampire-kind in danger, however, when he sucks some of Akasha's blood. For this audacious deed he must go into hiding.

So Lestat sails for America, moves to New Orleans, and creates his own little vampire family by turning first Louis and then Claudia. These newly turned vampires become frustrated with Lestat's domination of them. They try to kill him and think they have succeeded. Then they set off for Europe.

## Going to Hell

Lestat would have died, but because he has sucked the blood of Akasha, he is more powerful than other vampires. But he must bury himself for many years to recover. When he re-emerges in the 1980s, he becomes a vampire rock star and rocks the vampire world by threatening to reveal too much about vampire-kind to mere mortals. Unbeknownst to him, vampires from all over the world flock to his concert to prevent this from happening.

Meanwhile, Akasha has awakened and decides to rule the world with the help of Lestat. But her scheme is foiled by the vampire twins, Mekare and Maharet. Lestat has mixed feelings about this, since he loves Akasha even though he disapproves of her evil plan. In the long run for Lestat, it's simply another failed relationship.

Lestat undergoes more failures, too. For example, he has a chance to experience mortal existence again, but that turns out to be a bad idea. He also tries to avoid helping Memnoch the devil, but ended up playing right into the devil's plans. But despite his repeated failures and hardships over the course of several lifetimes, he becomes wiser and more powerful with each new experience.

# Made to Be Broken

Lestat typically follows his own impulses, whatever they may be. As a result, he breaks a lot of rules, but also introduces innovations that help vampires lead fuller, richer lives. Through it all, he succeeds in acquiring new powers and changing his nature. At the same time, he serves as an example to other vampires—sometimes an example to be followed, other times to be avoided.

# Blood Code

Here are some of the vampire rules that Lestat breaks over the years:

- ◆ Vampires must obey the leader of the coven or group to which they belong. (Lestat disobeys Armand.)

- ◆ Vampires must turn into vampires only those mortals who are equipped to cope with the dark gift. Those who would need too much help, including children, should not be turned. (Lestat turns Claudia, a little girl, into a vampire.)

- ◆ Vampires must not kill other vampires. (Lestat helps Akasha kill many vampires.)

- ◆ Vampires must keep their vampire nature and identity secret from mortals. (Lestat hates to keep his true nature hidden.)

# Breaking Free

Even though he often breaks rules, Lestat's actions have led to some good results. He is responsible for founding the Theatre des Vampires, in eighteenth-century France. The Theatre enriches vampire culture and helps get vampires up out of their coffins at night.

The Theatre is not only enjoyable for its own sake, it provides cover for the vampires who belong to it, enabling them to conduct their activities with more freedom. In fact, the Theatre enables vampires to bend the rule against revealing their nature to mortals by enabling them to be themselves while pretending it's all an act. Lestat took this idea even further as a vampire rock star in the 1980s, though most other vampires felt he went too far.

Lestat broke the rules by befriending mortals and by trading his dark gift to Raglan James for a chance to experience mortality again. Although James tricked him, the trade ultimately worked out well, since it enabled Lestat's mortal friend, David Talbot, to acquire a younger body. With his younger body, he was willing to become a vampire. Finally, Lestat even disobeyed the devil himself by escaping from Hell with the Veronica's Veil. But, as the devil Memnoch realized, this, too, would lead to positive results.

**Grave Mistake**

If you think you've read all the books by Anne Rice, you may be wrong if you've missed those she's published under the names Anne Rampling and A. R. Roquelaure. Actually, Rice has changed her name several times. Her parents called her Howard O'Brien. Howard, interestingly, was her father's name.

In addition to *The Vampire Chronicles*, Rice has written two books featuring vampire characters that are separate from the series, even though they have overlapping characters. These are *Pandora: New Tales of the Vampires* (1998) and *Vittorio: New Tales of the Vampires* (1999).

# Their Human Side

Despite their supernatural condition, Rice's vampires are very human in many respects. In fact, you might say their supernatural characteristics serve to emphasize their humanity by posing challenges and opportunities that require a lot of human spirit, sensitivity, and will in order to deal with them. Rice's vampires have more intense versions of the same kinds of problems and potential for solving them than mortals have. You get a poetic or symbolic sense of the nature of these problems from the book's account of the origin of vampires.

## In the Beginning

The origin of vampires, as Marius explains to Lestat, can be traced back to 4000 B.C.E, when Egypt was ruled by the powerful Queen Akasha. Akasha was violently opposed to local religious custom in which children ate some of the bodies of their parents after their deaths. She vented her wrath most strongly against the twins Mekare and Maharet, witches who had the power of summoning the demon Amel.

The twins were publicly raped and Mekare had her tongue cut off while Maharet's eye's were poked out. The punishment instigated a revolt in which Akasha was killed. As she died, however, Amel entered her body and transformed her into the first vampire. She felt a painfully strong thirst for blood, but found she could dissipate its intensity by turning others into vampires. She turned her husband, Enkil, and her husband's servant, Khayman, who then turned the twins, Mekare and Maharet who eventually destroyed her six millennia later (and ate her heart and brain, in keeping with the ancient custom!).

Until her death, however, the other vampires revered her and her husband as "they who must be kept." They hardened and became incapable of motion, but were preserved and guarded by the others down through the centuries. Talk about family heirlooms!

## Sounds Familiar

Given their human qualities, it's fitting that the origin of vampires, which Lestat was so eager to learn about from Marius, resonates symbolically with deep-seated human psychological pain. This is the sense of personal trauma that many people experience and internalize from an early age, and may spend the rest of their lives dealing with. The myth of the origin of Rice's vampires, in other words, works as a myth about the origin and significance of the troubled human psyche.

### Dead Giveaway

Rice's books have inspired a significant amount of scholarly criticism, much of which relates her fiction to the circumstances of her life. For example, some have suggested connections between Claudia, the child vampire in *Interview* and Rice's daughter Michelle, who died of leukemia at an early age. Other popular topics in Rice scholarship include homosexuality and religion. An especially original and insightful essay by Sandra Tomc relates the anxiety felt by Louis in regard to his blood thirst to issues of dieting and weight loss with which Rice and millions of other women have wrestled. (Tomc's essay appears in *Blood Read: The Vampire as Metaphor in Contemporary Culture* [1997] edited by Joan Gordon and Veronica Hollinger.)

Here's how Rice's vampire myth can be applied to the human predicament:

◆ **Eating dead parents.** Paradoxically, eating your parents can represent both making your parents a part of you—internalizing their authority—and taking power away from them. It is especially significant for children who have been "starved" by their parents—denied love, respect, or freedom in life—as Lestat was.

◆ **Punishing the twins.** Just as the drastic sentence imposed by the Queen prevented one from seeing and the other from talking, mistreatment of children can do permanent damage to their ability to "see" things clearly or speak about their feelings. This is a problem shared by many of Rice's vampires who long to see what it means to be turned and have a hard time explaining what it's like to others.

◆ **Possession by the demon, Amel.** Akasha was possessed by the very demon worshiped by those she sought to punish. And the demon prompted her to further bloodshed. People often hate in others what they most fear and hate—but cannot face—in themselves. Parents who punish their children excessively often hate in their children a trait they are afraid to face in themselves. Children, conversely, often adjust by admiring and identifying with that same trait. So Amel represents this dynamic of hatred and admiration present in both parents and children—the two-way street of demon worship and possession involved in parent-eating and child-punishing.

◆ **Blood thirst.** This is much like the hate and anger that can spread among people like a contagion—especially among family members who must live with, and rely on one another. Just as vampirism spreads from character to character in the *Chronicles*, so does animosity among vampires who are close to one another, including every vampire who gets close to Lestat in the first three books of the series.

◆ **Becoming a vampire.** The "dark gift" can represent the onus of the legacy of emotional pain and hatred some people must learn to live with, as well as their creative, and sometimes destructive, responses to it.

◆ **"They who must be kept."** If Amel is a living, active essence representing interpersonal conflict that spurs those he possesses on to new conflict and occasional resolution, the petrified bodies of Akasha and Enkil can represent the dead, stultifying aspects of the same conflict. Not only are the two vampire parents petrified, but the need to keep them burdens the entire vampire community.

# The Least You Need to Know

◆ Anne Rice has written the most influential vampire fiction since *Dracula*.

◆ The vampire condition is a "dark gift" involving heightened powers and senses as well as loss and deprivation.

◆ The vampire Lestat, Rice's most popular character, is selfish and arrogant, yet introspective and innovative.

◆ The mythlike origin of Rice's vampires resonates symbolically with the nature of human psychological pain.

# Chapter 20

# Undying Classics

## In This Chapter

- ◆ Classic vampire films
- ◆ *Nosferatu* and *Vampyr*
- ◆ Tod Browning's *Dracula*
- ◆ The Universal Studios horror films
- ◆ *London After Midnight* and *Mark of the Vampire*

Among the most classic of the classic horror movies are vampire films. Cinematic vampires were weaned on blood that was filmed in black and white. They learned to stalk in front of hand-cranked cameras and they cut their baby fangs mouthing in silent films. And after the better part of a hundred years some of these early picture-show predators remain among the most familiar and memorable images of vampires we know.

Sure, the movie technology used to film the old chestnuts has long since become obsolete. But the old vampire movies still give you that warm yet cold feeling of the wistful willies as nostalgia and fear combine to give you a lump in your throat and a pit in your stomach. They just don't make 'em like that anymore.

Yes, you can tell it's only a paper moon like the song says, but that moon is eerily full. So hang up the cobwebs, start the fog machine, prop up the tombstones, release the rats, and crank up the mechanical bat. Lights! Camera! Suction!

# Silent but Deadly

Most vampires are creatures of few words and long, deep, sinister looks. This makes them perfect silent film material. And while the silent screen vampires were serving up their most mesmerizing stares and evilest grimaces, early film directors were trying out cutting-edge creepy special effects, using the wizardry of infant film technology to evoke the supernatural menace of the vampire and show what mere words cannot convey.

## First in Fright

Whether or not they are interested in vampire movies for their own sake, most serious classic film buffs are interested in F. W. Murnau's weird, creepy gem of 1922, *Nosferatu: eine Symphonie des Grauens* ("Nosferatu: A Symphony of Terror"). This famous old flick is often hailed as a masterpiece of German expressionist filmmaking. It also happens to be the first film to bring a vampire to the screen that still survives (a Russian vampire movie was made previously, but has been lost) as well as the first movie version of the novel *Dracula*.

**Grave Mistake**

Not even vampires can transgress copyright laws with impunity. A judge found that Murnau's *Nosferatu* violated the copyright to *Dracula* held by Bram Stoker's widow and ordered it to be destroyed. Fortunately, at least one print of the film was preserved anyway.

Murnau's film moves the action of Stoker's story from contemporary London to the German town of Breman in the year 1838, the time and place of an outbreak of the plague. The vampire—called Count Orlock—brings the plague with him from his castle together with rats that live in the boxes of native soil he carries around with him. The Renfield character—known as Knock in the film—is scapegoated for the supernatural destruction and killed.

Only the Mina character—renamed Ellen—is aware of the real nature of the menace her town faces, thanks to her delicate feminine sensitivity combined with the fact that she does her homework and reads a book about vampires that her husband found in his hotel room. (Were you expecting a Gideon Bible?) She saves the day by sacrificing herself in order to trick Orlock into staying awake past dawn when the sunlight destroys him.

## Display of Talons

Murnau turns Stoker's novel into a cinematic fairy tale. All the towns-people of Bremen are heedless of the vampire warnings and they suffer as a result, but are saved in the end by the selflessness of a good and pure woman. Orlock the vampire is delightfully gremlinlike: tall and thin with bushy eyebrows, bald head, pointy ears, protruding nose, and ratlike teeth. But his most noticeable physical trait are his large hands with enormous claws instead of fingernails. They have yet to be out-done by any subsequent supernaturally evil clutches.

While the fairy-tale retelling and the appearance of the vampire make the film worth seeing, *Nosferatu* stands out for its use of bizarre and ingenious special effects. Not only are they visually fascinating, eerie, and poetic, they were created 75 years before computer graphics were developed. Here's a list that describes some of them:

- ◆ At the moment the Harker character—renamed Thomas Hutter—crosses over a bridge to Orlock's castle, the movie switches to negative film.

- ◆ Orlock levitates out of his coffin to his feet without moving a muscle.

- ◆ Orlock's carriage moves in fast motion and his coffins get loaded in fast motion, too.

- ◆ Orlock passes through a wall—while carrying one of his coffins.

- ◆ At dawn, Orlock disappears in a wisp of smoke.

*Nosferatu* was adapted as a big-budget talkie, *Nosferatu the Vampyre* (1979) by German director Werner Herzog and starring Klaus Kinski. More recently, *Shadow of the Vampire* (2000) pays tribute to Murnau's

**Cold Fact** _____

Orlock in the film *Nosferatu* is the first vampire to be killed by sunlight, thus inaugurating a new—and now time-honored—vampire myth. Dracula, in contrast, was weaker during the day, but was otherwise unharmed by the sun.

work by offering a fictional account of how it was made. John Malkovich stars as Murnau with Willem Dafoe as Max Schreck, the actor who played Count Orlock. In this new movie, Schreck is an actual vampire who preys on human victims during the making of the silent film. Although *Shadow* is not a timeless classic like *Nosferatu*, it is easier to find in video stores!

## Shady Characters

Another early experimental and artsy silent vampire film is Carl Dryer's *Vampyr* (1931), a surreal German feature about a man who visits a town under the spell of an elderly female vampire. (It is said the shades of executed criminals become the vampire's slaves.) Though evocative, the film doesn't have much of a plot. Like *Nosferatu*, however, it has some notable scenes featuring special effects.

For example, there are shadows that move around independently of the people who would ordinarily cast them. One shadow even shoots and kills a man. During a dream sequence in which the hero dreams of his own death, he walks around in ghostly form, thanks to double-exposed photography. When the vampire is eventually staked in her coffin, her face disappears, exposing her skull.

**Grave Mistake** _____

The picture credits to Carl Dryer's *Vampyr* say that the film is based on the story "Carmilla" by Sheridan Le Fanu. It's hard to see, however, even a remote connection between the two beyond the fact that both feature female vampires. Not only is it hard to see what story the film is based on, it's hard to see any story in the film at all!

# I Am Dlacoolah!

As intriguing and effective as the silent films are, they didn't do much to make "vampire" a household word. That job fell to Universal Pictures'

*Dracula* of 1931, directed by Tod Browning and starring Bela Lugosi in the title role. This was the most commercially successful of all of the 60-plus movies Browning directed and it set the standard for Hollywood horror, which Universal would continue to dominate for years to come.

## Instant Re-Play

Director Tod Browning spared himself the challenge of adapting Stoker's work directly by working instead with a theater-version of the story. *Dracula* was successfully adapted for the stage in 1924 by Hamilton Deane. Browning incorporated many of the plot modifications and much of the dialog from the play into his film. In addition, he also used some of the play's actors, most notably Lugosi. In addition, Dwight Frye played Renfield on stage and on screen, and Edward Van Sloane played Van Helsing.

Movie critics have found fault with the film for sticking too close to the play rather than developing the cinematic potential of the story. Throughout many scenes, the camera hardly moves at all, making for a stiff and slow-moving movie toward the end. The frequent close-ups of the glaring, staring Lugosi help, but the camerawork isn't exactly dazzling.

The film is also deficient in the special effects department. In fact, there really aren't any special effects to speak of, except for a squeaky, floppy vampire bat that hangs from a wire and flaps its wings when someone bounces it up and down from above. It would make a better baby toy than a prop in a horror film. Then it disappears and morphs into Dracula—off camera.

And the only blood the film shows on screen comes when Harker accidentally cuts his finger with a paperclip. All the juicy biting, sucking, and staking happen off camera and are left to the imagination. Slasher films were still a long way into the future.

> **Cold Fact**
>
> Lugosi's Dracula is meticulously polite even about the delicate subject of his own vampirism. After smashing to the ground a small mirror that Van Helsing has surprised him with (to show that Dracula casts no reflection), he apologizes and says, "I dislike mirrors. Van Helsing will explain."

## Perforating Performances

But although critics were nonplused, the film was a big success finan-
cially. Not only did movie fans pour into theaters to see it, but it didn't
cost too much to make. Not only were special effects costs low, but
Universal made the most of the movie set. While Browning and crew
were filming by day, a Spanish-language version of the same story was
being filmed at night.

Browning's *Dracula* is still well worth watching today, thanks to the
standout performances of the three veteran stage actors, who pretty
much carry the show. They give it weight and drama it wouldn't have
had otherwise. Lugosi is smooth yet commanding, and even though he
doesn't have fangs, he looks as though he could cut you with the creases
in his tuxedo. He remains the most dignified Dracula ever, even consid-
ering his occasional wry humor.

Van Sloane's Van Helsing is a sharp, cool customer who's so sure of his
status as a good-guy in the right that he doesn't waste his time being
nice to anyone—just patronizing to the frightened Mina and the somewhat dippy Jonathan. It's clear that this doctor can see what's going on
perfectly, regardless of his thick spectacles.

Best of all is Frye as the totally bonkers Renfield. He practically chews
the scenery and gets away with it. If you can imagine Pee Wee Herman
channeling for Sheena, Queen of the
Jungle you get something of the
idea. Frye would go on to play similar characters—the demented mad-
scientist's assistant, for example, in
other horror films.

And fortunately, these and other
actors get some pretty droll lines
that did not appear in Stoker's book.
Here are some worth mentioning,
culled from throughout the picture:

**Cold Fact** _____

Dwight Frye, who played
Renfield in Tod Browning's
*Dracula* went on to play a
bat-keeping mental case in
*The Vampire Bat* (1933) and
a hunchbacked lackey to a
vampire in *Dead Men Walk*
(1943). Neither film was
much of a success.

## Sound Bites

- Dracula to Harker: "I do not drink … wine."

- Van Helsing to his students: "The vampire attacks the throat. It leaves two little marks. White with red centers."

- Renfield to Dracula: "You will see that I get lives? Not human lives, but small ones. With blood in them!"

- Harker to Mina: "My, what a big bat."

- Martin, the asylum attendant to his wife: "They're all crazy except you an' me!"

# Monster Mill

Universal went on attempting to build on the success of *Dracula* with many more vampire and other horror movies. In fact, Universal Films was largely responsible for establishing not only Dracula, but Frankenstein, the Bride of Frankenstein, the Wolf Man, and the Mummy as horror movie icons. Universal made *The Invisible Man*, too, but it's hard to be an icon when you're invisible!

Anyway, moviegoers of the 1930s and '40s were so eager to see these creepy characters lurking and prowling on screen that Universal trotted them out, singly and in groups, in film after film. These pictures established and milked the Hollywood clichés of gothic horror, focusing almost not at all on sex and violence but instead on eeriness, implied dementedness, and nutty spectacle. Universal horror films were so state-of-the-art that the horror films of other studios largely imitated Universal's style.

**Grave Mistake**

Although most of Universal's vampire movies include at least some account of vampire myth and legend, not all questions are sufficiently explained. For example, a review in the 1945 *Hollywood Reporter* wanted to know how Dracula kept his white shirt so impeccably laundered after lying around in it in his dirt-filled coffin for so long!

## Family Vault

Check this checklist of movies featuring vampires produced by Universal:

- *Dracula* (1931). Universal Studios continued to use Lugosi and the Dracula image he created to plug its films for decades afterward. Eventually, the Lugosi estate won a lawsuit awarding them money for use of Lugosi's Dracula in Universal's promotions.

- *Dracula's Daughter* (1936). The film stars Gloria Holden as Countess Marya Zaleska, who falls in love with a mortal, despite her undeath and blood thirst.

> **Cold Fact**
>
> If you're into interesting pre-1975 Dracula trivia, a great source is the lovingly detailed *Dracula Book* (Scarecrow Press, 1975) by Donald F. Glut, which digs up all kinds of Dracula facts from movies, books, TV, and comics. Glut has also written sci-fi and horror novels and comics.

- *Son of Dracula* (1943). It stars Lon Chaney Jr., son of the real life horror-film icon. Dracula Jr. gets dusted in the end for hitting on another guy's girlfriend.

- *House of Frankenstein* (1944). Attempting to build on the success of their hit, *Frankenstein Meets the Wolf Man* (1943), Universal served up a whole houseful of monsters, including Dracula.

- *House of Dracula* (1945). Same monsters as before, different host.

- *Abbot and Costello Meet Frankenstein* (1948). And while we're inviting everyone else, why not bring in the hit comedy duo, too, especially since they're already under contract at Universal.

## Daddy's Girl

Not surprisingly, none of Universal's subsequent vampire efforts measured up to *Dracula*. Truth be told, the studio did a better job with its many Frankenstein movies. Even so, *Dracula's Daughter* stands out as a decent flick, notable for bringing an internally complex vampire to the screen. She's evil, of course, but she also has her tender side.

The action begins with Dr. Van Helsing arrested for the murder of an apparently innocent man named Dracula. The Doctor is caught red-handed with the murder weapon—a bloody stake. It takes him a lot of explaining to do to convince the authorities that he did not kill a human being, but a vampire. Not until a few run-ins with a lady vampire do they realize Van Helsing is right. Not only is Dracula's daughter a bloodsucking vampire, she has a magic ring that hypnotizes people.

Despite the blood thirst that drives her to prey on innocent people, she falls in love with good-guy Dr. Jeffrey Garth. She wants to become human and, failing that, to make Garth her willing companion as a vampire. He refuses, so she kidnaps his fiancée, Janet. But she still loves the young doctor. So, when her evil henchman tries to shoot him with a bow and arrow, she takes the shaft.

# Making His Mark

Universal Pictures was not entirely happy with the work of director Browning on *Dracula*, and didn't hire him to direct any of their other vampire features. But Browning didn't simply curl up and die. He went on to make many more movies, including the unusual cult classic, *Freaks*, featuring a large cast of veteran sideshow performers with various congenital aberrations. He also made another vampire film featuring Bela Lugosi: the horror whodunit, *Mark of the Vampire* (1935).

### Dead Giveaway

Tod Browning started out in show business as a carnival sideshow performer billed as "the Living Corpse." He would have himself buried and dug up two days later in front of an admiring crowd. After a stint in vaudeville he got acting parts under the famous movie director D. W. Griffith. He went on to direct films himself, including his best known pictures, *Dracula* and *Freaks*. *Freaks*, which featured actual circus "freaks," including dwarves, microcephalics, paraplegics, and quadriplegics shocked not only filmgoers, but the movie industry in general and was banned for many years. Backlash over the film all but ended Browning's career.

## London's Burning

Interestingly, *Mark of the Vampire* is a remake of the earlier silent film, *London After Midnight* (1927) also directed by Browning and based on the novel, *The Hypnotist*, which Browning wrote. The silent film stars Lon Chaney Sr., "The Man of 1000 Faces," in one of his most famous movie-makeovers: he appears as an alligator-toothed, top-hatted vampire. To make himself look just that much more bizarre, Chaney rigged up wires to pry his eyes open extra-wide—a painful measure for a subtle effect! The pain was not in vain, however; Chaney looks like he not only wants your blood, but is really going to enjoy getting it out of you!

If you'd like to see *London After Midnight* for yourself, you're not alone. All vintage movie fans know the feeling. Unfortunately, there are no surviving prints. It was last viewed by two movie critics in the 1950s before a fire in an MGM film vault destroyed the last copy several years later. It's a rotten shame, but permanent death by fire is an appropriate fate for a vampire movie as well as a movie vampire!

## Trick of the Trade

Browning's remake, though no substitute for the original, is worthwhile for its own sake. It features Lugosi as Count Mora and Carol Borland as his creepy vampire daughter, Luna. Together they do a lot of stately stalking on the grounds of the estate of the murdered Sir Karrell Borotyn. Browning pulled out all the gothic stops to make the set as creepy as possible, with plenty of fog and cobwebs hanging in the moonlit trees. And there are mechanical bats that are slightly less cheesy than the ones in *Dracula*.

In addition, there's a beautiful (and expensive) scene in which Luna flies and then descends to Earth on big white bat's wings. The spooky theatrics, vampires included, turn out to be part of an elaborate ploy on the part of Professor Zelan, played by Lionel Barrymore, to trick Borotyn's killer into confessing, which he does under hypnosis and to avoid getting attacked by the vampires. Crime does not pay! But acting does. The vampires were actors hired to scare the crook.

**Cold Fact** _____

Critics have suggested that the screenplay for *Mark of the Vampire* included indications that Count Mora and Luna committed incest and suicide, but that these details were censored by Universal Pictures as inappropriate in one of their films. One piece of evidence for this claim is the bullet hole Mora wears in his head throughout the picture that is not explained in the dialog.

*Mark of the Vampire* differs from *London After Midnight* in separating the characters of the hypnotist and the vampire. In the silent film, both parts were played by Lon Chaney. And, in *Mark of the Vampire*, Browning tried to build on his reputation as the director of *Dracula*. The film alludes to this in one of the closing sequences in which Lugosi packs up his bags, telling Luna that someday he will become famous for playing the part of a vampire!

## The Least You Need to Know

- ◆ F. W. Murnau's silent film, *Nosferatu: eine Symphonie des Grauens,* is widely considered a masterpiece of German expressionist film making.

- ◆ Tod Browning's *Dracula* was the most commercially successful of all of the director's 60-plus films.

- ◆ Universal Pictures led the horror movie industry by featuring name-brand monsters in film after film.

- ◆ Tod Browning's *Mark of the Vampire* is a remake of his own silent classic, *London after Midnight,* which has been lost to posterity due to a fire.

# Glossary

Here's a who's who of notable names in the world of vampires, including legendary, fictional, historical, and contemporary individuals, as well as a glossary of vampiric verbiage to help you expand your eerie eloquence.

**Akasha**  The Queen of the damned in Anne Rice's *The Vampire Chronicles*. She was an Egyptian queen who became the first vampire when the demon Amel took control of her soul and body.

**Allatius, Leo**  (Leone Allacci, 1586–1669). Greek priest who wrote what is apparently the first book on vampires ever published. The work describes the vrykolakas and indicates such beings may exist.

**Astral vampires**  The disembodied spirits of living people who send them out to prey on others. The phenomenon of astral vampirism was offered as an explanation for the Slavic vampire scare by occultist Franz Hartmann.

**Aswang**  A demonic creature of the Philippines said to live by day as an attractive Filipina, leading an apparently normal life. At night, however, she turns into a birdlike menace with a long, pointy tongue. It flies off to prey on victims, usually children, by sticking its tongue into them and slurping out their blood.

**Baby bat**  A young newcomer to the Goth scene. The term isn't necessarily a put-down, but it does imply a lightweight status.

**Baital**  Former dead person who resembles a small human with wings like a bat and a tail like a goat who may sometimes be found hanging upside down from trees in graveyards. A baital is a central character in the collection of Indian tales, *Baital-Pachisi*, or "25 tales of a baital." Most of these tales were translated by Sir Richard F. Burton and published in 1870 under the title, *King Vikram and the Vampire*.

**Bathory, Elizabeth** The sixteenth-century Slovak/Hungarian countess who is said to have made a practice of bathing in the blood of young virgins in the belief that this would keep her young looking. Her story has provided a kernel of truth behind a number of vampire films since the 1970s as well as several novels.

**Blood play** Also called blood sports and blood fetishism, is a sexual, spiritual, or expressive activity that involves cutting and blood. It is a form of sadomasochism and is sometimes tied in with body art: tattoos, piercing, brands, decorative scarification, and so on. Many, but not all, blood fetishists identify themselves as "real vampires."

**Born vampires** According to lifestyler lore, those who are naturally aware of their own vampiric nature and realize it from an early age.

**Bourgeoisie** Middle class, originally distinguished from the aristocracy on one hand, and the peasant class on the other. Many artists of the nineteenth century, as well as social critics of recent years, have expressed contempt for bourgeois complacency, conformity, and materialism.

**Calmet, Dom Augustin** French Benedictine monk and Bible scholar who wrote *Traite sur les Revenants en corps, les Excommuniè, les Oupires ou Vampires, Broucolaques de Hongrie, de Boheme, de Moravie, et de Silèsie* (Treatise on the Returned Dead, the Vampires and Vrykolakas of Hungary, Bohemia, Moravia, and Silesia, [1746]), the most exhaustive and widely read of all vampire books written up to that time.

**Carmilla** The creation of the Irish writer of short stories, Joseph Thomas Sheridan Le Fanu. She is a female vampire who preys on a teenage girl named Laura.

**Chiang shih** Vampirelike beings from China that arise as corpses re-animated by sunlight or moonlight.

**Chupacabra** Creature resembling a three-foot-long rat with wings and enormous teeth or, alternatively, said to have long quills running down its spine instead of wings. It has been said to have attacked and mutilated livestock in Mexico and surrounding regions.

**Cihuacoatl** A blood-drinking goddess of the Aztecs of Ancient Mexico. She was known as "the snake woman" and is traditionally represented as having two knives growing out of her forehead.

**Cihuateteo** Ancient Mayan (modern-day Mexican) monsters. They started out as women who died in childbirth and return from the grave to prey on living children by night. They resemble ordinary women except they are unusually pale.

**Clarimonde** The beautiful undead lover in Gautier's tale, *La Morte Amoureuse*. She represents a kind of muse for the decadent artist of the nineteenth century—a source of inspiration who leads him into down the path of sensuality.

**Corealis, Fiona** A blood player who has worked to focus public attention on blood play since age 19. She started the Blood Play Awareness Campaign in 1997 with two goals in mind: to counter the widespread perception that blood play is freakish and to encourage people to recognize the distinction between compulsive self-mutilation as an expression of self-hatred and blood play which can be creative and beautiful.

**Dakhanavar** Vampire from an Armenian legend who preyed on anyone rash enough to count the valleys around Mount Ararat where he lived.

**Dark gift** Everything that goes along with being a vampire in Anne Rice's *The Vampire Chronicles*, including indefinite existence, heightened perceptions, the power to turn others into vampires, and blood thirst. As you might imagine, it's a mixed blessing at best.

**Davanzati, Guiseppe** Italian archbishop and author of *Dissertatione Sopra I Vampiri* (Dissertation on Vampires, [1744]) reinforcing the view that vampires are unreal and that belief in them may be inspired by the devil.

**de Lioncourt, Lestat** The ambiguous, ambitious vampire hero of many of the vampire novels of Anne Rice.

*Deafula* Name of a 1974 film done in sign language for the deaf in which a theology student becomes a vampire and goes on the prowl after his classmates.

**Dracula, Count** The famous vampire villian in the novel *Dracula* (1897) by Bram Stoker.

**Dracula, Vlad Dracula Tepes ("the Impaler")**  The Wallachian prince who lived from 1431 to 1476 who is famous today as one of the inspirations behind Bram Stoker's fictional Dracula.

*Fin de siécle*  French for "end of the century," the aesthetic movement that took place at the end of the nineteenth century characterized by decadence and extravagance.

*Frankenstein*  The monstrous progeny of British author Mary Shelley, who wrote the novel as part of the famous ghost-story contest involving Lord Byron and John Polidori in 1816 in Italy. (Polidori wrote *The Vampyre* after this contest.)

**Ghoul**  An unearthly creature from the Middle East who eats the flesh of the dead. In Islamic countries, this is considered not merely gross, but deeply sacrilegious as well. Ghouls are demons that often masquerade as ordinary people and even marry unsuspecting princes or princesses until they are discovered and magically vanquished.

**Goth**  Originally referred to an ancient European tribe famous for sacking Rome. Only during the past two decades or so has the term been used to describe a fashionable subculture.

**Gothic literature**  A trend in eighteenth-century England characterized by eerie supernatural doings. Gothic architecture is an elaborate yet stark-looking medieval style.

**Haarmann, Fritz**  "The Vampire of Hanover" was a notorious blood-drinking killer who operated in Germany in the 1920s. He lured men to his home, raped them, bit them in the neck, and drank their blood. He was charged with committing over 20 murders, but was suspected of killing over 50 victims.

**Haigh, John George**  "The acid bath murderer" of London killed eight people during the 1940s and successfully escaped detection before finally being apprehended for his ninth murder. He typically shot or bludgeoned his victims in the head, cut open a vein in their necks, and drank a cup of their blood. Then he immersed the bodies in a vat of acid, effectively destroying the evidence.

**Hopping vampires**  Familiar to fans of Chinese martial arts/vampire movies, vampires that hop as a feature of their nonhuman, supernatural identity. They first appeared in the popular Hong Kong horror/comedy

*Mr. Vampire* (1986) and have been popping up ever since. If a good guy sees them, he can stop them in their tracks temporarily by holding his breath.

**Incubae** Female demons known to the European Middle Ages who stole in upon sleeping men by night and had sex with them.

**Kali** A Hindu goddess who takes the form of a hideous female sometimes represented with fangs. In addition, she has been worshiped with sacrifice, and is said to become intoxicated by drinking blood.

**Krafft-Ebing, Richard von** Pioneer in the field of psychopathology who noticed that many of the most bizarre and disturbing acts perpetrated by psychopaths were sexual in nature. He explained his view and compiled massive amounts of evidence to support it in a work called *Psychopathia Sexualis* (1886).

**Kurten, Peter** "The Vampire of Dusseldorf" was an infamous serial killer of the late 1920s who delighted in the blood of his victims, mostly young women.

**La Vey, Anton** Founded the Church of Satan, in 1966.

**Lamia** A Libyan princess who became transformed into a snake demon, said to kill children and seduce men.

**Langsuyars** Former women who died in childbirth and return to suck the blood of children. They wear their hair long to disguise a big hole in their backs.

**Lilith** Among the oldest known demons in world folklore and she's still going strong as a modern vampire and occult figurehead. She is obliquely referred to in the Sumerian *Epic of Gilgamesh*, which was written on clay tablets around 2000 B.C.E., but is best known from the Jewish Talmud. She was an important figure in Jewish legend throughout the Middle Ages, as we know in part from the many charms and amulets inscribed with magic formulas intended to keep Lilith away.

**Lugosi, Bela** Actor who played Dracula on stage and in the classic 1931 film. His depiction of the character became a horror movie icon and, eventually, a vampire stereotype.

**Marusia** Russian girl-vampire slayer from a vampire story collected and published in the mid-nineteenth century by Russian folklorist named A. N. Afanasiev.

**Mora** Eastern European versions of the demons known as succubae and incubae. The concept of the mora merged with vampire lore. Slavic legend sometimes distinguished between living and undead moras.

**Mummy** Any dead body that has been preserved from decay, either deliberately through embalming, or accidentally, as when a body is preserved in ice or in tar pits. The ancient Egyptians preserved the bodies of their rulers as mummies, apparently in the belief that this would enable them to live on in the afterlife.

**Necrophagia** Psychopathic urge to eat carrion and decaying corpses.

**Necrophilia** Psychopathic condition involving an erotic attraction to dead bodies.

**Paole, Arnod** A Serbian peasant and former soldier named from the town of Medvegia suspected of becoming a vampire after his death in 1725. His body and those of his suspected victims, was dug up and cremated.

**Penanggalens** Evil spirits that take possession of women and turn them into predatory witches. They fly around by uprooting their heads from their bodies with the guts attached, which dangle beneath them as they fly.

**Penny dreadfuls** Serialized horror stories that sold for a penny each in nineteenth-century England. They often included an illustration or two so, in a way, you could say they were an ancestor of the twentieth-century comic book or pulp magazine.

**Philinnion** A dead woman who returned from the grave for some post-mortem hanky-panky in a tale by the ancient Greek writer, Phlegon.

**Plogojowitz, Peter** Serbian peasant from the town of Kisilova, suspected of being a vampire in the eighteenth century after nine people got sick and died and claimed on their death beds that Plogojowitz came to them in their sleep and nearly strangled them.

**Polidori, John** The author of *The Vampyre*, the first vampire novel written in English. The story features the vampire Lord Ruthven, whose character is based loosely on Polidori's former companion, the famous Romantic poet, George Gordon, Lord Byron.

**Psychic vampires** Those who derive pleasure or spiritual nourishment from draining others of psychic energy. They may be supernatural creatures or worldly, manipulative people.

**Rake** A character type from Restoration (late-seventeenth-century British) plays and eighteenth- and nineteenth-century British fiction. Short for rake-hell (someone who seeks out infernal experiences), the rake is a selfish, profligate libertine who follows his libido instead of his moral compass.

**Rakshasas** Ghoulish, flesh-eating demons from India who haunt graveyards and interfere with the sacred rites of good people.

**Ramsland, Katherine** Anne Rice scholar and author of *Prism of the Night: a Biography of Anne Rice* (1992) and *The Vampire Companion: The Official Guide to Anne Rice's Vampire Chronicles* (1993). Since then she has become interested in real vampires and, more generally, the current fascination with the vampire myth.

**Ranft, Michael** Eighteenth-century German author whose work, *De Masticacione Mortuarum in Tumulus Liber* (Book of the Chewing Dead in Their Tombs, [1728]) refuted Philip Rohr's position that the dead are capable of chewing.

**Revenants** Beings that return from the grave, including spirits, ghosts, certain angels, zombies, and vampires.

**Rice, Anne** The hugely successful author of *The Vampire Chronicles*, featuring the impetuous vampire Lestat, as well as many others.

**Rohr, Philip** Seventeenth-century German author of *De Masticatione Mortuorum* (Of the Chewing Dead, [1679]), which describes the supposed ability of corpses to chew, and even eat their shrouds and parts of their own bodies.

**Ruthven, Lord** The vampire featured in the novel *The Vampyre* by John Polidori. His character is based loosely on Polidori's former companion, the famous Romantic poet, George Gordon, Lord Byron.

**Sadomasochism** The pleasure some people derive from inflicting and/or suffering pain. The term comes from the names of two novelists whose fiction describes inflicting and receiving pain, respectively, in erotic terms. The work of the French Marquis de Sade (1740–1814) emphasizes the joy of inflicting pain while Austrian Leopold von Sacher-Masoch (1836–1895) dwells on the pleasures of being hurt.

**Shaman**  A tribal healer and spiritual leader who often prepares for his vocation by exploring altered states of consciousness with the help of hallucinogenic drugs, sleep deprivation, or prolonged fasting. Having experienced these extreme states of being, he is thought to have privileged insight into the spirit world.

**Sire**  A vampire who creates another vampire by turning a human being.

**Soul eaters**  Vampirelike witches known to the Hausa tribe of Niger. As their name implies, they feed on human souls, causing their soul-deprived victims to waste away. They start off as ordinary human beings who swallow magic beans or stones that give them the power to steal other peoples' souls.

**Stock, Johann Christian**  Eighteenth-century-German author of *Dissertatio Physico de Cadaveribus Sanguisugis* (Dissertation of the Physical Traits of Bloodsucking Cadavers, [1732]), claiming that belief in vampires stem from hallucinations sent by the devil.

**Strix** (plural, *striges*)  Demon with a woman's head and the body of a bird of prey, capable of attacking sleeping infants and seducing men. The word, strix, which also means owl, appears to be related to *striga*, a Latin word that became the Italian word, *strega*, which is now used interchangeably with the English word "witch."

**Succubae**  Male demons known to the European Middle Ages who stole in upon sleeping women by night and had sex with them.

**Summers, Montague**  Renowned vampire scholar who collected and wrote exhaustively on everything he could find on the subject.

**Vampirology**  The study of vampires; a subdiscipline of demonology, which is older and has had more practitioners. Unlike demonology, which once enjoyed a certain degree of official support from the Church, vampirology has no major institutional underpinnings outside of fan clubs and research societies.

**Varney the Vampire**  The villain of the popular Victorian *"penny dreadful."*

**Vrykolakas**  A Greek vampire with essentially the same characteristics as the Slavic variety. The word comes from other words that may have meant "wolf pelt," or "werewolf." How or why this term came to be applied to vampires is uncertain.

**Xenophobia** The unwarranted fear of foreigners, a condition that gripped many Americans during the first half of the twentieth century. As vampires moved from legend into fiction and film, many came to embody this fear. Dracula, especially, represents a parasitic alien, arriving from foreign shores to multiply his own kind and deplete his new country.

**Zombies** Dead people who have been reanimated by voodoo magic of Haitian tradition. The word, zombie, comes from "nzambi," a Congolese word for spirit.

**Zoophagia** "Life-eating," the term used in the novel *Dracula* to diagnose Renfield's compulsion to eat bugs and other small animals.

# Index

# G